Growing Up
on The
Chocolate Diet

Growing Up on *The* Chocolate Diet

A Memoir with Recipes

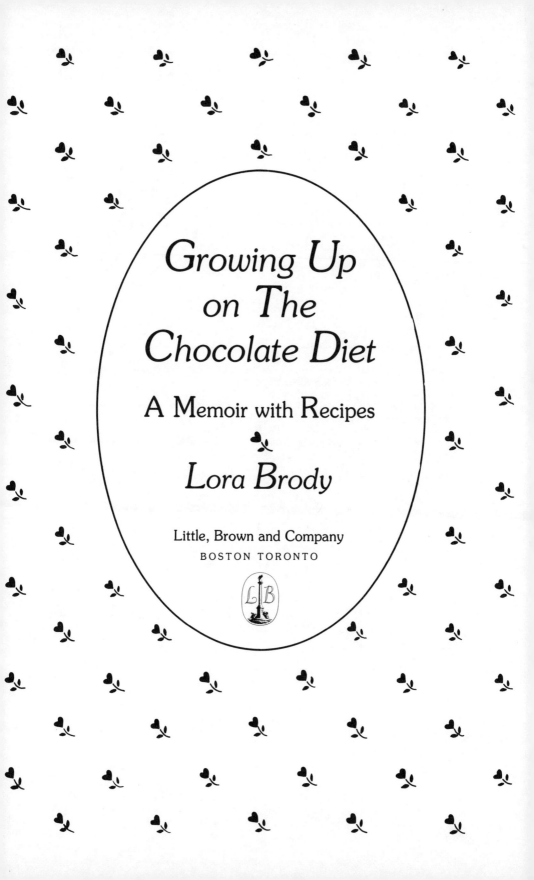

Lora Brody

Little, Brown and Company
BOSTON TORONTO

FIRST EDITION

The author is grateful to the following for permission to reprint previously published material:

"A Rose and a Baby Ruth" by John D. Loudermilk. Copyright © 1956, 1967, © renewed 1984 by Acuff-Rose Publications, Inc. Used by permission of the publisher. All rights reserved.

"Rigo Janci" from FOODS OF THE WORLD: *The Cooking of Vienna's Empire*. Copyright © 1968 by Time-Life Books, Inc. Used by permission of the publisher.

"A Marquis for the Millions" by Simone Beck, from *The New York Times Magazine*, October 14, 1973. Copyright © 1973 by The New York Times Company. Reprinted by permission.

"Famous Chocolate Refrigerator Roll" used by permission of Nabisco Brands, Inc.

Library of Congress Cataloging in Publication Data

Brody, Lora, 1945–
    Growing up on the chocolate diet.

    Includes index.
    1. Cookery (Chocolate)   I. Title.
TX767.C5B76   1985   641.3'374   85-5169
ISBN 0-316-10897-9

MV

Published simultaneously in Canada
by Little, Brown & Company (Canada) Limited

PRINTED IN THE UNITED STATES OF AMERICA

To my husband, David,
and my sons, Jonathan, Max, and Samuel

Contents

Acknowledgments

I had a wonderful time writing this book. The encouragement and loving support of my family and friends, the advice and assistance from colleagues and the members of the chocolate industry, and the enthusiasm and patient guidance of my publisher and agent combined with the delicious subject matter to inspire me.

I would especially like to thank the following people: Maida Heatter for all she taught me, Craig Claiborne for his amazing support, and Sandra Boynton for planting the idea. My mom, Millie Apter, who set the standard. My chocolate mentors: Malcolm "Uno" Blue of Nestlé's, Malcolm and Jean Campbell of Van Leer, Rudi Sprüngli of Lindt, Dennis DeDomenico of Ghirardelli, Gary Guittard and Kent Lyon of Guittard, Rose Levy Beranbaum, Adrianne Marcus, Milton Zelman of the *Chocolate News,* Rossario Caponetto of Ferrara, Ben Strohecker of Harbor Sweets, Walt Matheiss of Tobler, Joseph Datoli of Perugina, and Elaine Sherman, who is Madame Chocolate.

Thank you to the Chocolate Manufacturers of America for their vote of confidence and to Lenore Cooney and Diane McKeown of Dudley-Anderson and Yutzy for their guidance and promotional assistance.

Beverly Jones and Betsy Bisberg, who tested all the recipes lots of times and never, never complained, Colleen Mohyde, who retested several, and to Gertrude Goldberg, who came through with the right frosting recipe.

A million thanks to Debby Sachs and Sally Steinberg for their input and faith. To Miriam Sachs for her help with proofreading. To Howard Shapiro and Allan MacDougall for the words and music. To Germaine Gaudet, Katherine Ashenfelder, and Diane Dorfman, who kept the home fires burning and the baby marauder occupied. To Kim Stephens, who tamed the Apple and to Ralph and Audrey Wagner of Micro-Source Financial, who found me a printer that fit.

To Bob Kinkead and Ann Sullivan, who taught me most of what I know about food that isn't chocolate, and to Michael Apstein, who taught me how to say, "This is good, can I please have more?" in sixteen languages.

To my friends in the Women's Culinary Guild.

To Bill Primavera and Jay White of the Culinarians, who took a chance on an unknown.

To Bob Chadbourne, Bill LaPete, Paula Gross, Sandy Rivlin, and Rick Hornick, my photographers, who have the talent of Steichen and the patience of saints.

To Mel Rosenberg, The Brass Buff, and Around the Corner Antiques for props, and Bailey's of Boston for letting us use their store for pictures.

A very special thanks to both my agent, Helen Rees, and to all my new friends at Little, Brown and Company — especially my editor, Mary Tondorf-Dick, copyeditor Jean Crockett Ritchie, and art director Char Lappan. I would also like to thank Nancy Schwartz, Stephanie Holmes, David Goehring, Doreen DelRosario, Bonnie Sklar, Jacqueline Davey, Alan Fairbanks, and Lori Rowell, all at Little, Brown.

Introduction

Admit it. You saw the title and your heart lurched. Could it be? Is this for real? Eat chocolate and lose weight? With trembling hands you snatched this book off the shelf and feverishly flipped through looking for THE DIET. In *The Complete Scarsdale Medical Diet,* it's on page sixty-three, but Dr. Atkins made you wait until almost the end of his spiel. I hope this won't come as too much of a blow, but you seem to have forgotten that before Weight Watchers and Jane Fonda conspired to make thin "in," the word diet meant something else. According to Mr. Webster, diet means "the usual or regular foods a person eats most frequently," and more to the point, "anything that is habitually provided or partaken of." Maybe to you the word diet means cottage cheese and melba toast. To me it means chocolate layer cake, fudge brownies, and egg creams. While other kids were growing up on pizza and Coke, chili dogs and cheeseburgers, I was eating chocolate. All my life it has been my main ingredient — my passion, my love, and now, my livelihood. All my life I have been on The Chocolate Diet.

You are what you eat. The first time I ever heard that expression I laughed out loud. That's how completely the picture I conjured up in my head tickled my imagination. The possibilities for interpretations are so wonderful and so numerous. Does it mean if you eat beets for dinner you are a beet, or does it mean (philosophically) you think like, or have the outlook and personality of, a beet? Or, practically speaking, are your insides red, or is the chemical makeup or your blood now more akin to a beet's than last night when you ate lime Jell-O and your body took on the physical characteristics of lime Jell-O? Do men who eat lots of beef tend to be more masculine and are people who enjoy champagne more bubbly and sparkling than average? Do citrus lovers have an acid wit and are fish eaters great swimmers? Who knows? The idea that you can take on the characteristics (physical, philosophical, chemical, or personal) of what you eat is fantastic. It is possible to describe your whole life in terms of the food you ate and the subsequent person you became. The result would be a Life Menu of sorts. My Life Menu would go something like this: in my early years I was white bread (crusts off), brownies, chocolate cream pie, ice cream, candy bars, and tuna fish. In my postadolescent and college years I became garlic bread, pizza, spaghetti, hot fudge, chocolate-dipped doughnuts, Coke and chips 'n dip, and tuna fish. I spent my early married period as pumpernickel bagels, beef fondue, Shake 'n Bake, chocolate mousse, and tuna-noodle casserole. Then I became homemade bread, homemade soup, homemade baby food, homeground coffee, and tuna fish. Then I matured into French bread, bisque homard, côte de boeuf, carré d'agneau, haricots verts, and marquise au chocolat, and tuna fish. Right now I am chocolate brioche, chocolate tart, chocolate sponge roll, chocolate fondue, chocolate truffles, chocolate chip soufflé, chocolate cheesecake, chocolate ice cream, and for some relief, tuna fish.

As I look over my Life Menu I am struck by the fact that, while other things made appearances, chocolate (and tuna fish) were the stars. Now, since no sane person is going to buy a book of reminiscences about tuna fish, I will address the major and much-loved ingredient of my personality. If in fact you are what you eat I am a 114-pound bar of bittersweet chocolate.

I love chocolate. I love the way it comes wrapped in thin silvery foil and heavy-grade paper, and the way it is molded into little squares and signed with the manufacturer's name. I love the way it smells and the way it feels in my mouth. I love the fact that the same piece of chocolate has different tastes depending on where in your mouth you eat it. I love the fulfilling and important feeling you get when you eat it. I love the idea of chocolate. It is a special food that fits into no category or niche. It is in a category by itself.

There is, to my mind, no ingredient used in cooking as intensely satisfying and beautifully elegant as chocolate. It imparts a color, flavor, and texture to every recipe in which it is used that proclaim "Here is an important work of art." Its visual properties, its deep luster and gloss are magnificent. A fine chocolate glaze can rival the top of a mahogany Steinway grand piano for beauty.

Wherever I travel to teach, demonstrate, or promote chocolate, people always ask me the same questions: Do I really eat chocolate every day of my life? How do I stay so thin? Why isn't my skin a mess? Do I let my kids eat chocolate? What's my favorite dessert? What's the best chocolate to use? Is my mother a good cook? Where do I get my recipes? Can a dummy make this cake? How did I ever get a job as a chocolate consultant? How can they get a job as a chocolate consultant? I used to give short, straight answers to these questions, but the real answers aren't straight. They are funny, sad, ironic stories about people, places, and feelings. The recipes that accompany these stories are a collection of my all-time favorite chocolate things to eat. Some are my creation, some come from family and friends, and others from well-known cooks and celebrated restaurants. I consider them the chocolate crème de la crème and hope you will find them as inspiring and delicious as I do. Welcome to The Chocolate Diet!

Unless otherwise specified the recipes in this book call for: extra-large eggs, sweet (unsalted) butter, all-purpose flour that is measured after sifting, and unsweetened cocoa powder. While the recipes specify sweet, semisweet, or bittersweet chocolates, all three can be used interchangeably, depending on your taste preference. Unsweetened chocolate, however, cannot be substituted for sweetened chocolate. Some recipes may call for Dutch process cocoa, which simply means that during the processing a small amount of alkali has been added to neutralize the acidity, which makes the cocoa a deeper color and gives a more mellow flavor. I prefer cream cheese from the health food store for cheesecakes. It has fewer additives. I also favor the use of parchment for lining pans instead of wax paper. Sheets and circles of parchment can be purchased in cookware shops and by mail from Maid of Scandinavia, 3244 Raleigh Avenue, Minneapolis, Minnesota 55416 (800) 328-6722. Other suppliers to which I refer quite often are: H. Roth and Sons, 1577 First Avenue, New York, New York 10028 (212) 734-1110 for baking chocolate, whole and ground nuts, extracts, sour cherries, and marzipan. Madame Chocolate, 1940-C Lehigh Avenue, Glenview, Illinois 60025 (312) 729-3330 for many different brands of chocolate. They both have mail-order catalogues. In the back of the book is a listing of some chocolate companies and their addresses. While most will sell only large quantities (five hundred pounds), they can direct you to local sources.

Growing Up Chocolate

*I*t is a very sad fact that due to the bizarre eating habits of my immediate family, my mother was a closet cook. This talented lady had her wondrous culinary skills beaten into submission by a crew that routinely demanded such delicacies as twice-cooked roast beef (twice cooked at tremendous heat to insure that all traces of red had vanished), mashed potatoes — the lumpless variety that could, in a pinch, be used as a substitute for library paste — and hapless green beans and vulnerable peas boiled to the predigested state that nursing homes across the country aspire to. We insisted that everything on the table be cooked to the same nonthreatening color gray. That meant that it was really done. No live organisms or flavors to shock our taste buds out of their comfortably lobotomized state. We thought cocktail franks on frilly toothpicks were the ultimate in gustatory delight. Mom knew what was good, but we were too smart to let her lure us into eating fillet of sole that was cooked for any fewer than fifty minutes or flaccid spaghetti that had anything on it but instantly identifiable tomato sauce. We must have bought ketchup by the case. My brother used its magical corrective power to amend any subtle flaws that appeared on his plate — the dishes with major flaws were returned. Perhaps I am too hard on my family. After all, what was the rest of America eating in the fifties — those days before quiche, white wine, and red peppercorns? I'm sure they ate just like we did. Incinerated hamburgers and hot dogs, lasagne, Swedish meatballs, chicken (except in our house it was tuna) à la king. I always longed to know what Gidget's mother made her and Moondoggie for dinner. Certainly not tuna surprise or meatloaf and gravy.

There existed a very special category of food that transcended the usual insipid fare we forced Mom to dish up: comfort food. These were the dishes that made life worth living on raw, wet wintery days when the slush on the sidewalks leaked over the tops of your boots and soaked your feet, and the bitter wind chafed the back of your legs until they were red and sore. It was the food that made the mumps seem bearable, and the chicken pox less itchy. Eating these dishes made Sunday supper a joy, even though Monday morning and school anxiety loomed large. I know there is a school of thought that associates weight problems with using food for comfort. If they are right, I should weigh five hundred pounds, because during my school years, and to some extent now, the cure for any discomfort, physical or emotional, was dishes like fried salami and eggs served with light rye toast slathered with lots of butter. There should be enough butter to dribble down your chin when you take a bite. If you're ten years old it's okay to wipe your chin on your sleeve. Another great comfort dish (and a classic Sunday-night supper in our house while we listened to "Gunsmoke" and "Have Gun Will Travel" on the radio) was noodles mixed with cottage cheese and sour cream, accompanied by a big glass of ice-cold milk. Always make lots more of this dish than you think you will need. It somehow gets eaten — even cold the next day. The next two dishes made being sick worthwhile. One was bananas and sour cream and the other was hot peaches. You make hot peaches by pouring boiling water over ripe peaches and then peeling off the skins. Slice the peaches and sprinkle a little brown sugar on top. Served with a little heavy cream poured over the top, this is the cure for just about any kind of sore throat, cold, or general malaise.

Several years ago six friends and I got together for a nostalgia dinner. We each brought a dish from our childhoods that represented comfort and security. The menu was a trip in the time machine back to 1956, when there was no such thing as take-out, and fast food was a bologna sandwich on the run. (This bologna sandwich would, of course, have been wrapped in wax paper — Baggies being as futuristic as Cheez Whiz.) The family sat around a well-scrubbed speckled yellow formica table with metal trim, on yellow plastic-covered chairs that stuck to the back of your legs when you sat too long. Every time I have my legs waxed I think of those chairs. I remember how the table was too high to maneuver my knife and fork to cut the meat and the chair too heavy to move away from the table without a lot of notice from my parents when I tried to make the great escape before I had joined the Clean Plate Club. The nostalgia menu was fabulous: hot canned crab and Hellmann's Mayonnaise dip on Saltines for a little nosh before dinner, then a halved avocado filled with Kraft's French Dressing. This was followed by two extraordinary casseroles: one a delectable combination of spaghetti, tomato soup, canned shrimp, and bread crumbs; the other was the old classic, frozen green beans and cream of mushroom soup topped with canned onion rings. We also had chipped beef on toast, and meatballs cooked in (brace yourself) grape jelly — I think they were supposed to be sweet and sour. Our centerpiece was a magnificent lime-green Jell-O mold in the shape of a shamrock. It was layered with miniature marshmallows and maraschino cherries and garnished with rosettes of whipped cream, not Cool Whip. The ultimate travesty was dessert; I made mock apple pie from the back of the Ritz Cracker box. We washed the meal down with Dr. Brown's Celery Tonic and Chocolate Egg Creams.* When I brought some of the leftovers home, my children wanted to know why I didn't cook "this great stuff" all the time. I told them that they had their own nostalgia food — SpaghettiOs, Granola Bars, and Chocolate-Dipped Frozen Bananas.*

While Mom never gave up trying to get us to appreciate the finer foods in life (she once made cream of peanut soup, but managed to spill the entire tureen betwixt stove and table), she never had to do any arm-twisting to get us to gobble down her desserts. They were almost without exception masterful in conception and brilliant in execution. I learned my love of chocolate at the hand of a world-class savant. She would whip up delicacies like Chocolate Chip Cookies,* crisp and tender and full of butter and pecans and real pieces of chocolate, and Chocolate Cream Pies* with crusts so fragile and flaky it was hard to keep it on your fork, and filling so rich and chocolatey smooth that when it glided down your throat and into your stomach you felt like the wealthiest and certainly the most important person in the world. It caused your throat to say to your stomach, "Watch out, old buddy, something serious is coming your way." This amazing chocolate cream pie was my special birthday treat. It was always made in the same (enormous by necessity) Pyrex pie plate. The famous flaky crust (with a really thick thumb-dented roll around the top edge of the plate) was filled right to the brim with homemade chocolate pudding (mousse was at that time something that roamed the forests of Maine). Mom always waited until just before serving time to whip the cream for the top of the pie. She did it in a glass bowl, white on the inside and yellow on the outside. The bowl was chilled, as was the eggbeater she used. She would let me start beating (I'd have to kneel on a stool to reach), and when my knees and arms got tired, she'd take over. She would turn the handle of the eggbeater furiously fast for thirty seconds and then switch hands. Cream would spray out of the bowl and land in tiny white droplets on our faces and all over the counter. In those pre-ultrapasteurized days it was never a given that the cream would whip, so we would hold our breath until it was just possible to see the cream thickening at the sides of the bowl and lines on its surface left by the whirling eggbeater. Mom would let me beat slowly while she added a few table-spoons of sugar and a capful of vanilla. Then she would scrape the whipped cream onto the pie and, using a rubber spatula (which, in the tradition of Alexander Portnoy, I always thought was the Yiddish word for rubber scraper), dip and swirl the cream into place. We had to act fast now because the skinny birthday candles would sink up to their wicks in the whipped cream. They leaned at crazy angles as we rushed to light them before they were swallowed up. As the birthday girl, I was allowed to eat as many pieces as I wanted — I believe five was my record — washed down, until the age of seventeen when I discovered the wonders of coffee with chocolate, with several tall glasses of ice-cold milk. I have been hard-pressed in my adult life to come up with as delicious and satisfying a birthday treat.

Another tradition in our house was to invite my current grammar-school teacher to lunch. This auspicious occasion usually took place in May and was the focus of much attention and nervous energy on my part. Every time I see the bumper sticker that says "Question Authority," I wish that someone had suggested it to me in grade school. To me the teacher (principal, school secretary, custodian — any school-related employee) was an undisputed power in my life. So cowed and awed was I by their position that they could have told me to eat chalk and I would have. To have a personage such as this eating in my house with just my mother and me as company was tremendously anxiety-producing. I was torn between wanting something I never got in school, the undivided attention of this person whom I held in such high esteem, and the fear that this divine creature would exhibit some horrible human frailty like having to use the bathroom. The prospect of instantly elevated status among my peers was the overriding motivation. I got to report back to them every minute detail of the event. What did the teacher and I talk about when we walked to my house? What did she say to my mother (about me)? Did she drink milk or coffee? Did she remember to put her napkin on her lap? Did she eat everything? Did she have seconds? And, most important of all, did she go to the bathroom? I like to think that the pressure on the poor teacher was monstrous.

We always had the same menu. Good thing I was promoted every year because if we had had to have one teacher back twice we would have been in real trouble. We ate tuna salad sandwiches (Bumble Bee of course) with little bits of chopped celery and lots of mayonnaise (Mom held the onion in case the teacher needed to kiss someone right after lunch) on black (pumpernickel, if you will) bread with optional iceberg lettuce and sliced tomatoes. We also had coleslaw, Kosher dill pickle spears and three-bean salad, real lemonade for me, and iced coffee for the grown-ups. You may wonder at the lack of sophistication in this menu. Please understand that the aforementioned were my very favorite foods in the entire world — should my revered teacher eat anything less than what I considered the best? Also, keep in mind that we had about forty minutes to chow down this delicious repast — this was school lunch hour, after all.

Ah, dessert. Here was a real treat, simple as could be and (at least to the mind of a little kid dying to impress her teacher) delectably scrumptious. It was the

Famous Chocolate Refrigerator Roll* from the back of the Nabisco Famous Chocolate Wafers box. The combination of semifrozen whipped cream and chocolate cookies was, and still is, unbeatable.

The teacher was sent back to school with a generous goodie bag filled with my mother's Famous Fudge Squares.* Our selection of dishes and the lunchtime ambience must have made the grade because we never had a teacher who either declined the invitation or failed to treat me with a little more respect after eating at our house.

Chocolate Egg Cream

The recipe for an egg cream is sort of a touchy subject. First of all, you are put upon to explain to the uninitiated that there are no eggs in egg creams. Then you have to come to grips with the fact that everybody who makes egg creams makes them their own way, and no two ways are exactly alike. I suspect I'll be deluged with letters from outraged New Yorkers who, upon having read my recipe for egg creams, will question everything from my intelligence to my sanity. Well, remember, even though I live in Boston, I was once a New Yorker. I didn't learn how to make egg creams from a correspondence course. I learned from an old guy who ran a newsstand/candy store on Broadway between Eighty-first and Eighty-second streets. So, if you don't like this version, take it up with him.

First you get a tall glass. The taller the glass, the more chocolate egg cream you get to make. Into the bottom of the glass pour a couple of fingers of Fox's U-Bet Chocolate Syrup. Yes, yes, yes. You may substitute if you can't find Fox's U-Bet, but bear in mind, it won't be authentic. After you finish pouring the syrup, check to see if anyone's looking, then lick the syrup that has dripped down the side of the jar. Next, fill the glass a little more than halfway with cold milk. DO NOT use skim milk. Now, this is the part that takes a little coordination: you will also need a long-handled spoon and a seltzer bottle. A seltzer bottle is not a bottle of Perrier or Canada Dry Sparkling Water. It's that big glass bottle that weighs a ton that takes cartridges in the top and has a handle that squirts out seltzer water. You definitely need a seltzer bottle to make egg creams. Okay. Long-handled spoon in one hand, seltzer bottle in the other. Squirt a healthy blast of seltzer into the glass and quick as a bunny stir like mad with the spoon. So, what are you waiting for? You did a great job! Drink, already.

Chocolate-Dipped Frozen Bananas

This delicious confection makes a wonderful child's birthday party treat.

SERVES 8

4 large, firm bananas
12 ounces semisweet or milk chocolate
  chips
¼ cup solid vegetable shortening
Approximately 1½ cups of one or more
  of the following toppings:
Sweetened flaked coconut, lightly
  toasted

Toasted hazelnuts, chopped
White Toblerone bar, chopped
Reese's Peanut Butter Cup,
  chopped
Chocolate sprinkles

Halve the bananas crosswise and stick a thin wooden dowel or chopstick halfway into the flat cut side of each piece. Place the bananas on a wax paper–lined cookie sheet and freeze them for 20 minutes.

Melt the chocolate chips together with the shortening either in a glass bowl in the microwave oven or in a small metal bowl set over a pan of gently simmering water. Stir with a whisk until the mixture is melted and very smooth. Allow it to cool slightly.

Spread one third of the topping or toppings of your choice onto another wax paper–covered cookie sheet.

Dip the bananas one at a time in the chocolate, using a rubber spatula to coat them entirely. Allow the chocolate coating to begin to set (30 seconds–1 minute) before rolling the bananas in the topping spread on the cookie sheet. Freeze until ready to serve. Let the bananas thaw for 2 minutes before serving.

Mom's Chocolate Chip Cookies

MAKES 48–52 COOKIES

¾ cup (1½ sticks) unsalted butter
1 cup dark brown sugar, firmly packed
½ cup granulated sugar
¼ cup water
1 extra-large egg
2 teaspoons vanilla extract
1 cup all-purpose flour, measured after
  sifting
½ teaspoon salt

1 teaspoon cinnamon
½ teaspoon baking soda
½ teaspoon cloves
1½ cups (8 ounces) semisweet
  chocolate chips
1 cup pecans or walnuts (5–6 ounces),
  broken into large pieces
3 cups quick-cooking oats

Preheat the oven to 350 degrees with the rack in the center position of the oven. Grease three cookie sheets with vegetable shortening. Either by hand or in an electric mixer on low speed, cream the butter, sugars, egg, water, and vanilla. Add the rest of the ingredients. Use a soupspoon to form mounds set 1 inch apart on the prepared cookie sheets. Bake 12–15 minutes, turning the rack once back to front during the baking. Remove from cookie sheet immediately to cool on a rack.

If you find the bottoms of the cookies are burning, use two baking sheets, one on top of the other.

Famous Chocolate Refrigerator Roll

SERVES 12

1 teaspoon vanilla extract
2 cups heavy cream, whipped, or 1
  (8-ounce) container frozen whipped
  topping, thawed

1 package Nabisco Famous Chocolate
  Wafers
Chocolate curls (optional)

Stir vanilla extract into whipped cream or frozen whipped topping; spread 1½ to 2 cups on wafers; put wafers together in stacks of 4 or 5. On serving platter, stand stacks on edge to make one roll; frost with remaining whipped cream or topping. Chill 4 to 6 hours. Or, freeze until firm; cover with plastic wrap. Thaw 1 hour in refrigerator before serving. If desired, garnish with chocolate curls.

To serve:

Slice diagonally at 45-degree angle.

Famous Ice Cream Roll

This version of the Famous Chocolate Refrigerator Roll is made with ice cream and your choice of topping. See end of recipe for a list of suggested ice cream flavors and toppings.

SERVES 8–10

1 package Nabisco Famous Chocolate
  Wafers
2½ pints ice cream, softened slightly
1½ cups heavy cream, whipped with 2
  tablespoons sugar and 1 teaspoon
  vanilla extract
Garnish

Tear off a 2-foot piece of heavy-duty aluminum foil and place 6 chocolate wafers end to end in a line down the center of the foil. Use an ice cream scoop to place a small amount of ice cream on top of each wafer. Press another row of wafers on top of the ice cream. Repeat with the remaining ice cream and wafers, ending with a row of wafers. Use a rubber spatula to smooth any ice cream that has oozed out onto the sides of the roll. Wrap the foil tightly around the roll, twist the ends, and freeze the roll for at least 3 hours.

One or two hours before serving unwrap the roll and place it on a serving platter. Frost with the whipped cream, sprinkle with the garnish, and refreeze until ready to serve.

Ice cream and garnish suggestions:

Pistachio ice cream, unsalted pistachio nuts, chopped

Mint chocolate chip ice cream, chocolate-covered mints

Strawberry ice cream, strawberry sauce, and fresh strawberry slices

Chocolate ice cream, hot fudge sauce, and chocolate sprinkles

Butter almond ice cream, slivered almonds, toasted

Coffee ice cream, chocolate coffee beans

Mom's Chocolate Cream Pie

To make a pie crust as flaky and delicious as Mom's, it's important not to overwork it. The crust will be very crumbly and barely hold together. Don't be tempted to mash it to make it stick.

SERVES 8

For a single 10-inch crust:

1 egg yolk
1 tablespoon white vinegar
Ice water
2 cups all-purpose flour, unsifted

1 tablespoon sugar
½ teaspoon salt
¾ cup solid vegetable shortening

In a small bowl combine the egg yolk, the vinegar, and about 2 tablespoons of ice water. The total liquid mixture should not exceed ⅓ cup. Mix the dry ingredients in a large bowl and cut in the vegetable shortening — preferably with a pastry cutter or two forks. The mixture should resemble coarse meal. Slowly dribble the liquid into the mixture while incorporating with a fork. With the hands, work into a ball, cover with plastic wrap, and chill one hour.

Preheat the oven to 450 degrees with the rack in the center of the oven. On a lightly floured board, roll out the dough and place it in the pie plate. The easiest way to do this is to fold the dough in half and then in quarters, then lift it into the plate and unfold it. Crimp the edges. To bake, cover the pastry with foil and place pie weights or beans on the foil. Bake 6 minutes with the foil on, then remove the foil and bake another 6 minutes. The crust should be well browned — check for unbaked spots before removing from the oven. Cool completely before adding the filling.

For the filling:

4 extra-large egg yolks
1 scant cup granulated sugar
4 tablespoons all-purpose flour
1 ounce (three tablespoons) cornstarch
4 ounces semisweet chocolate, chopped

2 ounces unsweetened chocolate, chopped
1 teaspoon vanilla extract
2½ cups milk

For the garnish:

1 cup heavy cream
3 tablespoons confectioners' sugar
1 teaspoon vanilla extract

Grated chocolate
Maraschino cherries (optional)

In a small bowl mix the egg yolks, sugar, flour, and cornstarch, adding one or two tablespoons of milk just to make a paste.

Scald the remaining milk and add it to the egg/flour mixture.

Place this mixture in a saucepan and whisk constantly at medium heat until it begins to boil and thicken. Cook for one minute. Taste a bit to make sure the flour taste is gone.

Off the heat, add the chocolate and vanilla and stir until the chocolate melts and is incorporated.

Pour the filling into the prepared crust and refrigerate.

To serve:

Whip the heavy cream with the confectioners' sugar and vanilla. Smooth on top of the cooled filling.

For added decoration, grate chocolate on top. If the birthday person is under 10, also add maraschino cherries.

Mom's Fudge Squares

We used to call these fudge blocks — so rich and dense were they. They were the perfect marriage of brownie and fudge.

It's better to do these by hand — not in a mixer.

For the squares:

1 stick (4 ounces) sweet (unsalted) butter at room temperature	¼ teaspoon baking powder
1 cup granulated sugar	2 ounces unsweetened chocolate, melted
1 extra-large egg	½ cup milk
1 cup all-purpose flour	1 teaspoon vanilla extract
	½ cup walnuts, chopped

Preheat the oven to 350 degrees with the rack in the center position. Butter an 8 x 8-inch pan.

Cream the butter with the sugar and the egg. Add the sifted dry ingredients and then the melted chocolate. Do not overbeat. Add the milk, vanilla, and nuts, stirring just to blend. Bake 30 minutes. While the squares are baking, prepare the frosting.

For the frosting:

2 tablespoons instant coffee	1 ounce unsweetened chocolate, melted
¼ cup boiling water	1 teaspoon vanilla extract
1 generous cup confectioners' sugar	
1 tablespoon sweet (unsalted) butter at room temperature	

Dissolve the instant coffee in the boiling water. In a medium-sized mixing bowl combine the sugar, butter, chocolate, and vanilla. Stir in the coffee.

Remove the squares from the oven and let them sit at room temperature for 5 minutes; then pour the frosting over the squares and let them cool completely before cutting.

Ice Cream

When I was a child, ice cream was a treat that wasn't taken for granted as it is today. We never kept ice cream in our house. It was something one went "out" to get and then only on a very hot summer Sunday afternoon. It was the reward for enduring something my parents euphemistically called "a little drive." Talk about hell on wheels. . . . Since these excursions predated air conditioning or rear windows that opened, or that were at least low enough for a very short child to see out of, the ordeal held all the appeal of crossing the Sahara in a coat closet. One of the luxuries that our 1949 Pontiac did have was a radio. This caused a great deal of in-transit conflict because my brother and I wanted to listen to "The Shadow" and "Johnny Dollar," but Dad wanted to hear the ball game or the opera. Tremendous fights would ensue involving great rivers of tears, angry pouting, and kicking the back of the front seat on the kids' part, and aggravated yelling and idle threats (the standard mode of discipline in our house) on Dad's part. Mostly Dad and *Aida* won, and it was many years before I could attend the opera without somehow feeling that I had lost an important battle. However, on rare occasions (when it was an opera that Dad didn't really love or the Red Sox were getting schlonged), we got to listen to our hero's announcer ask, "Who knows what evil lurks in the hearts of men?" When he said in his deliciously lugubrious voice, "The Shadow knows," I got chills up and down my spine.

There wasn't really a tremendous selection of ice cream places. Perhaps there were three good ones, so of course none of us could agree on which one to go to. More cause for conflict (at five hundred decibels). A driver's license not only makes it legal for a person to zip around in an automobile — it also makes that person the supreme ice cream parlor chooser. One could marginally influence

Dad's decision by either being really obnoxious, threatening insanity, fits, car sickness, etc., if you didn't get your choice ("BUT, I NEEEEED IT," delivered in a practiced whine, was the stock phrase), or by making your sibling cast his vote for your choice by giving him a swift and deadly nuggie in his upper arm.

My all-time favorite place was called Judy's. It was located fifteen miles out of town on a lovely New England country road lined with severe, white Congregational churches and well-kept village greens, usually sporting a war memorial or a gazebo for band concerts, or perhaps a tiny duck pond.

Judy's was an unassuming free-standing little brown wood building with a tiny porch in front. Inside was a counter with red vinyl stools that spun around with a grinding screech and afforded an industrious child a dizzying ride. It was quite a few years before my legs were long enough to reach the ground to push off to a full spin. I had to be content with the momentum I got by pushing my palms against the counter with my arms held straight out. Every once in a while I got a really good send-off and would shut my eyes tight while I spun around. I tried to guess which wall of the restaurant I was facing before I opened my eyes. This was not a big place as ice cream parlors go. There was just one room plus a little alcove. The walls were knotty pine, as were the booths that lined them, and the windows had white country curtains and lots of big dead flies caught inside the screens. There were several tables in the middle of the room, but the best place to sit was at one of those booths so you could play "Love Me Tender" and "Tammy" on the jukebox. The seats, like the stools, were covered with red vinyl, which was mended in places with a slightly different color red Mystic Tape that had begun to peel up around the edges and expose its sticky underside. The menus were a single page covered with thick, yellowed plastic edged with a thin strip of black cloth, stained with countless flavors of ice cream, and sticky with butterscotch and hot fudge. While we were waiting for the waitress to take the orders I made it a point to check that the hundreds of pieces of used gum were still stuck to the underside of the table. I remember the revulsion I felt when I first discovered them and tried to imagine who could be so crude and unmannerly to do something this vulgar to a place I considered one stop short of paradise. I recall wanting to tell on these criminals — but I didn't want to be the one to let the waitress know — what if she got really upset and screwed up our order so that I ended up with marshmallow (yuck) instead of whipped cream? I kept the grim secret, hoping the management would discover it on their own. And I made it a habit never to chew gum at Judy's lest they think I was the culprit.

I always ordered the same thing: hot fudge sundae with Peppermint Stick Ice Cream,* whipped cream, and nuts. As much as I loved their chocolate ice cream, the combination of hot fudge and peppermint always won out. Since one of my parents usually got a chocolate cone and let me have lots of licks, I had the best of both worlds. My brother favored strawberry milk shakes. My ice cream came in a regulation thick-sculpted glass sundae dish. The sundae maker at Judy's was an artist. No hot fudge dripping down over the sides here. There was a respectable ratio of ice cream to hot fudge so that you didn't run out of one before you were finished eating the other. The hot fudge, which was spooned both in the bottom of the dish and over the two generous scoops of ice cream, was really hot so that it melted part of the ice cream when it was poured on top. This meant I didn't have to wait too long and mush too much to get ice cream soup—the desired consistency. The ice cream itself was pink in color with tiny bits of hard green peppermint candy throughout. (Preppy before its time.) It was creamy rich and so smooth. The peppermint flavor came across loud and clear, fresh and clean. The combination of those flavors and the deep, dark soulfulness of the hot fudge was like a perfect marriage arranged by a matchmaker blessed with tremendous sensitivity. The whipped cream was squirted out of a stainless steel pressurized can in a tidy, but generous, rosette. Chopped (unsalted) pecans were sprinkled on the whipped cream and a plump, juicy maraschino cherry (not the puny cocktail kind) with a long stem went on the very top. The trick in eating this masterpiece was to gently dig down into the glass and extract a spoon laden with all the ingredients: ice cream, hot fudge, whipped cream, and nuts. Of course, unless the person making the sundae had gone berserk with the nuts, you would run out of chopped pecans first. I ate my sundae very slowly (aggravating my father to no end—he seemed to inhale his ice cream cone so that it was gone before I had even finished my cherry), hoping that the ice cream would melt by itself and I wouldn't have to start "playing with it," as my mother disdainfully termed the maneuvering I did with my long-handled spoon to make ice cream into "soup." Now that I have children who love to do the same thing to their ice cream I can understand how it made my mother crazy.

No matter how careful I was about trying to deliver the ice cream directly into my mouth from the spoon I always ended up with two dubious dessert dividends that occupied my interest for the entire ride home. One was a chocolate mustache that my mother instructed me to wipe off my face. It seemed that no matter how vigorously I applied my napkin, the back of my wrist, and my tongue, there always remained a tiny vestige of chocolate on my mouth. It seemed to love me as much as I loved it. The other problem was sticky hands. I hated sticky hands. No matter how small the amount of stickiness I would obsess about it. Licking it off made it worse. Rubbing with a napkin made the paper stick to my skin. I would marvel at my parents. Not only could they manage to eat and drink and not get their faces dirty, they never seemed to get sticky hands. My hysterical pleas for a pit stop went unheeded. Since my parents never had the sticky hands problem they couldn't begin to know what agony it was for me to endure the ride home in the sweltering car with fingers that stuck to each other and had to be peeled apart.

Today when you shop for ice cream you have to chose between generic and designer brands. You all know the difference. The generic you get in the supermarket. It comes in a half-gallon rectangular box and has one of those perforated pull strips that are supposed to make it easy to open the lid but never work quite right and the entire side of the box gets ripped open in the frenzy to get at the ice cream. The corners usually leak and the top of the box has a strange and inedible skim on it — actually you can scrape this skim off with your upper teeth but once you get it in your mouth you tend to want to spit it out. A typical generic flavor is vanillachocolatestrawberry. With your eyes closed it is absolutely impossible to tell one flavor from the other. When generic ice cream melts you are left not with a puddle of flavored liquid but an insipid pool of foam. This is because of a dubious invention called "overrun," which is the process of pumping air into the ice cream while it is being churned and frozen. You are left with the visual impression that you have more ice cream than you really do.

Designer ice cream, on the other hand, comes in cylindrical heavy-duty cardboard or plastic containers that are just short of one pint. There is usually Danish writing on the back, plus a map of some Scandinavian country, even though the product is made in the Bronx. The lids fit snugly down and around the top of the carton and the ice cream stuck to the top of the lid is easy to lick off and is downright tasty. A typical flavor would be Bananarumhazelnut, or Intensely Coffee. The real giveaway of designer ice cream is that it is impossible to serve it directly from the freezer (as opposed to generic, which one could scoop with a used Dixie Cup). People who can't bear to wait are given to running the serving spoon under scalding water before trying to scoop. Manufacturers of this kind of ice cream have the good sense to leave the air out, which, of course, accounts for its dense consistency.

Another kind of ice cream, which I like to refer to as the Down-Home variety, is manufactured in old-fashioned ice cream churns set (along with all that unsightly prerequisite rock salt) in storefronts of affluent communities all across the country, where they happily grind away, sounding like a root canal in progress. This is the place where endlessly long lines of salivating ice cream lovers get to revert back to their early childhoods through a custom called "mix-ins." This involves taking perfectly delicious usually naturally flavored high-quality (not to mention high-priced) ice cream and making a mishmash by adding stuff like broken bits of Reese's Peanut Butter Cups, Oreo cookies, nuts, M & M's, coconut, chopped Heath Bar, and the like. Now, this is an idea that I think should have surfaced years ago. This conglomeration is then topped by any number of sauces (hot fudge being, of course, the best) and REAL whipped cream made with cream from a real cow.

***

The real curse of middle age is that an almost forty-year-old body doesn't incinerate calories quite as effectively as a twelve-year-old body. So, with great reluctance, I've had to start to limit my intake. It helps not to keep ice cream in the house. See how things tend to go full circle? When I want great ice cream I usually make it myself, and as I lick the last bit of hot fudge scraped from the very bottom of the dish, I think longingly of Judy's.

The Good Humor Man

Every day at four o'clock
I hear a tinkling bell,
And then I know that soon I'll see
The Face I love so well.

Fifteen cents is all it costs
To see my heart's desire.
I'm going broke, but what the heck!
He sets my soul on fire.

Whatever do I see in him?
Heaven only knows.
Perhaps it is his teasing eyes.
Perhaps his sunburnt nose.

Now at last I see him —
White uniform, deep tan.
I guess everybody knows it:
I love the Good Humor Man.

L.A.B. 1963

In 1963 every girl in my high school was in love with Frankie Avalon and Conway Twitty. I had the hots for the Good Humor man. They went to record hops and waited for boys to ask them to dance to "At the Hop" and "Put Your Head on My Shoulder." I hung out on street corners waiting to hear the familiar bell and to catch sight of the square white truck. I must admit that I fell in love with Toasted Almonds and Chocolate Malts (two delicious kinds of Good Humor bars) and then the infatuation spread to the supplier of these treats. I guess it was like a heroin addict falling in love with her pusher. His name was Joe and he was a football player at the state university. He was terrifically good-looking — tall and broad-shouldered with a strong, rugged Italian face, deep brown eyes, an as yet unbroken nose that was always sunburned and peeling, long black eyelashes, dimpled chin, beautiful skin, gorgeous teeth, unruly black curls, and the sweetest shy smile — much too good-looking ever to be interested in old tomboy me. He was dressed completely in white, from his official Good Humor jacket to his white bucks — the Dr. Kildare of the ice cream set. All the girls at school had noticed him too, and were beginning to take precious time away from their gum-wrapper chains and Bobby Rydell fan club meetings to buy ice cream. Since I knew I didn't have a chance at the pusher I concentrated on the goods, with only a furtive longing glance at Joe. At first I would meet his truck at school, and then after a few weeks (around the time he had begun to notice the girl who faithfully bought two ice cream bars every day and always had the right change) he began to stop at my street corner. Slowly I began to engage him in conversation and before I knew it I was spending large chunks of my afternoons (time that was earmarked for Latin and algebra) lounging against the Good Humor truck, making small talk with the driver.

School got out for the summer and I had to go to work. I seriously considered giving up my job as counselor at a local day camp. The bus got me home at 3:30 and Joe usually came to my street corner at 3:00. The first day of camp I began to suffer withdrawal and separation anxiety even before I got out of bed. My sweet little campers must have thought Attila the Hun was in charge. With heavy heart I boarded the great yellow homebound bus. After a long, hot ride the bus turned the corner of my street — what did I see ? Great Balls of Fire! Parked directly in front of my house (and blocking the driveway, as my father quickly pointed out) was Joe and his Good Humor truck. All that exact change must have paid off. He had rearranged his schedule so that I could have my fix.

It was a blissful summer full of long perfect hot sunny days and mellow and softly agreeable nights. I had the best of both worlds. During the day at camp I could be the head child in charge of lots of little children. Carefree fun was the order of the day. Cutting and pasting crumbly leaves and moss to construction paper, buddy checks, and water balloons, camp fires, and hide-and-seek in the woods were what we lived for. We shouted, we sang, we had tickle fights. But in the bus on the way home I got ready for my other life. That bus was to me what the phone booth was to Clark Kent. Physically I couldn't do too much with what I had. I mostly prepared mentally. I thought of funny things to say, practiced to be more like the kind of grown-up girl I fantasized Joe might want to have a more "serious" relationship with. I can't imagine what I thought the next step could be — a tour of the truck's muffler system? He had taken to spending more and more time parked in front of my house. I would sit on the fender of the truck and we would gab. Actually, he wasn't much of a talker. I would recite all the funny things I had thought of on the bus ride home. Every time he laughed at something I said, I felt like I had scored a touchdown. He said he thought I was really smart. I thought he was the most delicious thing I'd ever seen, but would die before I told him so.

The beautiful days of the summer whizzed by. More and more I found myself wearing my grown-up afternoon personality at camp. One day my braids became a French twist. This change was greeted with extreme hilarity by the other counselors, but with real awe by my six-year-old campers, who said they had never seen anything so fancy in the hair department. There was immediate pressure on me to fix all my little girl campers' hair in that style. I let my stubby nails grow and horrified my mother by sneaking her razor and shaving my legs. "Now, you'll have to do it all the time!" she admonished me. I even went to the extreme of trading in my blue jeans for a skirt and my grubby sneakers for sandals.

By the end of August the conversations on the fender of the Good Humor truck were longer, more relaxed, and involved a bit more than my telling funny stories and his laughing at them. Joe began to talk about going back to college, football, and other strange and unfamiliar things like pep rallies, canteens, and homecoming. College life might have been a ritual that took place on Mars for all I knew about it. The week before school started a truly unexpected thing happened. My Good Humor man asked me out on a real date. To the movies. The date was for Saturday night. Novice that I was I started getting ready on Tuesday. By Saturday afternoon I had worked myself into such a frenzy of anxiety that my parents threatened to put me in the freezer to cool me down. I tried on dozens of outfits — mine, my mother's, and several of my friends' entire wardrobes. He was coming at 8:00. From 5:00 until 7:30 I paced, gargled with mouthwash, checked my face, my clothes, my underarms, to make sure the smell-well was working. I practiced smiling in the mirror, introducing him to my parents, and I agonized about the BIG question: where to sit in the car? Obviously I was going to sit in the front seat. But where in the front seat? In the era before bucket seats the choices were overwhelming. One could hug the door (the passenger door, that is) and run the risk of being thought a real prude. Or you could sit right next to the fellow — thigh to thigh, so to speak, but that was much too pushy for the first date. After all, I didn't want him to think I was fast. There remained this ambiguous area in front of and around the radio (if, please God, he had a radio). There was a very subtle difference between sitting on the volume-knob side of the radio and sitting on the tuning-knob side. When in doubt sit exactly in the middle of both knobs.

At precisely eight o'clock the doorbell rang. I had decided beforehand that I would answer it and spare Joe the disapproving once-over my father was sure to give him in view of the fact that he was (a) my very first real date, (b) four years older than I, (c) in college, (d) sold ice cream for a living, and, finally, (e) wasn't Jewish. I figured a quick (and much practiced) intro would suffice for the parents. When I opened the door I became confused. There stood a shortish boy, hair neatly combed, wearing a brown tweed sports jacket, chinos, and brown tie shoes. In the driveway was a green Valiant. Where the hell was my beloved in white bucks? Where was his boxy white chariot? Who was this guy shuffling shyly, tongue-tied and slightly stoop-shouldered, on my front porch? Since the Good Humor man was the only one who had booked me for this particular Saturday night I figured it must be my hero in disguise. We suffered through a quick parental howdy-do and walked toward his car. I was close to tears. I had been duped. Cheated and bitterly disappointed. I felt like I was on a blind date, sitting (directly in front of the radio) in this unfamiliar car with this stiff and silent boy.

We went to the drive-in to "see" *King Solomon's Mines* with Stewart Granger. In the present era of guilt-free sex I'm not sure what people do at drive-ins. In my day there was really only one thing to do at the drive-in and it wasn't eating popcorn. As we headed into the parking lot I was feeling morose and doubly cheated. I certainly wouldn't have minded going to the make-out mecca with Joe of the white uniform and refrigerated truck, but here I was with this complete stranger who expected me to neck with him. Let me say, at this point, that philosophically I was not opposed to a little practice kissing with a good-looking guy. After all, how many Saturday-night dates had I had before this (only one and that was to a confirmation dance with a boy who was so short that his nose ran on my neck when we danced)? It wouldn't look so bad in my social résumé and it would give me something to gossip about when my more socially advanced girlfriends were bragging about their summer conquests. I have to say, try as I did, the thrill just wasn't there. I had, like so many women before me, fallen for the uniform, not the guy.

Joe went back to college the next day. A rather stout, unkempt fellow, who was taken to chewing smelly black cigars, took over his route. For a long time afterward my heart leapt every time I saw a Good Humor truck, and each time I see an old rerun of *King Solomon's Mines* I think of Toasted Almonds, Chocolate Malts, and Joe the white knight.

Old-Fashioned Peppermint Stick Ice Cream

Months of experimenting, dozens of eggs, pounds of candy, and gallons of heavy cream went into the formulation of this recipe. My family and friends, dedicated lovers of peppermint stick ice cream, begged for relief after the fortieth try. The final results, in my humble opinion, are well worth the thousands of calories consumed and the pounds gained. This is ice cream at its creamy richest and heavenly smoothest. Because the peppermint flavor and the sweetening come from the candy used, it is essential to buy high-quality peppermint candies made with real (not artificial) peppermint extract. I use peppermint pinwheels (hard, round red-and-white candy) purchased from a local candy shop. Candy canes are acceptable if they have a strong enough peppermint taste. Both types of candy are made both with real and artificial flavoring — so be careful when you buy — all you have to do is taste one to know the difference. I made this ice cream in both an Italian "gelati" maker and an American electric White Mountain ice cream machine. The latter made a much more authentic American-type ice cream with a higher overrun (amount of air incorporated), which is really what good old-fashioned peppermint stick ice cream is all about.

MAKES 1 QUART

12 ounces good-quality hard
  peppermint candy (1¾ cups)
1 13-ounce can evaporated milk

4 extra-large egg yolks
2 cups heavy cream

Place the unwrapped candy between two pieces of wax paper and tap each one once with a hammer to break it into several small pieces. Try not to pulverize the candies. Discard the wrappers. Combine 8 ounces (1¼ cups) of the candy with the evaporated milk in a small bowl, reserving the rest of the candy for later. Cover this mixture and refrigerate 8 hours or overnight.

Whisk the egg yolks together with the cream in a small saucepan and cook over low heat, stirring constantly until the mixture thickens slightly and coats the back of a spoon. Strain and cool. Combine the custard with the evaporated milk mixture and process in an ice cream machine. Add the reserved candy when the ice cream is beginning to freeze and hold a shape.

5-Star Hot Fudge

MAKES 3½ CUPS

8 ounces bittersweet chocolate
2 ounces unsweetened chocolate
2 cups heavy cream
½ cup dark brown sugar, firmly packed

3 tablespoons sweet butter, cut into
  small pieces
2–3 tablespoons rum (optional)

Chop both chocolates into small pieces.

Cook the cream in a 1½-quart saucepan until it is reduced by half a cup. This will take approximately 15 minutes over moderate heat. The cream tends to boil over very easily, so watch it closely.

Add the brown sugar and continue to cook until the sugar dissolves.

Remove from heat and add the chopped chocolates, stirring until they melt.

Add the butter and stir until it is melted and incorporated.

Stir in the optional rum.

This sauce will thicken when refrigerated. If it becomes too thick for your taste then reheat it gently in a double boiler or in a microwave oven. It will keep refrigerated for three weeks (depending on the expiration date of the heavy cream you used), or you can freeze it.

You can make a milk chocolate version of this sauce by substituting the same amount of milk chocolate for the bittersweet. If the milk solids separate out when you add the chocolate to the hot cream (the mixture will look curdled), process the mixture for a minute in either a blender or food processor.

Magnolia Street

My father's three sisters and their families lived in a big red two-family house on Magnolia Street in Hartford, Connecticut. My father's parents had lived in this house when they were alive, as did my parents for the first decade of their marriage. The first five years of my life were spent here, and although my memories of this early time are very dim, I can recall feeling well loved and very well fed.

The house was filled with huge pieces of dark-stained mahogany furniture. The sofa and chairs were covered with well-worn, dark green velvet, the kind you could draw lines in with your finger. There was a massive dining room set that consisted of a table that could hold twelve comfortably, a dozen dining room chairs (of which there were never enough when the whole family was gathered for dinner — I always had to sit on the telephone table), and a lowboy that had lots of drawers of all different sizes and depths. What those drawers did hold (aside from the prerequisite silverware, serving pieces, tablecloths, napkins, and other table paraphernalia) were several boxes of Barton's Assorted Chocolates. It usually took me ten seconds from the time I entered the house to sniff out which drawer held the candy. The other extremely memorable pieces of furniture were the little end tables on either side of the couch. They had long, shallow drawers that held several worn and mismatched decks of playing cards that were held together with knotted elastic bands. These were the kids' canasta (and later on, strip poker) cards. The other very important thing this drawer held and that was set on top of the table in a heavy crystal bowl on Wednesday, the adults' bridge night, was bridge mix. Bridge mix was better then. Nowadays when you eat bridge mix you are sure of getting stuck with those boring malt balls and Raisinets instead of peanuts and cashews. It's really tricky trying to dope out what's inside the chocolate covering, but in the Magnolia Street days you could be sure of fishing out at least two peanuts and cashews for every malt ball and Raisinet.

All the houses on the street were two-family arks with large two-decker porches in front. The porches at the street level were open, but the second-story porches were screened and almost every one boasted a behemoth, in the form of a glider sofa, suspended on creaking springs and covered with mildewed floral-patterned vinyl. It didn't smell great, but it did smell familiar and comfortable. Every house had a small front yard with at least one magnolia tree in it. In the early spring, just after the first crocuses and daffodils bloomed, our dowdy street was transformed by these trees into a wondrous fairyland. First, giant white buds appeared almost overnight on the trees. It looked as if an enormous flock of snowy cockatoos had invaded our street and taken up residence in the branches. Then, huge, brilliant white blossoms streaked with pink and maroon opened, releasing a fragrance so sweet and fresh that people walked around with eyes half closed, noses up, sniffing and smiling great broad smiles of relief because spring had come and the world smelled good.

After my father and mother moved to their own apartment, my three aunts and their families continued to live in this house. My aunt Esther, my uncle Leo, and their two children (my favorite cousins) lived on the first floor of the house. My aunt Rose and her husband, Uncle Herman, lived on the second floor, which they shared with my aunt Sarah, who also had a bedroom suite in the converted third-floor attic. I lived for Friday evenings, when my father would drive me over to Magnolia Street, where I would spend the weekend, staying until Sunday afternoon. Oh, how my aunts Sarah and Rose rolled out the red carpet every weekend. First order of business was dinner, which was never anything weird or the least bit threatening. Friday night equaled chicken. Usually roasted, some-times oven fried. Mashed (yum) potatoes with lots of butter and salt and pepper, maybe a few cooked carrots or a string bean or two — not that I would have to eat them if I didn't want to. I never had to eat the chicken skin, either. My aunts gave in to my finickiest gustatory whim — they even cut my meat and buttered my bread for me. Not only that — get this — I got to drink chocolate milk (the real homemade kind) with a straw that bent. Often there was chocolate pudding with whipped cream for dessert, or chocolate ice cream. Or better yet, my uncle Herman would have bought some great junk food like Hostess cupcakes, Devil Dogs, or Twinkies. The fact that my aunts fell all over themselves indulging my fussy eating habits made me impossible to live with at home during the rest of the week. I'm sure the main reason my parents were so delighted to have me spend every weekend away was so that they could have some time off from the responsibility of the care and feeding of Her Royal Highness.

My aunt Sarah never had any children of her own and my aunt Rose's stepson didn't live with her. As a result, their nieces (my cousin Leah and I) were all the more special to them. Because the major portion of their lives was taken up with nonchild-related work, they had almost unlimited patience (well, at least Rose did) and energy for us. When I think back it seems incredible that their entire weekends were devoted to making me think I was the best-loved little girl in the world.

After dinner, Rose and Sarah would wash the dishes and I would help dry them. Then the three of us would snuggle together (wrapped in a dazzling green, orange, purple, and black crocheted afghan) on the sofa and watch TV. The box of Barton's Assorted made an appearance during these periods, and Rose and Sarah were both very good sports about letting me spit out the candies with the jelly or coconut insides.

I always got to stay up hours after my regular bedtime. It wasn't until after the late movie that Sarah and I would go up to the third floor to bed. I loved Sarah's rooms. There was a spotless bathroom that smelled of cleanser and bath oil and shampoo. In the bathroom was a cabinet full of exotic and expensive potions and lotions, makeup, nail polish, oils, perfumes in atomizers with funny bulbs to squeeze, tiny brushes, squat jars full of rich, heavily scented cream with gold foil labels and French writing on them. There was a wonderful black leather, red-trimmed nail kit that closed with a tiny zipper. It contained several different kinds of miniature scissors, a metal nail file, a cuticle stick, and a tube of white stuff to put behind your nails to make them look clean. Underneath was another cabinet full of neatly folded, fluffy pastel-colored towels. Sarah had a living room of sorts, but since she really lived downstairs when she wasn't bathing or sleeping, the room contained only a closet, a bureau, and an ironing board. Her bedroom was furnished with a pair of twin beds and a small bookcase. She slept in the bed near the window and I slept in the bed near the bathroom — just in case. After we got into bed and before we fell asleep we had a special few minutes together. We held hands across the space between the beds and Sarah and I would sing. We would always sing the same songs: "I'm Forever Blowing Bubbles," "Bicycle Built for Two," "Take Me out to the Ballgame," "Mollie Malone," and "The Lorelei." I used to tell her that when I was a grown-up married lady I would have three daughters and name them Daisy, Mollie, and Lorelei.

Our Saturdays were just as much fun. After breakfast (the sugar-fortified cereal my mother refused to buy), I listened to "Junior Miss" on the big Motorola radio, and I would watch Sarah give herself her weekly manicure. She did it with the same care and attention that I'm sure Michelangelo gave the Pietà. Then we would wait for the driver education gentleman to show up. Sarah was in her forties when she decided she wanted to learn how to drive. Because everything she did was first class, she hired a guy from a first-class driver ed school to teach her via private lessons . . . hundreds of private lessons. Every Saturday morning at 10:00, he would pull up in front of the house in his big white Chevy Impala. It was the cleanest car I had ever seen — which was a good thing because being clean was very important to my aunt Sarah. She would be all dressed up when she went down to take her lesson. For a long time the family was sure she had a thing going with the driver ed man. Sarah had a steady Saturday-morning date with this patient gentleman for nearly two years. I believe she failed her first (of many) road test after six months of weekly lessons — that's how long it took her to get up her nerve to take the test. She did get to a point after a year and a half when she felt comfortable taking passengers along on her lesson. I got to ride in the back and eat M & M's and wax bags full of bridge mix. My older cousins ordered me to bring back information about the suspected affair between teacher and pupil, but since I had no idea what to look for, and since I couldn't see over the back of the front seat, my observations were useless. After several years of intense drilling on the fine points of parallel parking, hand signals, and U turns, my aunt (to our great astonishment as well as hers, I am sure) passed her test and received her license. The very next day she went to the local Chevy dealership and bought the exact same white Impala in which she had learned to drive. I don't know if the driver ed man got a commission, but we all agreed that he deserved one.

The rest of Saturday was devoted to the movies. Either I would go with my cousins to the local theater, whereupon en route they would torment me with threats that the Creature from the Black Lagoon had hotfooted it off the movie screen and was lying in wait for me in the bushes up ahead, or better yet, my aunts would take me on the bus to downtown Hartford, where we would have lunch before the movie. I had three favorite places for lunch. The first was the Spaghetti Palace. Here I could have my all-time favorite Italian dish: spaghetti with plain butter sauce, hold the cheese, and Chocolate Tortoni Torte,* a house specialty. My next favorite place was the basement cafeteria of one of the large department stores. They had (and still do) the finest tuna fish sandwiches made outside of my mother's kitchen. They also served fantastic coleslaw. This sumptuous repast was washed down with a cherry Coke. I always had their Brownie Tart à la Mode* for dessert. The third restaurant was visited only rarely because it was in another league from these first two. It was on the third floor of THE department store in Hartford: G. Fox. It was called the Connecticut Room, and until I was really grown up and on my own, it was one of the fanciest places I had ever eaten in. We usually ate there once a year around Christmastime, so that we could combine a special lunch with a tour of the beautiful Christmas decorations in the store's windows. It was a very special treat for me. I remember the good-natured (imagined, probably) hustle bustle of the holiday shoppers, and the smell of snow in the air. I remember when it got really cold waiting for the bus to take us into town, my aunt Rose would stand in back of me, open her fur coat, and wrap me up inside with her. At the entrance of the Connecticut Room there was a little desk for the hostess and a velvet rope suspended between two stanchions, behind which a long line of ladies, standing in groups of twos and threes, shopping bags in arm, would wait for their tables. My aunt Sarah (whose compulsiveness and hatred of being kept waiting I am delighted to have inherited) always had a reservation, so, like royalty, we swept to the front of the line, and amid the glowering looks of the hungry waiting ladies, were seated right away. The room was large and very elegant with lots of black marble that was accented by the pink linen tablecloths and napkins. There were heavy cut quasi-crystal water goblets that required (at least on my part) two hands to lift. The waitresses always recognized my aunts and that made me feel tremendously important. As much as they implored me, my aunts could not get me to waver one iota from my set menu. I would have a tuna fish sandwich (and what a fancy sandwich it was, made with decrusted thin white toast cut into four squares with a tiny frilly toothpick stuck into each square). With the sandwich I would drink a Shirley Temple that the bartender would decorate with several maraschino cherries. Naturally, the best part was dessert: a big dish of the creamiest, richest Chocolate Ice Cream* in the world. The little princess was in heaven.

I loved going to the movies in town with my aunts. We always went to first-run shows. Some of them were a little racier than my parents would have liked; once my aunts took me to see *Cat on a Hot Tin Roof*. I was ten at the time and was bored to death for most of it, but I did manage to wait till we got home and the whole family was around to ask what Paul Newman and Elizabeth Taylor were going to do in bed after the movie ended. Even though we had just had a substantial lunch my aunts always stopped at Fannie Farmer's to buy a pound of dark chocolate almond bark and several pieces of chocolate walnut fudge for us to eat during the movie. We usually went to the Strand Theater, which had red velvet seats and the biggest screen I had ever seen. When the witch from *Snow White* looked in her magic mirror and cackled her terrible laugh it was doubly scary because she looked about as big as the Empire State Building. If the movie was a sad one (like *The Red Shoes*) we would all cry together while we munched, and if the movie was a happy, exciting one (like *An American in Paris*) we would laugh and munch. If the movie was particularly scary or had really scary parts we somehow consumed the candy much faster. We wiped out all the almond bark during the "Night on Bald Mountain" part of *Fantasia*.

As the three of us rode the homebound bus at the end of the afternoon we talked about our favorite movie stars. I always wanted to grow up to be Elizabeth Taylor or Audrey Hepburn or Margaret O'Brien. My aunts always wanted to marry men like Tyrone Power and Cary Grant. I think my aunt Rose really lucked out because my uncle Herman does bear a striking resemblance to Cary Grant.

None of us was hungry for a real dinner so we usually had some comfort food like Campbell's cream of tomato soup and Milk Crackers and butter, or macaroni and cheese. Saturday night we had a standing date with Matt Dillon and Kitty, Chester and Doc. And then to bed.

Sunday mornings meant sleeping late, reading the funnies (without having to fight with my brother over who would get the page with Dick Tracy first), and Aunt Rose's famous soft scrambled eggs, pumpernickel toast with sweet whipped butter and raspberry jam, homemade hot chocolate,* and great-smelling Maxwell House coffee for the grown-ups. After breakfast I would crawl under the dining-room table and read. My aunts kept assuring me that I would ruin my eyes reading in the dark, but given the genetic makeup of my extended family the damage had been done prenatally, and reading in the dim, warm comfort of my special place couldn't have made much difference. If it was summertime I would read on the screened-in porch while swinging back and forth on the glider sofa. From the sofa's bowels and underpinning came high-pitched squeaks and low grinding groans that were repeated with monotonous regularity with each movement back and forth. The noises never bothered me, so immersed was I in the latest adventures of the Bobbsey Twins and Nancy Drew.

My glorious weekends came to an end when my father picked me up in the afternoon. I was silent and a little grumpy on the ride home. The trip back to reality is usually tough. He would always ask, "So, what did you do this week-end?" I would always reply, "Nothing." There was just no way to put into words all the joy and warmth and feeling of being completely loved that my aunts filled me with every weekend. I think he understood.

Brownie Tart à la Mode

SERVES 8–10

For the tart:

12 ounces semisweet chocolate, cut into small pieces	⅓ cup plus two tablespoons flour, measured after sifting
3 tablespoons sweet (unsalted) butter	¼ teaspoon baking powder
3 extra-large eggs	6 ounces pecans, coarsely chopped
1 cup sugar	6 ounces semisweet chocolate,
1 teaspoon vanilla extract	chopped into medium-sized chunks

Preheat the oven to 350 degrees with the rack in the center position. Butter a deep 10-inch pie pan. It's helpful to use a glass pie plate, so you can see if the bottom is getting too brown.

In a small metal bowl set over a saucepan full of gently simmering water, melt the chocolate and butter together, stirring occasionally until the two are blended and smooth. Remove from heat to cool slightly.

In the large bowl of an electric mixer, beat the eggs and sugar until the mixture is light and fluffy. Add the vanilla.

Sift the flour together with the baking powder and fold it into the egg/sugar mixture. Mix only until blended.

Fold in the nuts and the chocolate chunks. Spread into the prepared pie plate and bake for 30 minutes. The batter will completely fill the pie plate, but won't overflow into your oven. Do not overbake. Cool, but do not refrigerate.

To serve:

Cut the pie into wedges, place a scoop of your favorite ice cream on top (with this dessert, mine's peppermint stick), and top with the following hot fudge sauce:

SERVES 8

6 ounces bittersweet chocolate, cut into small pieces	½ cup sugar
3 tablespoons sweet (unsalted) butter	2 tablespoons light corn syrup
1¼ cups milk	1 teaspoon vanilla extract

Place the chocolate and butter together in a small bowl set over gently simmering water. Stir until they melt. Mix the milk and sugar together in a medium-sized saucepan. Cook over moderate heat, stirring with a wire whisk, until the milk begins to simmer and the sugar dissolves completely. Reduce the heat to low and add the melted chocolate and butter and the corn syrup. Continue to cook over low heat, stirring constantly for several more minutes. Add the vanilla off the heat. Cool slightly.

Chocolate Tortoni Torte

This long, low, rectangular loaf has three chocolate sponge layers surrounding a creamy toasted coconut and almond filling.

SERVES 8–10

For the layers:

8 extra-large eggs at room temperature, separated	1 cup sugar
10 ounces semisweet chocolate, chopped	⅔ cup ground almonds
	1 teaspoon almond extract

Preheat the oven to 350 degrees with the rack in the center position. Cover a heavy-duty jelly-roll pan measuring approximately 17 x 11 inches with a sheet of parchment. Melt the chocolate in a small bowl set over a pan of gently simmering water. Stir, and when melted set aside to cool slightly. In the large bowl of an electric mixer beat the egg yolks with ½ cup of the sugar until they are very thick and light-colored. Stir in the almonds, the chocolate, and the almond extract. In a separate bowl beat the egg whites, slowly adding the remaining ½ cup of sugar. Continue beating until the whites are stiff and shiny. Fold one large spoonful of the whites into the yolks to lighten, then pour the rest of the yolks on top of the whites and fold together. Spread on prepared pan. Bake 15–17 minutes, until the top is dry and springs back when lightly pressed. Cool in pan. Use a small sharp knife to cut around the edges of the pan to release the cake. Place a sheet of parchment or wax paper over the cake and a cookie sheet over that and invert. Peel the paper off the back of the cake. Use a ruler and long sharp knife to divide it into three layers the short way. If your pan was 17 x 11 inches you would then have three 5⅔-inch layers. Prepare the filling.

For the filling:

¾ cup (2 ounces) ground almonds
2 cups (6 ounces) sweetened flaked
  coconut
2 cups heavy cream, very cold
½ cup confectioners' sugar, sifted

2½ tablespoons dark rum
1 teaspoon almond extract
2 extra-large egg whites at room
  temperature
2 tablespoons granulated sugar

Toast the coconut and almonds in a large Teflon skillet over high heat. Shake the pan vigorously back and forth, making sure the coconut and almonds are in constant motion. An alternative method is to toast the almonds and coconut on a jelly-roll pan in a 350-degree oven for 10–15 minutes. It is very important to keep checking and stirring the mixture during the toasting. Cook until most of the flakes and nuts are golden brown.

In a chilled bowl, using chilled beaters, whip the cream until it is very stiff. Be careful not to whip it into butter. Add the sugar and rum and blend in. Mix in the almond extract.

Beat the egg whites, and when they turn opaque, sprinkle in the sugar and continue to beat until they are stiff and shiny. Fold the beaten whites into the whipped cream. Fold in 2 cups of the toasted coconut and almonds, saving the rest for decoration.

To assemble:

1½ tablespoons unsweetened cocoa
1½ tablespoons confectioners' sugar

Sift the cocoa and sugar together and set aside. With the aid of a wide spatula or cookie sheet, transfer one cake layer onto a long cake plate. Spread a little less than one-third of the filling on the layer and gently place another layer on top. Place a little less than half of the remaining filling on it. Place the last layer on top and use the rest of the filling to frost the top and sides of the cake. Sift the cocoa/sugar mixture on top of the cake. Cut 5½-inch strips of wax paper and lay them on the diagonal at 1-inch intervals on top of the cake. Sprinkle on the reserved toasted coconut and almonds, then carefully remove the wax paper strips. Press the remaining coconut/almond topping onto the sides of the cake. (An alternative method is to frost the cake, omit the cocoa and sugar, and simply sprinkle the top with the coconut/almond mixture, pressing the remaining topping into the sides.) Freeze the cake for at least three hours or overnight.

To serve:

Allow the cake to sit at room temperature for 15–20 minutes before slicing.

Milk Chocolate Ice Cream

For this sinfully rich dessert use your favorite kind of milk chocolate — either plain or with nuts or fruit. I've made this ice cream using Hershey's Golden Pecan bars, milk chocolate Toblerone, Nestlé's Crunch bar, and Cadbury's Fruit and Almond Bar. I have also used the divine plain milk chocolate that Lindt makes so well. Whatever you use just keep in mind: if it tastes good enough to eat then it will taste great in this ice cream.

MAKES 1½ QUARTS

12 ounces milk chocolate
4 cups heavy cream
4 extra-large eggs

½ cup sugar
2 teaspoons vanilla extract

Chop the chocolate into half-inch chunks and set aside. Pour the cream into a large (2-quart) saucepan and heat over moderate heat until it begins to simmer. Meanwhile, either by hand or using an electric mixer, beat the eggs and the sugar in a medium-sized bowl until a ribbon forms. Slowly pour the hot cream into the eggs and beat. Pour the mixture back into the pan and cook over low heat, stirring constantly, cooking only until the mixture coats the back of a spoon. Do not allow the mixture to boil. Off the heat, add the chocolate and stir until it melts completely (this will take more time and effort than dark chocolate — milk chocolate is harder to incorporate into hot liquid).

Cool the mixture, then freeze in an ice cream freezer.

The Best Hot Chocolate

There is really a difference between hot chocolate and cocoa. Cocoa (the ingredient) is made from what remains from the chocolate liquor (that's the technical term for unsweetened chocolate) after all the cocoa butter has been pressed out. The remaining dry cake is then ground into cocoa powder. The drink made with cocoa powder, sugar, and hot milk is delicious, but for an even richer (rich enough to be dessert) concoction, try this easy recipe:

MAKES FOUR 12-OUNCE SERVINGS
8 ounces (1 cup) heavy cream
8 ounces semisweet or sweet
  chocolate, broken into small pieces
3 cups milk

Scald the heavy cream in a small saucepan. Off the heat, add the chocolate and stir until the chocolate melts. Divide this mixture among four large (12-ounce) mugs. Heat the milk until small bubbles appear around the edges and a skin starts to form on top. Remove the skin and pour the milk into the mugs. Stir the hot chocolate and serve immediately with a dab of whipped cream, marshmallows, or marshmallow topping.

Candy

*B*etween the ages of five and twelve I spent every single Saturday afternoon at the movies. Important parts of the movies are very vaguely remembered — the giant squid from *Twenty Thousand Leagues Under the Sea,* Elizabeth Taylor's magnificent violet eyes and high, sweet voice in *National Velvet,* and the terror I felt when Bambi's mother was shot. Mostly what sticks in my memory is what I ate during those matinees. The candy selection at the Lenox Theater in Hartford, Connecticut, was, at least to a child with limited spending potential, enormous. It was housed in a big glass case that was usually smudged and streaked from too many children pressing their noses and pointing their fingers against it in an effort to make their selections known. I always started with Junior Mints to eat during the cartoons. This was back when there was an inner white waxed-paper liner in the box. That was a classy touch that I miss today. While Mickey and Minnie Mouse ran in and out of holes in the walls and Mighty Mouse saved the day I ate my Junior Mints very slowly — biting a tiny ring of chocolate from around the outer edge and then letting the whole thing melt in my mouth. I tried to make the box last through Pluto; Huey, Dewey, and Louie; and the Road Runner and into the first half of the feature movie, but usually I wasn't too successful. The only good substitute for Junior Mints was Nonpareils, except I was never sure how to pronounce the name and had to point and hope for the best. Once the candy lady misunderstood and gave me (ugh) Nibs instead. For the second half of the movie I had a number of favorites: Jujubes over Dots (because they lasted longer, didn't stick to your teeth as much, and didn't come in black), Necco Wafers, Red Hots, Chuckles, Spearmint Leaves (although they got sort of boring before they were gone), Sugar Babies, Jordan Almonds, and Tootsie Rolls. Other heavy contenders were Raisinets, Mike and Ike, Good and Plenty, and Milk Duds. These things all lasted a really long time and didn't get all over your hands. For the final moments of the show I always had a chocolate candy bar. It was agony deciding which one I would have: Snickers (loved those peanuts), Almond Joy (the chocolate coating was markedly superior), O! Henry, 5th Avenue, Three Musketeers, Milky Way, Heath Bar, Mr. Goodbar, Nestlé's Crunch, or SkyBars. I like to think my meager allowance was in some small way responsible for the college educations of several Mars executives' offspring. I know for a fact that the extent of my candy indulgence was directly responsible for my dentist's Mercedes 450 SL.

I did not limit my candy eating to darkened movie theaters. I would frequent our local Fannie Farmer (no mean feat since it required a forty-minute bus ride with two transfers) and buy pieces of chocolate fudge pecan log (chocolate nougat in the center with pecan halves pressed around the outside). Fannie Farmer also sold chocolate truffles. Not the chi-chi kind Bloomingdale's sells for thirty dollars a pound, these were small rectangular bars with two layers of creamy, smooth dark chocolate and a layer of milk chocolate sandwiched in between. I think the only other ingredient besides the two chocolates was lots of heavy cream. I would sit in the very back of the bus on the way home and spread my coat out on the seat right next to me so no one would be tempted to sit there (chocolate pervert that I was), and as I luxuriated in the taste of the candy I felt as well off as if I had bought a mink coat.

Naturally, the best candy was the stuff I didn't have to shell out my hard-earned allowance for. This took the form of gold foil-wrapped chocolate coins we got for Hanukah, solid milk chocolate Easter eggs "those lucky kids" brought to school and could sometimes be persuaded to share with us nonbelievers, and, best of all, the five-pound box of Russell Stover Assorted Chocolates that Dad's firm sent home every Christmastime. I divided the Russell Stover into three categories: really good stuff, the okay stuff, and the stuff that was instantly spit out into the sink. The first category contained the pink nougat, nut-filled, dark chocolate–coated all-time winner. Everyone in my family knew that if they got that piece they had to give it to me, and they were encouraged to make their first bite very tiny just in case. Today when I see a box of Russell Stover, I automatically start scratching the bottoms of the dark, rectangular pieces in hopes of finding this kind. Included in this category was anything with peanut butter, toffee, and the pink creams. (Remember as a child thinking pink was a flavor?) The middle (or just-acceptable) group contained all the other creams, plain chocolate-filled, and marshmallow. The totally unacceptable (yukky, as we termed it then) candies were those filled with jelly, coconut, marzipan, or cherries. Thank God tastes change because marzipan and chocolate-covered cherries are now two of my most favorite things in the world to eat.

Whitman's Sampler created a marvelous solution to the dilemma of the unknown centers. On the inside of the lid of their beautiful box was printed the name and filling of each piece of candy, indicating its position in the box, so that when you raised the lid there was a detailed battle plan all spelled out.

Now that I'm a little too old to indulge myself quite so openly I rely on others to supply me with candy. You can understand why it will be a sad sad day for me when my children declare themselves too old to go trick-or-treating. I know for a fact that I make up through raiding their hauls for what I missed out on as a kid at Halloween. I would get raisins and apples, a cookie or two, perhaps some candy corn, and a few Life Savers. The only chocolates were Hershey Kisses, and precious few of them too. I think my scant collection was a result in part of the parsimonious nature of our neighborhood plus the limited amount of time I was allowed to ring doorbells.

It was strange that a fairly economically upscale suburban neighborhood like I grew up in after we moved from Magnolia Street gave such meager offerings to the trick-or-treaters. The worst house was the one right behind ours. The only thing that kept us kids going back year after year was the delicious burning feeling of self-righteous indignation we got when the lady of the house would give us each one (and only one) Life Saver, or one of those hideous hard fruit candies with the soft, sour insides that you never knew about until it was too late to spit it out. She also used to give out old ribbon candy and candy canes left over from Christmas. The gang tossed around various ideas about how to get back at her. The ideas centered mainly on her daughter, who was older than we by enough to look down her nose at what she considered scuffbag, déclassé ragamuffins. We had to wait a long time, but when the opportunity presented itself, it was fantastic. The following June the daughter in question was having her debutant party in her backyard. The party was going strong in the late hours of the night. My friends and I pulled all that nasty candy from where we had hidden it the previous October, under socks and behind outdated volumes of the National Geographic, and put it together with tiny pieces of gravel from the street in front of my house. We wanted to dress completely in black, but how many kids did you know in the early sixties with anything black in their wardrobes, so we settled for brown and navy blue. We painted our faces black with shoe polish (what a lovely surprise we had when we tried to wash it off) and took off from behind my house, slithering on our bellies like Marine commandos. We wiggled right up to the property line and gazed in astonishment at the girls in their lovely white gowns and long gloves illuminated by the pink-and-blue Chinese lanterns hanging from the trees. I wasn't too interested in boys then, so I can't tell you how they looked. The band played a gentle waltz and the couples danced around the yard, some dangerously close to where we lay in wait. My friend Arthur Kelly (now a police chief in Maine) threw the first piece of candy. It hit the dimpled white arm of one of the debs. She let out a very refined little screech and grabbed the wounded area, looking around angrily for the offender. I let loose next with several Life Savers and pieces of gravel. The Life Savers didn't go far, but the stones hit their marks. More screeches, now less refined, as the tiny missiles landed with sharp stings on bare backs and exposed ankles. When Georgie MacGuiness hit one of the boys in the eye with a sour ball we figured it was time to pull out. By the time Halloween rolled around again we were too old to go trick-or-treating.

When my children go out trick-or-treating on Halloween they bring home the most wonderful candy, which I, conscientious mother that I am, have to sample to make sure it is not loaded with rat poison and razor blades. Reese's Peanut Butter Cups, Toblerone Bars, Chunky Bars, miniature Hershey Bars, not to mention much of the selection from my movie matinee days. It didn't take long for the kids to wise up and start hiding their candy. At first I could locate it, but then, when they got more creative (like having their friends keep it at their houses), I knew I had to start negotiating. The first concession I had to make was to allow my children to take shaving cream with them when they went trick-or-treating, then I had to promise not to tell the orthodontist that they ate the Kraft's Caramels and the Sugar Daddys. I had to let them stay out an extra hour so they could collect surplus candy for me, and, finally, I had to promise never never again to humiliate them by renting that gorilla suit and going trick-or-treating myself. Believe me, these compromises were well worth their weight in candy.

Camp

I t was my mother's famous goodie bags sent from home — not my athletic ability, my lanyard weaving talents, nor my eager-beaver, gung-ho personality — that made me a star at camp. Besides the famous c.c. cookies (which because of their delicate consistency arrived in several thousand tiny pieces) there were Chocolate Rum Nut Balls,* Chocolate Peanut Butter Balls,* Chocolate Meringue Drops,* tiny bittersweet brownies referred to as Mom's Brownies,* plus another kind of chocolate bar called Surfer Squares.* One chocolate treat that the camp supplied was Some-Mores. Now, I realize that not everyone went to a girls' overnight camp and may draw a blank at Some-Mores. I think the only thing you missed by not going was the off-chance that you might have gone to my camp and would have had the opportunity (if you were really nice to me) to taste some of Mom's goodies. Quite frankly, there are few things on this earth to match the pettiness, meanness, and downright nastiness of a bunch of eleven-year-old girls. Better you should learn about this magical, delicious treat from me now in the comfort of your home (where you don't have to worry about some creepy kid throwing an ice-cold water balloon at you over the bathroom door or short-sheeting your bed), rather than being initiated the rustic way, which involves toasting marshmallows with one hand and scratching poison ivy and mosquito bites with the other. There are two versions of Some-Mores, the traditional and the updated. Both are chocolate sandwiches held together with a toasted marshmallow. The traditional version is made with graham crackers and Hershey Bars. The updated version (which I think ranks right up there) uses Carr's Wheatmeal Biscuits and Tobler Tradition. Sandra Boynton has christened these "Encores."

Chocolate Rum Nut Balls

With any luck these gems were in my camp CARE package.

MAKES 4 DOZEN

6 ounces (½ cup) evaporated milk
6 ounces (½ cup) chocolate chips
2½ cups vanilla wafers, crushed

½ cup sifted confectioners' sugar
1¼ cup walnuts, finely chopped
¼ cup rum

In a heavy-bottom 2-quart saucepan combine the evaporated milk and chocolate chips. Cook over low heat, stirring constantly until the chocolate melts. Remove from heat and add the vanilla wafers, the sugar, ½ cup of the nuts, and the rum. Mix thoroughly. Let the mixture stand at room temperature for 30 minutes. Form into 1-inch balls and roll the balls in the remaining nuts. Refrigerate about 1 hour or until firm.

Chocolate Peanut Butter Balls

These made the whole camp experience worthwhile!

MAKES 5 DOZEN

2 cups sifted confectioners' sugar
1 cup dry-roasted unsalted peanuts, chopped
¼ cup graham-cracker crumbs
¼ cup chocolate wafers, crushed

¾ cup chunky peanut butter
1 cup (8 ounces) sweet (unsalted) butter
24 ounces chocolate chips
½ cup vegetable shortening

Combine the sugar, peanuts, graham-cracker crumbs, and crushed wafers in a medium-sized mixing bowl. In a medium-sized saucepan set over low heat, melt the peanut butter and butter. Stir until blended. Pour the melted peanut butter mixture over the dry ingredients in the mixing bowl and stir until combined. Form in 1-inch balls.

In a medium-sized bowl set over gently simmering water, melt the chocolate chips together with the vegetable shortening. Stir gently to blend. Remove from heat and, using a wooden skewer or fork, dip the balls into the chocolate. Place them on wax paper to set.

Chocolate Meringue Drops

MAKES 24–30 COOKIES

6 ounces chocolate chips
2 extra-large egg whites
½ cup sugar

½ teaspoon vanilla extract
½ teaspoon almond extract
1 generous cup walnuts, chopped

Preheat the oven to 350 degrees with the rack in the lower third but not the bottom position. Cover two heavy-duty cookie sheets with parchment.

Melt the chocolate chips in a small bowl set over a pan of gently simmering water. Beat the egg whites, adding the sugar slowly, until they are stiff but not dry. Using a rubber spatula, stir in the melted chocolate, the flavoring, and finally the chopped nuts. Drop by spoonful onto the parchment and bake for 12–15 minutes, until the tops are dry. Do not overbake.

Mom's Brownies

MAKES 24–32 BROWNIES

8 ounces unsweetened chocolate, cut into small pieces
1 cup sweet (unsalted) butter, cut into pieces
4 extra-large eggs
1 cup granulated sugar
1 cup dark brown sugar, firmly packed
2 teaspoons vanilla extract

1 cup all-purpose flour, sifted before measuring
¼ cup unsweetened cocoa
2 cups (approximately 20 ounces) pecans, coarsely chopped
1 cup (8 ounces) semisweet chocolate chips

Preheat oven to 350 degrees with the rack in the center position. Using butter or solid vegetable shortening, grease a 13 x 9-inch pan. Melt the chocolate and butter in a small metal bowl set over a pan of gently simmering water, or melt them in a glass bowl in the microwave oven. Cool slightly.

Beat the eggs, both sugars, and vanilla on high speed for 10 minutes. Fold in the chocolate/butter mixture and stir until well mixed. Add flour and cocoa and mix just until dry ingredients are incorporated. Do not overbeat. Fold in nuts and chocolate chips.

Spoon the batter into the prepared pan and smooth with a rubber scraper. Bake for 30–40 minutes, taking care not to overbake. Cool in pan before cutting.

Surfer Squares

Want to assure your child a happy summer-camp experience with lots of friends and attentive counselors? Send along a CARE package full of these goodies. They are a supermoist brownie. No mixing bowls needed!

MAKES 18–24 SQUARES

6 ounces butterscotch chips
6 ounces chocolate chips
¼ cup dark brown sugar, firmly packed
¼ cup (4 tablespoons) butter
1 extra-large egg
¾ cup all-purpose flour

¼ teaspoon salt
1 teaspoon baking powder
1 teaspoon vanilla extract
1 cup miniature marshmallows
½ cup walnuts, chopped

Preheat the oven to 350 degrees with the rack in the center position. Butter an 8-inch-square pan. In a medium-sized, heavy-bottom saucepan, combine the butterscotch chips, the chocolate chips, the sugar, and the butter. Cook over medium heat, stirring constantly, until the chips and butter melt and the mixture is smooth. Remove from the heat and cool slightly before adding the egg. Mix well. Sift together the flour, salt, and baking powder and stir into the melted mixture in the saucepan. Stir in the marshmallows, nuts, and finally the vanilla extract. Spread the mixture into the prepared pan and bake for 25–30 minutes. Cool completely before cutting into squares.

Mun Kickel (Poppy Seed Cookies)

This is the only nonchocolate recipe in this book, so you can bet it's pretty special. This is a rather plain-looking and complex-tasting cookie that has a long history in our family. Legend has it that my father's mother taught my mother how to make these cookies, and to this day my father insists that his mother's were better than the ones his wife makes. Of course, my family thinks that mine don't hold a candle to the ones my mother makes. Be that as it may, when we visit my parents, the first thing we do, right after exchanging hugs and kisses, is tear into the kitchen to grab a handful of fresh-baked mun kickel.

MAKES 36–48 COOKIES

3½ cups all-purpose flour
3 teaspoons baking powder
1 teaspoon salt
1 scant cup poppy seeds
4 extra-large eggs
1 cup sugar

1 cup vegetable oil
¼ cup orange juice
1 teaspoon vanilla extract
Cinnamon sugar (made by combining
  1 cup granulated sugar with ¼ cup
  ground cinnamon)

Preheat the oven to 350 degrees with the rack in the center position of the oven. Grease two heavy-duty cookie sheets with Crisco or other solid vegetable shortening. Sift together the flour, baking powder, salt, and poppy seeds into a large bowl. Make a well in the flour mixture and add the eggs, sugar, oil, orange juice, and vanilla. Mix well with your hands. Divide the dough in half and knead one half for about 5 minutes, adding more flour if necessary to make it soft but not sticky. Roll the dough on a floured board to a thickness of ¼ inch. Cut with a juice glass dusted with flour. Sprinkle the tops of the cookies with cinnamon sugar. Place the cookies on a greased cookie sheet and bake for about 20 minutes or until they are very lightly browned. Repeat with the remaining dough.

The Reunion

We had a quarrel, a teenage quarrel,
Now, I'm as blue as I know how to be.
I can't see you at your home
I can't even call you on the phone.

So I'm sending you this present,
Just to prove I was telling the truth.
Dear, I believe you won't laugh when you receive
This rose and a Baby Ruth.

"A Rose and a Baby Ruth" by John D. Loudermilk

*I*n my high school, popularity was unfortunately not based on one's ability to bake a wicked brownie. Great chocolate chip cookies did not take the place of straight white teeth and big breasts. Direct access to the world's best chocolate layer cake did not mean a thing in a world where popularity was measured in terms of "neat clothes," "cool cars," and going steady with the captain of the football team. The prom queen and her court had interchangeable names like Maureen, Noreen, and Doreen. There were also Darnel and Arnelle. Once wholesome Catholic names, now synthetic fibers. Let's face it, cheerleaders with big breasts, nice teeth, naturally curly hair, and names like Mouseketeers got dates, I didn't. (I have a feeling these girls gave out things that were a lot more interesting to sixteen-year-old boys than brownies.) Being short and skinny with braces and glasses and having the poise of a fifth-grader, I was basically ignored by all my heartthrobs. Too bad I didn't go to high school in the late sixties, when my

Twiggyesque shape would have been the one to envy. The heartthrob who avoided me with the most unstudied expertise was a boy named Skipper Kauffman. Cute preppie type. How I adored him. Unlike the other boys, who just ignored my furtive crushes, Skipper (What the hell kind of a name is that for someone who aspired to be secretary of state after Princeton?) went out of his way to be insulting. He made it very clear that he had no wish to waste his time and energy on anyone sporting anything less than a 36C. He was so nasty. I hated him. I loved him. I did my best to console myself (and increase my girth) on Saturday nights by doing an informal five-city survey of great hot fudge sauce. I secretly cursed this creep along with the rest of my ignorant classmates and vowed that someday I would run into them all again when the cheerleaders' gigantic breasts would be sagging down around their knees and Skipper and his cohorts would have beer bellies and bald spots. I would be the one who was noticed. After graduation we all went our separate ways. I began to obsess on THE REUNION. I knew I had fifteen years to make it big.

Other neurotics entertain their shrinks with sad tales of repressive mothers and compulsive fathers, kinky uncles and jealous siblings. For fifteen years my psychiatrist made a small fortune listening to my fantasies about my high-school reunion. I would be the most beautiful, the most successful, the most happily married, the best mother, the best-adjusted, the most-poised alumna ever graduated from my high school. I would have, of course, written several best-selling volumes of fiction, been on the cover of *Time* magazine, won a Pulitzer Prize, and traveled all over the world. My children would have all been accepted at Ivy League schools (even though they were only in elementary school at the time — Harvard was dying to get them). I would, of course, be terribly gracious as my classmates gathered around me, gasping in surprise at the metamorphosis. Yes, I'd be gracious to everyone except Skipper Kauffman. I would glance at his bald spot (and potbelly) and mutter something about how some people age better than others. I did actually have another completely different fantasy about the reunion. I would go with another woman and pretend she was my lesbian girlfriend. But I realized no one would "get" it.

I cannot say that fifteen years went by in the twinkling of an eye. By the time THE INVITATION came I had managed to work out a lot of nasty feelings that I had about my high-school years. That is not to say, however, that I had given up the idea of going back home and putting on the dog. Many of my fantasized successes were still in the planning stage, but I certainly had a much better sense of self now, not to mention contact lenses and straight white teeth. I suspected that most of my old classmates had stayed closer to home than I had. I just hoped to hell they had seen my name in the *New York Times*.

The reunion was to be held at an Italian restaurant in Hartford that was famous for its chocolate desserts. Having dinner at this place was indeed an added bonus. (Although I was sure I'd be too nervous to eat anything.)

I spent the six months prior to the affair getting my body ready (I figured that my mind had already been serviced during all that therapy). I ran eight miles every day, I did hundreds of sit-ups. I consumed dangerous quantities of vitamin E for my skin and hair. I gagged down unflavored gelatin for my nails, and I limited my chocolate intake drastically in case it did turn out to be true that my beloved food caused acne. I did consider plastic surgery (you know, just for those first very faint wrinkles around my eyes) but opted to spend all the money on THE DRESS, which I made a pilgrimage to New York City to buy. Henri Bendel was delighted to take my small suitcase full of money. I made my husband, David, take out a second mortgage to buy a suit that had to be stored in the safe deposit box when it wasn't on his back.

The night of the event arrived and as we pulled into the parking lot of the restaurant my heart was pounding like a pile driver and my mouth was parched with terror. What if all those other graduates had spent the same amount of time, effort, pain, and anguish on this thing that I had? What if they looked better than I? What if no one cared that I was somebody now? What if no one noticed? Dear God, I prayed, just this once let fantasy become reality. In retrospect I am appalled at the amount of power I allocated to these people, who probably were as insecure as I was. Chin up, head high, in I marched. God came through. I couldn't believe my eyes. The first thing I noticed was that the prom queen and her court (all dressed in matching aqua polyester separates) still had breasts, but boy oh boy, they had hips too. Hips that endured through three strings of ten-pin bowling every Wednesday afternoon. Too many helpings of Sara Lee at those Tupperware parties. Gravity had not been kind to those enviable breasts, either, which now were closer to waist than shoulder. The royal clique was as cool to me as they had been fifteen years ago, but I realized it was less a result of their disliking me than it was our having so little in common that we had absolutely nothing to talk about. Revelation. I did make a mental note that several had children old enough to have been conceived on graduation night. They giggled and gossiped among themselves just as they used to, and the circle was tightly closed just as it was fifteen years ago, but somehow I was hugely relieved to find myself on the outside. I met several people whose faces I vaguely remembered. At first no one recognized me and when they did they expressed great amazement at the change. They were warm and seemed genuinely happy to see me and thrilled at my successes (yes, they do read the *New York Times* in Hartford). Everyone I saw exclaimed over my metamorphosis—"Boy, have you changed" was the phrase of the evening. One nice man told me that he had always admired me because I was "different." I asked him if he had any idea how lonely "differ-

The Reunion

ent" was. I wasn't ready to pat myself on the back quite yet. The acid test would be Skipper's reaction.

Two things happened simultaneously. The waiter placed my dessert in front of me (It was an enormous and delicious-looking piece of Chocolate Pecan Ice Cream Roll*), and Skipper Kauffman walked into the restaurant. (He was always late to class, too, leaving me in misery for the first quarter of each Latin class — would he come? Would I have to suffer through the agonizing boredom of this much-loathed class without having him to gaze at?) Well, I am delighted to report that it is possible for time to stand still. I was looking at a ghost from 1963. Literally nothing about this person had changed, including his height. He must have stopped growing in twelfth grade because I was taller than he by several inches. He was wearing (I kid you not) his same old preppy uniform — chinos, madras shirt, felt belt, Shetland cable-knit sweater with suede elbow patches, and Weejuns. He looked like my baby-sitter. He glided toward our table, working the crowd. As he approached I gobbled a little bit of the wonderful chocolate dessert. It was like rubbing a lucky coin or rabbit's foot for courage. He said hello up and down the table and when he got to me it was obvious that he didn't know who I was. I stood up (towering over him I was able to see his bald spot) and shook his hand. This incredulous look came over his face. He began to sputter my name. Meanwhile his (small-breasted) wife, who had read my name tag, began to go on about how she had heard about me, seen me on TV and in the newspapers, made all my recipes, etc. "Skipper, why didn't you tell me you knew her?" gushed the wife. Well, in fact, the jerk hadn't known me — he could have, but didn't. "Skipper," I said, squeezing his hand a little tighter, "tell me, are you still a prick?" I sat down and finished my dessert. I never felt the need to go to another reunion.

Sweet Georgia Brown

Chocolate Pecan Ice Cream Roll with Bourbon Caramel Sauce

Are you ready for a quick trip to paradise? A dense chocolate sponge roll surrounds a filling of butter pecan ice cream. The whole thing is topped with toasted meringue and pecans and is served with the most intensely rich and buttery-smooth bourbon caramel sauce. Both the cake and the sauce can be made several days ahead. Save the meringue for the last minute.

For the cake:

8 ounces semisweet chocolate, chopped
7 extra-large eggs at room
  temperature, separated
⅔ cup sugar

3 tablespoons cocoa
2 pints (4 cups) best-quality butter
  pecan ice cream, softened slightly

Preheat the oven to 350 degrees with the rack in the center position. Line a 17 x 11-inch heavy-duty jelly-roll pan with parchment. Melt the chocolate in a small bowl set over a pan of gently simmering water. Stir until smooth, then remove from the heat to cool slightly. Beat the egg yolks with half the sugar until they form a ribbon when the beater is lifted from the bowl. On low speed, add the cocoa and then the melted chocolate. In a clean bowl, with clean beaters, beat the egg whites with the remaining sugar until they are stiff but not dry. Fold the whites into the chocolate mixture and spread the batter in the prepared pan. Bake for 12–15 minutes, reversing the pan once front to back halfway through the baking. Cool the cake in the pan and then place another piece of parchment over the cake and a cookie sheet on top of that. Invert the cake and peel off the top parchment. Use a pair of scissors to trim the edges of the cake so they are even. Spread the cake with the softened ice cream, and with the long side of the cake nearest you, and using the bottom parchment as an aid, roll the cake up. Don't worry if it cracks during the rolling — it won't show. Wrap tightly with plastic wrap and freeze in the coldest part of the freezer until it is frozen solid. Prepare the bourbon caramel sauce.

For the sauce:

2 cups sugar
1 cup water
Few drops of lemon juice
2 ounces (4 tablespoons) sweet
  (unsalted) butter at room temperature,
  cut into pieces

½ cup heavy cream
¼–⅓ cup bourbon — depending on
  how powerful you want the sauce to be
2 teaspoons vanilla extract

In a heavy-bottomed 2-quart saucepan, bring the sugar, water, and lemon juice to a boil, stirring only until the sugar dissolves and the syrup is clear. Boil on moderate heat until the syrup begins to take on an amber color. This will take 15–20 minutes. Watch it very carefully because it burns easily. You want it to be a rich caramel color. If your eyes begin to sting when you smell it — take it off the heat! Stir in the butter, bit by bit, and then the heavy cream, the bourbon, and the vanilla. The mixture will bubble up with each addition — that's why it's important to use a large pan to cook this sauce in. If you're not going to use the sauce right away, cool it a bit, then pour it into a jar and store it in the refrigerator. You can reheat it in the microwave or in a saucepan over low heat.

Meringue topping and assembly:

1 cup dark brown sugar, firmly packed
¼ cup water
6 extra-large egg whites at room
 temperature

1½ cups (12 ounces, approximately) pecans, finely chopped

Prepare this topping just before serving. Preheat the broiler. Remove the plastic wrap from the cake roll and place it on an ovenproof tray and return it to the freezer (if it doesn't fit, the refrigerator's okay—if you work fast). Mix the brown sugar and water in a small saucepan. Stir over high heat until the sugar dissolves, then boil without stirring until the syrup reaches 225 degrees on a candy thermometer. Meanwhile, place the egg whites in a mixing bowl and beat with the mixer on the lowest speed. When the syrup is ready, place the mixer on high and slowly dribble the syrup over the egg whites. Continue beating at high speed until the meringue is stiff and shiny. Use a rubber spatula to fold in the chopped pecans. Using a long, flexible metal spatula, spread the meringue over the cake, concentrating most of the meringue on top. Don't be too fussy about making it smooth —it actually looks better with swirls. Place the cake under the broiler about 4–5 inches away from the element (if the rack position is too high for the cake to fit, then lower it to the center position). Leave the cake under the broiler until the meringue is browned—like the top of a lemon meringue pie. Keep watching it—it doesn't take long!

To serve:

Cut slices thick enough (1½ inches at least) so they can stand upright. Drizzle some sauce over each slice and pass the rest of the sauce separately.

Grandma Ida and the Straight "A" Chocolate Layer Cake

I wish I could say I met my husband-to-be over chocolate. It just isn't so. I can say, however, that I went to a girlfriend's house one day, met her older brother, who was home for the weekend from college, fell in love instantly, and was invited to stay for supper, at which a wonderful chocolate cake was served. So, true love preceded chocolate by a mere hour or two.

My mother-in-law is a very smart lady. She is also a pretty good judge of what makes people tick. Her specialty is instant (which is swifter than snap) judgment. More often than not her appraisals are right on target. In all her years of sizing up people, their characters, motives, and the like, she had only made one serious mistake. She should have looked a little more carefully at the giggly fifteen-year-old girl who had accompanied her daughter home from school that fateful day. If she had been on the ball, she would have locked her son in the basement until I left.

While I had not yet made any great inroads in the pursuit and seduction of boys my age, I was no fool. Not for one moment did I think I could, with my present lack of almost everything that might attract an older man, interest this guy. However, I did a spontaneous mental reevaluation of the standards by which I judged men from then on. The competition never even had a chance. I also decided that no matter how long it took and how hard I had to work this was the one I wanted. I figured it was in the best interest of the potential of this as yet nonexistent relationship that I not let on about my feelings, so I limited my conversation to more giggles and intense blushing.

When we sat down to eat I knew I was going to be in serious trouble. Not only did this family conduct a rational and lively conversation at the dinner table, everyone was expected to eat everything on their plates. Picture, if you will, this nightmare scenario: the Tuna Queen meets avocado and grapefruit salad with blue cheese dressing. They all waited politely until everybody was served (we never waited at our house, but I was a quick learner), and then everyone dug in with great gusto exclaiming over the delicious taste of the dish. Not only was I expected to eat something I didn't like or didn't know the name of, I was supposed to be gracious to boot. I managed to gag down most of it by not breathing while I was eating, so I couldn't taste anything. I also drank copious amounts of water to hasten the evil stuff down the hatch. You would have thought I was being tortured with castor oil instead of a delectable combination of fruits and vegetables. The real killer for me was the obsessional thoughts I had about the blue cheese dressing. Oh, God! Eating mold. You have to realize that if by some horrible twist of fate I was the one who discovered the blue fuzz-covered orange stuck way back in the refrigerator drawer, I would scream hysterically until a more-hardened adult came by to remove the offensive object — and not into the kitchen garbage can either; it had to go outside, into the trash barrel, where I wouldn't run the risk of seeing it ever again. This woman wanted me to eat dressing that had cheese with mold on it. That I did, in fact, get it down was a testament to the strength of the feeling I had for her son. I knew there was no way I would get another invitation to this house and this table if I didn't chow down this grub. My salvation came with the next course, which was roast chicken. At least I could identify the food on the plate. The problem was that everybody else at the table was eating the skin, a component of chicken that had never passed through my lips. Could I pretend I had a rare and fatal allergy to chicken skin? And brussels sprouts? There were not enough roasted potatoes on my plate to stick on my fork along with the skin and sprouts so I could at least have something else in my mouth. I tried to ration the potatoes as best I could so that I would end up with enough neutral matter to balance out the bad stuff. There was no lettuce to hide anything under. The result was that I spent almost the entire meal studiously carving up everything on my plate into tiny pieces. My future in-laws, who had never seen anyone do this before, thought I was quite strange. I think the tendency to treat food this way must be genetic because I see my sons do it, and while I can feel for them, it still makes me furious. Thank goodness my behavior didn't discourage my hosts from inviting me back again, because it was in this home that I began to have my culinary and gastronomic horizons broadened, and got the added bonus of having the opportunity to keep tabs on my future husband.

Everyone else at the table had gobbled up their chicken and then sat with their empty plates in front of them. Well, not exactly empty; each plate held a few well-gnawed bones. They all sat looking at me and I realized they were waiting for me to finish so they could clear the table and bring on the next instrument of culinary torture. In silent panic I ran some great lines through my head that would explain my plate still being partially filled with minced pieces of chicken skin and mangled brussels sprouts:

"This was so delicious I'd like to bring the rest home to share with my family."

"Ever since Uncle Zeke had his fatal heart attack after eating brussels sprouts I just can't seem to get them down."

"The Novocain I had last week hasn't worn off and I'm having a hard time chewing the chicken skin."

What I actually did was mumble, "I'm full."

I actually hoped that they had a policy of not giving dessert to bad children who didn't finish their dinner. I could just imagine what lay in wait in the kitchen to polish me off. The worst possible thing would be baked custard. The next worst would be stewed fruit. With my luck we would probably have both. I guess the gods had decided that I had suffered enough, because when my mother-in-law-to-be (I knew, she didn't) reappeared from the kitchen, she was holding not a bowl of stewed fruit, or dishes of baked custard, but a china cake dish with a beautiful chocolate layer cake on it. The cake had two high layers and was covered with thick swirls of light chocolate icing. She began to serve the dessert and I realized that I had a credibility problem. After all, wasn't I the one who only moments before was so full I had to send my plate back to the kitchen with most of my dinner on it? Everyone else at the table had a big slice of cake. I was the only one yet to be served. My mother-in-law-to-be gave me a hard look and said, "I don't like to waste food. Are you sure you have room for this?"

"I sure think so," I said.

"Well, I'll give you half a piece. Next time you come here to dinner you eat everything on your plate and we'll see about the other half."

The cake was heaven. Light and airy, soft as a cloud. The frosting was sweet and creamy and as delicious as the cake itself. I would have killed for another piece but figured that violence wasn't the right way to attract the man of my dreams, who was sitting across the table from me, eating a whole piece of cake. You better believe that the next time I was invited to dinner (and the many, many times after that) I licked my plate clean in anticipation of dessert. I learned to conquer fears of pot roast, stuffed cabbage, borscht, and even avocados and brussels sprouts, all in the name of true love and lust for Ida's son and her chocolate layer cake. I christened it the Straight "A" Cake* because it scored so high and because I had to work so hard to get a piece.

It was a very long courtship. It took me a good three years just to get the message across to him that there was something besides his mother's great chocolate layer cake that compelled me to hang around his house. Good thing

The Straight "A" Chocolate Layer Cake

51

subtlety wasn't my strong suit because I would still be eating pot roast. Since he and the state of Connecticut considered anyone under eighteen jailbait, and since he was a big shot college man and I was only a high school kid, our first dates usually included a cast of thousands: his sister, his three best friends, and his enormous hyperactive collie that his sister had won in a Name the Lassie Puppy Contest.

Things improved tremendously when I got to college. First of all, I was finally old enough. Old enough for what, you may ask. Not much. Remember, this was the very early sixties and I was very definitely a product of that uptight NATO morality (No Action, Talk Only). I really believed it when my mother and Dear Abby said "Nice Girls Don't." I was so stupid, of course nice girls did, they just never talked about it like they do now. Anyway, dating my intended (I knew, he didn't) at college was a hell of a lot better than doing it at home. Since we were now both in New Haven, I didn't have to plan my invitations to his mother's house around his school vacations, and I didn't have to share him with family, friends, and crotch-sniffing dog.

Young people in the fifties and sixties who weren't having sex tended to do a lot of strenuous outdoor activities. We swam, we skied, we skated, we took long walks. Great quantities of mediocre food and cheap wine seemed to help too. We lived on spaghetti with garlic butter accompanied by Italian bread with garlic butter washed down with gallons of cheap wine. The alternative favorite menu was two eggs, over light, dark rye toast, a side of bacon, and home fries. This delectable repast was consumed in a place called the Duchess Diner, which I hope still exists in New Haven. Besides pasta, garlic, and eggs, the other thing we lived on was Howard Johnson's hot fudge sundaes. If we felt rich we would each have our own, but if it was near the end of the month we "proved our love" by sharing. One sundae, two spoons. I tried to be subtle about eating most of the hot fudge, but then I noticed that he really only cared for the ice cream. It was the Jack Sprat syndrome — a perfect match.

It was an idyllic existence marred by only two blemishes. Skiing and garlic bread are great but they don't take the place of you-know-what, and I was fast approaching the age by which popular convention dictated that every respectable girl worth her salt should be married. He took the news of my intentions better than I expected. The coma lasted two weeks and the residual shock subdued him long enough for me to have most of the plans made by the time he came around.

Straight "A" Layer Cake

SERVES 8–10

1¾ cups cake flour
1 teaspoon salt
1 teaspoon baking soda
1½ teaspoons baking powder
½ cup milk
3 ounces unsweetened chocolate, cut
  into pieces

1 cup sour cream
¾ cup (1½ sticks) sweet (unsalted)
  butter at room temperature
1 cup sugar
⅔ cup dark brown sugar, firmly packed
2 teaspoons vanilla extract
3 extra-large eggs

Preheat the oven to 350 degrees. Set the rack in the center position. Grease two 9-inch round cake pans, cover the bottoms with a circle of parchment or wax paper, grease the paper, and then dust the pans with flour. Knock out the excess flour.

Sift the flour, salt, baking soda, and baking powder three times and set aside.

Scald the milk and add the chocolate, stirring until the chocolate has melted and the mixture is smooth. Cool completely. Stir in the sour cream. If the chocolate is too warm and the mixture seizes when the sour cream is added, warm it over a low heat to loosen.

Cream the butter and both sugars until light and fluffy. Mix in the vanilla. Add the eggs one at a time, beating until each is incorporated. Add the flour alternately with the chocolate mixture, mixing only until the ingredients are incorporated. Do not overbeat!

Pour into the prepared pans and bake for 35–40 minutes or until the edges start to pull away from the sides of the pan and a cake tester comes out clean. Cool in pans 15 minutes. Unmold onto cake racks to cool completely. Prepare the Chocolate Melt-Away frosting.

For the frosting:

2 cups confectioners' sugar, sifted
½ cup milk
2 extra-large eggs
Pinch of salt

½ teaspoon vanilla extract
4 squares unsweetened chocolate
6 tablespoons sweet (unsalted) butter

Combine the sugar, milk, eggs, salt, and vanilla in a metal mixing bowl. Set the bowl over another, larger bowl filled with water and ice. Melt the chocolate and butter together in a double boiler and then add it to the first mixture. Beat with electric or rotary beater until the icing is thick enough to hold a soft peak. Use immediately.

The Straight "A" Chocolate Layer Cake

To assemble:

Place one layer on a cake plate with four strips of wax paper under the edges. Spread one-third of the frosting on this layer. Cover with the top layer. Cover the top and sides with the remaining frosting.

Chocolate Weddings Then and Now

I have a nagging desire to get married again. Not to a different man, the one I have is still just about perfect. I want to do the wedding part again and do it my way. What did I know when I was twenty and getting married? I don't think I had ever been to but two weddings in my life. I told my parents I wanted only three things my way and they could do the rest. I wanted to design my own wedding gown, I didn't want hard liquor at the reception, and I wanted a chocolate wedding cake. They fought me on every count.

"Just go and try on a few gowns. You'll change your mind."

"I'll feel stupid. I'm not the bride type."

"If you're not the bride type, why are you getting married? I take that back, your father and I are thrilled you're getting married." (You bet they were, to the nice Jewish law student.)

I had secretly gone to the bridal salon at G. Fox and tried on a gown. Actually, I had to hang around a long time before the saleslady got the idea that I was there to do more than check my profile in her sixteen gilded mirrors. No one ever told me that you had to wear nylons and bring your mother just to try on fancy white dresses. Since I had no idea what style I wanted I blindly stabbed at a gown hanging on a rack. It was encased in enough cotton shrouds and plastic wrapping to do justice to King Tut, so it was hard to see what I selected before it was excavated. When the last of the plastic fell away and I saw the giant puffed sleeves and plunging neckline I knew it wasn't exactly me. If I were some six-foot-tall debutante with a long blond pageboy and diamonds in the vault I would have been okay. This dress was not exactly the thing for the breastless, hipless wonder midget. I just couldn't bring myself to give the saleslady the satisfaction of seeing me in this dress. So I made her leave while I tried it on. Do you have any idea how much those things weigh? Not only that, there are thousands of hooks and eyes and snaps and tiny hidden zippers and underpinnings. I felt like I was wrestling with a pair of drapes and the contents of a sewing box. I finally got the thing on and fastened after a fashion. The image of myself in the mirror made me giggle at first and then I was convulsed with great whoops of laughter. I looked just like one of the Munchkins from *The Wizard of Oz*. The dress I designed myself did raise some eyebrows when I walked down the aisle. It was made out of a beautiful white-and-gold sari, very simple with not one hook or eye or tiny hidden zipper. I think it weighed all of four ounces. My relatives had quite a time trying to figure out the significance of my not wearing pure white.

My father won the next point. He insisted not only that his business associates and our friends and relatives needed hard liquor to enjoy my wedding but that he and my mother couldn't get through it on champagne alone. I conceded.

"I never heard of a chocolate wedding cake. Why can't you have fruitcake like everyone else?"

"I know you never heard of it, but I want one, and you know everyone hates fruitcake. People make a lot of money selling those disgusting fruitcakes. They know nobody will eat them, so they can charge a fortune to make tiny little cakes that will serve hundreds of fruitcake-hating wedding guests."

"Nobody makes chocolate wedding cakes."

"I'll find someone to make it."

"What will people think?"

"About a caterer who makes a chocolate wedding cake?"

"No, about a stubborn girl who wants a chocolate cake at her wedding when every other bride in the entire universe has a pure white cake." (Note the use of pure here.)

"My friends will be happy because they love chocolate cake. Your friends will think that I'm not a virgin because the cake is brown. And they'll be happy because they'll have something to talk about."

"Don't talk dirty."

Imagine an entire generation of neurotic women who thought virgin was a dirty word.

I did find a Kosher caterer to make my chocolate wedding cake. Too bad it was so awful. I think he used vegetable shortening or margarine instead of butter. The real disappointment was that he frosted the cake with white royal icing (I had asked for chocolate icing, but I think my mother must have slipped him a twenty not to do it). The combination of the dry, crumbly tasteless cake and the hard, sugary icing created a pretty unremarkable dessert. My mother saved the top of the cake in her freezer and tried to serve it to us on our first anniversary. I demanded chocolate cream pie instead.

So, now you can see why I wanted to do it again my way. I have not, as yet, had the chance to do it for myself, but as a caterer I have shared the thrill and agony of hundreds of weddings. They sure are different now. Whoever hears about a twenty-year-old girl getting married these days? Nowadays the parents of the bride and groom are guests, just like everybody else at the wedding. The bride and groom make all the plans, all the decisions, and the parents seem relieved of the burden. I can see now that I was way ahead of my time because hardly anybody serves hard liquor anymore. Champagne and white wine seem to make everybody very happy. Where once prime rib ruled as king of the menu, pheasant roulade now reigns. And I sell only chocolate wedding cakes.

When I gave up my catering business I found the only thing I missed was the vicarious joy I received from other people's weddings. Dinner parties I could live without. So, I continue to make chocolate wedding cakes. The cakes have between three and five tiers, are covered with a satiny smooth, shiny dark chocolate glaze, and are decorated with white roses and baby's breath. They are fairly time-consuming and expensive, but not terribly difficult to make. They are beautiful to look at and wonderful to taste. It is a labor of love well worth the effort. Since I think everyone should have the opportunity to have a fabulous chocolate wedding cake, and since I can only turn out twenty or so a year, I will teach you how to make one.

Chocolate Wedding Cake

To make a three-tiered cake to serve 50 people:
The recipe below makes one 9-inch layer. To make a three-tiered wedding cake consisting of three round layers — 6-inch, 9-inch, and 12-inch — you will need four times the following recipe: half the recipe for the top, one recipe for the 9-inch, and 2½ times the recipe for the 12-inch. The easiest way to do this is make the 9-inch first. Then, if you have a heavy-duty machine, double the recipe, putting the entire batter into the 12-inch pan — but don't bake it yet. Make another single recipe; put half into the 6-inch pan and the other half into the 12-inch pan.
Be sure to use heavy-duty baking pans. Springforms are okay. It is not necessary to grease them, but it is essential to use parchment to line the bottoms of the pans. The 6-inch layer will bake for 15 minutes, but the 12-inch may need 3 or 4 minutes more. Take care not to let the top burn. I usually place a cookie sheet under the 12-inch layer while it's cooking — to protect the bottom from burning.

For one 9-inch layer:

1 pound (16 ounces) bittersweet
  chocolate, cut into small pieces
5 ounces sweet (unsalted) butter, cut
  into small pieces
4 extra-large eggs at room temperature

1 tablespoon sugar
1 tablespoon all-purpose flour, unsifted
½ teaspoon bitter almond or almond
  extract

Preheat the oven to 425 degrees with the rack in the center of the oven. Line a 9-inch layer pan with parchment paper.

Place the chocolate and butter in a metal bowl set over a pan of gently simmering water. Stir together until melted. The mixture will harden at first and then smooth out.

Place the eggs and sugar in a large mixing bowl and beat with a wire whisk or whip attachment of an electric mixer until they become light in color, turn thick, and triple in volume. This will take at least 15–20 minutes by hand and 5–10 minutes with a heavy-duty mixer. Add the flour and mix it in.

Add the chocolate mixture to the egg/flour mixture and stir in well — the mixture will deflate somewhat; make sure there are no traces of egg to be seen.

Pour into the prepared pan and bake 15 minutes. Remove from oven and let the cake cool in the pan right-side up (do not invert) on a cake rack. When the cake has cooled down a bit, place it in the freezer and allow to freeze until solid.

To remove from pan:

Spin bottom of pan over gas or electric burner on high for a few seconds until the cake is loosened. Invert onto a cardboard disk.

These layers may be kept frozen until you are ready to assemble the cake. Wrap them well in several layers of plastic wrap and foil to protect from freezer burn. Defrost still wrapped (so the moisture collects on the paper, not the cake) for at least one hour before glazing.

To glaze and assemble:

Have ready:

A 15-inch flat cake plate, an 8-inch and a 5-inch heavy cardboard disk, wax paper, plastic straws, scissors, chocolate glaze, frosting spatula.

For the glaze (more than enough for 6-, 9-, and 12-inch layers; you will have glaze left over):

3 cups heavy cream
30 ounces bittersweet chocolate, cut
  into very small pieces. My favorite for
  this cake is Tobler Tradition.

In a medium-sized saucepan scald the cream (heat until tiny bubbles form around the edges of the pan). Add the chocolate and stir very gently until the chocolate melts and the glaze is smooth and shiny. It is very important not to beat or overmix this glaze, which would form air bubbles and mar the finish of the cake. Allow the glaze to cool while you get the cake ready to glaze.

Place the 12-inch layer on the cake plate that is resting on a lazy Susan. Slip strips of wax paper under the edge of the cake to protect the plate from the glaze. Stick one plastic straw into the center of the cake, make a small snip on the straw with the scissors to mark the depth of the layer, and then pull it out. Cut the straw through at the snip mark, and then, using this piece as a measure, cut ten lengths of straw the same size. Push these pieces of straw into the cake to form a circle 4 inches from the center. This will support the next layer. Be very careful that the straws are not higher than the layer itself.

Place the 9-inch layer on the 8-inch cardboard circle and repeat the straw process, but form them in a circle 2 inches from the center. Place the 6-inch layer on the 5-inch cardboard disk.

Pour about 1½ cups of glaze on the bottom layer. Using the frosting spatula smooth the glaze over the top, while you turn the lazy Susan with the other hand. Let a small amount of glaze go over the sides. Use the spatula held flat against the sides to smooth the glaze on the sides while you turn the lazy Susan. Try not to fuss too much with the glaze — remember, most of the top is covered by the next layer and you can easily hide imperfections on the sides with decorations or fresh flowers. Immediately slip the wax paper out before the glaze hardens.

Slip the lazy Susan out from under the layer and place it under the 9-inch layer. Glaze this layer and then the 6-inch.

Here's the tricky part: place the 9-inch layer (still on the cardboard circle) flat on your hand (it's easy to pick up if you slip a metal spatula under it). Stand on a low stool so you are slightly above the bottom layer. Eyeball the center of the cake and gently slip the 9-inch layer on top of the 12-inch layer. You probably won't be dead center. You can push it a tiny bit with the frosting spatula, but unless you're really off center, don't bother. No one will notice. Now that you're an expert you shouldn't have any trouble positioning the top layer in the same way.

Let the glaze dry completely. The best place to store this cake (it can be made up to two days in advance) is a cool, dark room. Don't refrigerate it, because the shine from the glaze will disappear.

I decorate my cake with white roses and baby's breath. I place tiny rosebuds resting on a rose leaf around the layers and then place three perfect white roses and a sprig of baby's breath held together with a white satin ribbon on top.

Make sure to tell the person who is cutting the cake to remove the straws as they cut.

If you need to feed more than 50 people I suggest you make several extra 9-inch layers. These are the easiest to make and to serve. The extra layers can be served from the kitchen. Count on each 9-inch layer serving 12–15 people.

Fruit à l'Armagnac au Chocolat

(Chocolate-Dipped Armagnac-Soaked Prunes or Apricots)

When we were married my father gave us a bottle of thirty-year-old Armagnac. This very special kind of brandy is produced in a region of southwestern France. The funny-looking brown bottle with the fancy label and curved neck was relegated to the back of our liquor cabinet (which was also the broom closet and laundry depository) in Brooklyn. After all, what did we who thought White Russians and Rusty Nails were what you washed your cheese spread down with know about brandy. It survived the move to Boston in its unopened state. When our friend and wine expert Michael Apstein laid eyes on it with great delight we figured the time had come to give it a try. It was heavenly. Too bad Dad hadn't given us a case of the stuff! We held on to the bottle as long as possible, doling it out during only the most important occasions and only to our dearest friends. Finally there was just about one quarter of a cup (or one brandy snifter) left when I thought about combining this ambrosial liquid with its magic warming power with my favorite food. How could I miss? The combination of prunes and Armagnac is a famous one and rightfully so. The addition of chocolate only makes a good thing better. If you're not a prune fan, try the apricot version.

MAKES 12

For the fruit:

10–12 jumbo pitted prunes or dried apricots (approximately ¼–⅓ pound)   **¼ cup Armagnac**

Place the prunes or apricots or a combination of the two in a small bowl.
    Pour the Armagnac over the fruit and cover the bowl with plastic wrap. Let the fruit soak in the liquor at room temperature several hours or overnight.

For the chocolate coating:

**½ cup heavy cream
6 ounces bittersweet chocolate, cut
  into small pieces**

**2 tablespoons Armagnac reserved from
  soaking the fruit (see instructions
  below for straining the fruit)**

Scald the heavy cream in a small saucepan. Off the heat, add the chocolate and stir gently until the chocolate is melted and the mixture is smooth. Set aside to cool slightly.

To assemble:

7 ounces marzipan or almond paste
12 pleated foil or paper cups 1 inch
high with bottoms measuring 2
inches across

Roll the marzipan or almond paste between two pieces of plastic wrap or wax paper until you have a square that roughly measures 9 x 9 inches and is $\frac{1}{16}$ of an inch thick.

Place the fruit in a strainer set over a small bowl. Reserve the strained Armagnac. Stir the 2 tablespoons of reserved Armagnac into the chocolate coating. (Drink the rest.)

Set the foil or paper cups on a tray and use a teaspoon to place enough chocolate coating in each one to cover the bottom.

Remove the top sheet of plastic wrap from the marzipan or almond paste and arrange the fruit on it so that each piece of fruit is 2 inches apart and 1 inch from the outer border. Cut squares around each piece and wrap the marzipan around the fruit, completely enclosing it. Place the fruit seam side down in the prepared chocolate cup. Repeat with all the fruit. Carefully spoon the remaining chocolate coating over the marzipan-covered fruit. Refrigerate for several hours until the chocolate is set.

I Can Cook

Shortly after our wedding (two hours after, to be exact) we left for our new life together in New York. We left in my mother's 1959 station wagon, which was loaded to capacity with wedding presents (which included no less than four fondue sets—more about those later), furniture (including my bedroom set, which my parents couldn't wait to get out of my bedroom so they could turn it into a guest room—ironically, David and I were their most frequent visitors), food left over from the wedding so my mother wouldn't have to worry about my new husband starving while I learned how to cook, and four friends who lived in New York and wanted to save the bus fare home.

I'd been to New York before: Empire State Building, Museum of Natural History, Statue of Liberty, Metropolitan Opera House. Where I had never been before was Brooklyn, where we were going to live. We dropped our friends off in Manhattan and proceeded over the Brooklyn Bridge. Some friends!—we found out soon enough that as much as they loved our company they had a policy of not crossing water to come to see us. We pulled up to a slightly dilapidated apartment house that boasted an un-uniformed doorman, slumped over, sound asleep, with his chair tilted back at a precarious angle against the wide-open door of the building. Up the block I was at first delighted to see a movie theater. At closer inspection I changed my mind. The double bill at the Sin-Art (men $5, ladies free) was *Hawaiian Thighs* and *The Spy Who Came*. I began to hope that the Sin-Art's male clientele didn't come tiptoeing past our slumbering doorman looking for young lovelies to share the action. Our two-and-a-half-room apartment rented for $125 a month. We arrived during cockroach jamboree week, but that wasn't too much of a problem because we had forgotten to buy light bulbs, so unless you stepped directly on one of the nasty critters you hardly knew they were there. We spent our honeymoon evening trying to reassemble the bed we had taken from my parents' house. Picture, if you will, two manual defectives, hot, tired, and getting very grouchy, floundering around in the pitch-black, trying to avoid stepping on cockroaches the size of German shepherds, attempting to assemble a pile of lumber that needed only six boards and a Phillips screwdriver to become a nuptial bower.

"Are you sure this is the right kind of screwdriver?"

"I said I think it is. I mean, when I looked at it the last time, when it was light out, I think it had that funny bottom with the little grooves. Can't you tell by feeling the bottom?"

"I'd rather be feeling your bottom."

"Don't talk dirty." Bottom joins virgin and hits a new low.

David decided that if he threw the screwdriver at the wall with all his might and it went in, then it was a Phillips. It was too dark to find it after it bounced off, so we went to sleep on the mattress on the floor. I felt a little like Fay Wray, but instead of having to fret about one huge creature sweeping me up and carrying me away, the dirty work, I feared, would be done in segments by the swarms of hideous insects doing a stepped-up tango on the floor near the mattress. We had just gotten settled when some depraved maniac began to torture babies in the alley outside our bedroom window. My husband of twelve hours jumped up, but not to call the police to report these evil goings-on, but to pour some water into a kettle and put it on the stove to boil. He grabbed the whistling kettle, yelled for me to raise open the window screen, and, like a madman, raced over and dumped the scalding water into the alley. Are these grounds for annulment? I didn't realize he didn't want a family, but there are more subtle ways to say you don't like babies.

"Cats."

"Cats were torturing babies?"

"No, no. Cats in the alley. The females scream like that when the males want to mate."

Carousing cockroaches and cats who were into S and M. Welcome to New York. Perhaps we could get them all lifetime passes to the Sin-Art.

It took a while for me to get used to my new life in the big city. Since David spent almost all his time at work or at law school, I was pretty much left up to my own devices. I was not well trained in the domestic arts, but the roaches and I conspired to keep the place pretty neat. I spent the summer exploring the city, learning how to use the subway. There is more to using the subway than figuring out where you want to go and surrendering your token (which back then cost fifteen cents). You have to learn how not to look at people on the subway. It took a little while for this to sink in and a little while to figure out why all these sleazy types would come and sit next to me and even follow me out of the train. Just because they leer at you doesn't mean you have to be polite and smile back. Hartford manners do not apply in New York City.

I needed the subway to get to Manhattan to check out great places to shop for food and, more important, to buy chocolate. I would go to Ninth Avenue in the thirties to Manganaro's to buy fresh mozzarella cheese and spinach pasta. I would go to Houston Street in the Lower East Side to Russ and Daughters for smoked fish, dried fruit, the honey candy that my father loved, and especially for the long shoestrings of red-and-black licorice that lasted such a long time. Next to Russ and Daughters was the funny bread and egg store run by orthodox Jews. The women looked so pious and solemn that I always felt a little uncomfortable and out of place — especially in my miniskirt. They had the best black bread, with the thickest, chewiest crust, and the moistest bialys filled with sweet onions and a few poppy seeds. Around the corner was the pickle place where you pointed to the appropriate barrel and a jolly, white-aproned gentleman fished out a gigantic, shiny green half-sour pickle for you. Even though he wrapped it in several layers of white deli paper, the people sitting on either side of you on the subway ride home knew just what you were carrying. It was then to Little Italy for hard anise cookies and fresh sweet sausage, and perhaps a cannoli or cream horn and a cup of capuccino at Ferrara's.

Naturally, most of my time was spent looking for great chocolate. In this effort I spent hours cruising the avenues of the Upper East Side of Manhattan. I would spend one entire day on each avenue, casing each bakery and candy shop before making a final decision. I had one experience early on that taught me that my food budget did not allow me to burst into a store like I was Auntie Mame in Tiffany's at Christmastime: I found myself on Lexington Avenue, several blocks uptown from Bloomingdale's. There was this teeny little bakeshop tucked in between a boutique that sold handbags from Florence (Italy, not Schwartz) and an antique shop that seemed to specialize in Ming dynasty soap dishes. Something should have told me that I was in the high-rent district. In the bakeshop's tiny case there were only three or four items. I wondered how they could stay in business offering such a small variety. See, I had not yet learned about less being more. The brownies were small, but looked delicious. The pecan rolls were minuscule, but irresistible. The woman on line in front of me (the one in the full-length sable coat) ordered a dozen of each and put it on her store charge account. My turn. I ordered three of each and patted myself on the back for my monumental self-control. The saleslady wrapped up my goodies and said, "That will be seven twenty-five." No wonder the sable lady charged it; who would want to walk around with enough cash to pay for twenty-four pastries if six cost $7.25? I really just about dropped dead. My weekly food budget was fifteen dollars, and this was only Tuesday. I couldn't say I changed my mind, please take them back. That would be too humiliating. I was going to have to eat this one, literally. So I shelled out the cash with as much graciousness as I could muster. We carbohydrate loaded for the rest of the week: macaroni and cheese, baked beans, and cheese sandwiches. Of course we had great (if not tiny) desserts. That's how I learned, from buying what we from then on referred to as "the second-mortgage brownies," that less is indeed more.

My parents had season tickets to the Metropolitan Opera. I lived for those days when they would come to New York because it meant I got to pick the restaurant and they got to pay for dinner. The lemon chicken at Pearl's Chinese Restaurant was all the rage then. Dad's love of Chinese food and his American Express card meant we made an appearance at Pearl's minutes after Mimi Sheraton pronounced it THE place to dine. Dad also had this fondness for Ruby Foo's. My hip New York friends (the ones who wouldn't cross water) thought that it was a scream for us to eat at the place where they had spent their post-high-school prom hours drinking sloe gin fizzes and Mai Tais with little paper umbrellas sticking out of the glasses. I always loved the little twinkling stars in the ceiling and I was sad when they redecorated the place.

My very favorite place of all is gone. La Comedie was, I believe, the largest French restaurant in the United States, if not the world. It was an old, well-established place located near Lincoln Center that served, what was to my fairly unsophisticated palate, the most delicious and elegant food I had ever eaten. It also boasted the makings of a chocolate lover's paradise. In each of the many dining rooms was a two-layered dessert cart covered with a white tablecloth. On the top level of this cart were fruit tarts, usually some génoise and butter cream creation, and assorted petits fours. In the center was the showstopper. It was a gigantic glass punch bowl filled with chocolate mousse. It was the most ethereal chocolate dessert I had ever tasted. The mousse was foamy, but not so airy that it lacked substance. It had a sophisticated bittersweet taste that was very different from the cloyingly sweet mousses I was used to. I think it was the first mousse I had ever eaten that wasn't stabilized with gelatin. The waiter, when given the go-ahead, would dip two big silver serving spoons into the bowl and put a big scoop of mousse onto a gold-rimmed dessert plate. Then, miracle of miracles, he would reach under the white tablecloth to the lower level of the cart and bring out yet another huge bowl, of crème Chantilly. Another silver serving spoon, another scoop, always placed right alongside, never on top of, the chocolate mousse. The karma between this mousse and me was perfect, so perfect that I substituted the phrase "chocolate mousse" for my TM mantra. The waiter hovered nearby in case (are you kidding?) I wanted more. The bad news is that La Comedie closed and I never got the recipe for that mousse. The good news is that Simone Beck's Marquise Glacé au Chocolat* is a dead ringer for it.

Simone Beck's Marquise Glacé au Chocolat

This is the richest, smoothest, deepest chocolate mousse I have ever tasted. It can be eaten garnished only with a dab of freshly whipped cream, or used to fill the Name Cake on page 172. If you dislike the taste of coffee, omit it, and add plain water to the chocolate.

SERVES 10

10 ounces semisweet chocolate, chopped
2 tablespoons instant coffee
¼ cup boiling water
4 extra-large eggs, separated
6 ounces sweet (unsalted) butter at room temperature, cut into small pieces

Pinch of salt
⅔ cup sugar
¼ cup water

Put the chocolate in a metal bowl set over a pan of gently simmering water. Dissolve the coffee in the water and pour it over the chocolate. Stir to blend.

When the chocolate has melted, stir in the egg yolks one at a time until the mixture thickens slightly after each addition. Keep the heat of the water in the pan underneath the bowl at a low simmer so that the chocolate/egg mixture does not boil.

Remove the bowl from the hot water and add the small pieces of butter, one at a time, stirring after each addition to melt the butter before adding the next piece.

Place the egg whites and the pinch of salt in the bowl of an electric mixer.

Place the sugar and water in a small saucepan and bring to a boil, stirring until the sugar dissolves. Boil without stirring until it registers 220 degrees on a candy thermometer.

Start beating the egg whites at high speed. When they turn opaque (this should take only 30 seconds or so), begin to pour the syrup into the bowl in a steady stream. Beat the meringue until it is shiny and firm.

Using the lowest speed on the electric mixer fold the chocolate into the meringue. Turn into a two-quart serving bowl and chill.

The Trianon

Sixteen years ago, my husband and I lived in Brooklyn Heights. Our neighborhood was a charming area, full of fancy, wonderfully furnished townhouses, occupied by charming, sophisticated, and obviously successful people. My husband and I were not quite in this league. Actually, as we took in the view from the four windows in our one-room apartment — a sweeping panorama of brick walls — we looked upon ourselves as soon-to-be-successful. Rich we weren't, but we were hopeful.

To keep in shape for the day when we would be rich, once a month we practiced being members of the upper crust. My husband, David, the aspiring lawyer, would take the subway to Manhattan's Upper East Side, to a shop called Colette's Pâtisserie, where he would lay out $7 (back then that was almost 50 percent of our weekly food budget) for a chocolate cake called the Trianon.* Lora, the aspiring editorial assistant, would not make the pilgrimage to Colette's to purchase the Trianon because Lora was scared to death of Colette. Colette was a sour-faced, ill-tempered Frenchwoman (no, I cannot bring myself to call her a lady). She was the kind of French person who convinced many Americans never to set foot on French soil. One didn't have to cross thousands of miles of ocean to be insulted by a Frenchman. All one had to do was take the Lexington Avenue IRT to Sixty-sixth Street and walk one block east.

The fact that people couldn't throw down their $7 fast enough was in itself a testimonial to the chocolate cake that Colette made. David would tuck his treasure under his arm and hotfoot it back to Brooklyn, where we would double-bolt our door, take the phone off the hook, and proceed to devour the entire cake, garnished solely with a quart of ice-cold milk. The apartment house could have burned down, and I'm sure we wouldn't have noticed. This cake took second place only to great sex.

The cake itself was loaf shaped. It was about seven inches long and four inches high. It was very plain-looking. The top sank in during baking and Colette filled in the sunken part with chocolate curls, which always were smashed by the time the cake got home. There was no frosting or glaze. It looked pretty much like a chocolate brick. It tasted like fantasy become reality. The outside was crusty (tenderly crusty), a bit crunchy on the teeth. Then came a slightly dry, almost coarsely grained texture. And finally, dead center was a silky smooth, creamy, melt-in-your-mouth-coat-your-arteries, oh-my-God chocolate essence. I've seen grown men cry over this cake. One cake would usually serve eight normal people. But if we had any of our chocolate-loving couples over to dinner, and I felt wealthy enough to serve the Trianon, we would have to buy two. There was never any left over.

During the Trianon awareness stage of my life I was not a cook. Frozen fish sticks (burned on the outside and raw on the inside) were my forte. Be that as it may, I vowed that I would learn how to make Colette's cake. The nasty expression on her face and the ungenerous look in her eye made it clear that one did not simply ask for the recipe. Actually, I had heard tales of those unfortunate souls who were dumb enough to ask. She physically escorted them to the door, all the while screaming at the top of her lungs about what barbarians and ingrates they were. No way was I about to set myself up for public humiliation like that, chocolate cake or not. I set about to duplicate the dessert in my own kitchen (the culinary closet was more like it). The project seemed doomed to failure from the start. The basic problem was that I couldn't cook. I made three or four feeble attempts to re-create this bit of heaven on earth and then threw in the dish towel.

Five years later many things had changed. We had left New York for Boston, David was out of law school and had graduated from the soon-to-be-successful phase of his career to the hot new lawyer in town, and I had traded in my dreams of making it big as an editorial assistant for dreams of making it big in the food world. I was making a decent living selling cookies to Bloomingdale's. Those of you who are familiar with the kind of cookies that Bloomingdale's sells realize these were not your run-of-the-mill sugar cookie. They were meringue mushrooms that I made using the fabulous recipe in *Maida Heatter's Book of Great Desserts*. They were wonderful-tasting cookies that looked exactly like real mushrooms. At first I made them just for friends and family, but then it occurred to me that there might be a living to be made in meringue mushrooms. I trotted off to Bloomies, mushrooms and husband in hand. Up to the pastry counter I marched and demanded to know who made "all this stuff" (I gestured with sweeping arm to the collection of goodies in the cases). In the kind of condescending tone Bloomingdale's salespeople learn during their training sessions, the clerk replied that they had their sources from around town and around the world. I pulled out my basket of mushrooms and the clerk swallowed his smirk. He called the buyer in, who said they'd take a couple dozen on consignment and would let me know how they sold. We went home and I made David call Bloomingdale's and say he heard that they were selling Lora Brody's meringue mushrooms and could he order ten dozen. Family influence notwithstanding, the item was a huge success and for the next four years I faithfully delivered fifty-dozen meringue mushrooms to Bloomingdale's every week.

Naturally, I wrote to thank Maida Heatter for her help in changing the course of my life (not to mention the interior decoration of my kitchen — it was redone in sticky white goo that hung from the lights, encrusted the work counter, and made the phone stick to your hair). She responded with a wonderful and supportive letter, and a great correspondence was born. We wrote back and forth, sometimes three and four times a week. We called each other long distance more times than the mushroom income could justify. As expected, the main focus of these calls and letters was our favorite food — chocolate. One day when I was writing to Maida, I had a déjà vu of that wonderful cake we had consumed with such lust in New York years before. Had she ever tasted or even heard of such a cake, I asked. I tried to describe it, but even though I could recall the taste of the cake as clearly as if I had eaten a piece yesterday, I found it was difficult to put the taste into words. Even so, Maida got the message. Yes! Yes! Yes! She and this cake had quite a history, she wrote in her return letter. It seems that years ago when Maida lived in New York City, she discovered the cake and, like us, became obsessed with getting the recipe. She tried much harder than I ever did. She would send her handsome and charming husband around to the shop to invite Colette to dinner at Le Pavillon, take her to the theater–anything to worm the recipe out of her. With all her typical charm, Colette showed him the door, leaving no expletives deleted. Undaunted, Maida began to hang around outside the shop. She was convinced that the secret of the cake lay in the kind of chocolate Colette used. Can't you just picture this elegant, well-dressed classy lady slouching around outside this chi-chi East Side store, waiting for a delivery of the goods? A chocolate voyeur! Ironically, she did manage to find out the brand of chocolate used in the recipe. It was Van Leer's. The bad news was that this piece of tasty knowledge didn't help to crack the recipe.

Maida would buy dozens of the cakes and ship them to friends, food writers, bakers all over the world. But no one had the answer. Maida sent me an enormous file of correspondence, notes, and recipes that represented ten years' worth of research to try to unlock the secret of this amazing dessert. I bought fifty pounds of Van Leer chocolate and went to work. I would bake four and five cakes a day. I started with a recipe that I thought was close and changed it a measurement here, an ingredient there, with every baking. Sometimes I scrapped the whole recipe

The Trianon

69

and started with another as my base. I used my family and friends as guinea pigs. The problem there was that they were totally undiscriminating — they loved all the variations. The truth was that I wasn't even close.

I had met Julia Child several times and found her to be very approachable and certainly interested in culinary conundrums. So I called her with this one. Indeed, Julia was interested in this dubious project, and so I sent her both Maida's file and mine too. I should add that while we were doing all this test-baking, we had a constant supply of the Trianon on hand, shipped straight from the source. Julia's first reaction to the bought cake was that it wasn't the same as the one she had tasted from Colette's many years ago. Julia felt quite strongly that the chocolate wasn't the same quality. I was reluctantly inclined to agree with her assessment. I was also inclined to tear my hair out and push my fist through a wall. Not only was I trying to re-create a totally illusive item — I was trying to re-create something that existed only in my memory.

After several frustrating months of work, Julia published her version of the Trianon (which she called Le Gâteau Victoire au Chocolat Mousseline) in her cooking column in *McCall's* magazine. It wasn't the Trianon but it was darn good. Even better was Julia's gracious mention of me in the article, which made my mother the most popular woman in her bridge club.

Months passed and many pounds of chocolate were invested in the name of unlocking the secret of the Trianon. To no avail. Then a great tragedy occurred.

David and I always made a practice of stopping at Colette's when we were in the City. One reason was to purchase a couple of cakes, the other was to see if there was any hint that the passage of time might have mellowed the dear lady. Not that I expected her to volunteer any information, but perhaps she might let a clue slip my way. On one of our pilgrimages, another woman who worked in the shop was behind the counter when we got there. I summoned up my courage and asked if Colette was around and, if so, could I say hello. The woman rolled her eyes heavenward and sort of crossed her hands on her ample bosom and said, "Colette is no longer with us." David said, "She quit?" I kicked him hard in the shin. I wanted to weep from frustration. I was sure that the recipe to this cake would never be mine. I just knew Colette took the secret to her grave and most likely was resurrected each night to bake it in her kitchen — just so she wouldn't have to trust it to her survivors.

We headed back to Boston in a deep depression. (To be really truthful, I was the one in the deep depression. David, the wise one, had moved on to the quest of the perfect crème brûlée.) The fact that this "post-Colette" cake we brought back from New York with us wasn't nearly as good as the others made the outlook even bleaker.

I found a version of the cake that was pretty good (not the real thing, though) and for the next five years sold it in my catering business under the name Trianon. I truly despaired of ever finding the real recipe. Then one day the most amazing thing happened. My friend Dian Smith, a talented writer who lives on Manhattan's Upper West Side, wrote to say that she and her husband, Bob, had, just the night before, been to dinner in the apartment of an attorney in their building. For dessert he served a chocolate cake that reminded Dian of the cake I had described to her when I was searching for the illusive Trianon recipe. The gentleman, whose name was Larry Rodman, called the dessert Larry's Chocolate God. He said he got the recipe from a young woman who got it from her aunt, a Frenchwoman named Colette, who owned a bakery on Third Avenue. The aunt made her niece promise not to share the recipe until she (the aunt) had died. I got dial burn, so fast did I race to call him up. He said he was sure the baker/aunt in question was indeed the same Colette I had been courting unsuccessfully all these years. He generously shared the recipe with Dian and me. It tasted and looked just like the real McCoy — and it wasn't even hard to make! The search was over; the recipe was mine at last.

The Trianon

Isn't it wonderful that even though this recipe was so difficult to come by, the cake itself is not so terribly difficult to make?

SERVES 12 NORMAL PEOPLE OR 8 CHOCOMANIACS

12 ounces bittersweet or semisweet chocolate, cut into small pieces	**1 cup sugar**
	5 extra-large eggs, separated
10 ounces (2½ sticks) sweet (unsalted) butter, cut into pieces	**Pinch of salt**
	1 cup cake flour, sifted before measuring

Preheat the oven to 325 degrees. Position the rack in the lower third of the oven.

For this cake to be "authentic," it must be baked in a loaf pan with an 8-cup capacity. If the pan is too large the cake will be flat. Too small and it will rise too high and get too crusty. To measure the capacity of your loaf pan simply pour water into a measuring cup and pour it into the pan, keeping track of the number of cups you poured. The pan I use measures 10¼ inches long, 4 inches wide, and 3¼ inches deep.

Coat the sides and bottom of an 8-cup loaf pan with a generous layer of butter. Line the bottom of the pan with parchment and butter the parchment. Do not use vegetable shortening.

Melt the chocolate and butter in a metal bowl placed over a pan of gently simmering water. Stir with a wire whisk until both ingredients are melted and blended. Add the sugar and continue to stir, over heat, for two minutes. Remove from heat and stir in the egg yolks one at a time, mixing until each is incorporated.

In a clean metal bowl, with clean whisk or beaters, beat the egg whites with the salt until they are firm and hold soft peaks, but are still shiny.

Stir one large spoonful of the whites into the chocolate mixture to lighten. Pour the rest of the chocolate mixture over the whites. Sift one-third of the flour over this mixture and begin to fold. When the flour is incorporated, sift on another third, continue to fold, sift on the remaining flour and fold until the flour is incorporated and no whites are visible.

Pour into prepared pan.

Bake 50 minutes. Check the cake after 30 minutes. If the top appears to be browning too much, place a piece of tin foil over the top of the cake.

The cake is done when the top has risen an inch or so above the pan and it is crusty and browned. The cake should be firm and not wiggle when the pan is moved. Turn off the oven and close the door. Let the cake sit in the oven another hour.

Remove the cake from the oven and place it on a rack to cool completely. Do not be tempted to speed the cooling process by refrigerating the cake — you'll never get it out of the pan. Loosen the sides of the cake with a small knife and place a cookie sheet on top of the cake and flip the pan and the sheet over. Remove the pan. The cake will be *very* fragile. Wrap it in plastic wrap and foil — it's better to wait a day or so before serving the cake — but if you can't wait, be prepared for the cake to crumble a bit when you slice it.

To serve:

Slice and serve with unsweetened whipped cream and (if you're not a purist) raspberry sauce made by pureeing a package of frozen raspberries. It is not necessary to defrost the raspberries before making the puree.

It is possible to freeze this cake, although the freezing does change its personality.

Learning to Entertain or I Was a Corporate Bride

When David graduated from law school he joined a fancy Wall Street law firm. The oriental rugs in the lobby of this firm cost more than our combined college tuitions. The second week after he joined the firm we were invited to a black tie dinner dance at the Pierre Hotel. I wore my wedding dress and a severe case of hives. I was a vision in pink, white, and gold. I had never been to a formal dinner with my husband, so you can imagine my disappointment and feelings of panic when I found out that I wasn't going to get to sit next to him. I was seated between a talkative, opinionated real estate lawyer with terrible bad breath, and a politician who was so famous that even I had heard of him. It was agony talking to the lawyer — he kept pushing his face closer to mine as I kept backing away. I was being overcome by his breath when I whipped my head around in desperation to talk to the politician. The fear of not being able to hold my own in conversation with this esteemed person wasn't nearly as bad as the fear of humiliating myself by passing out into my soup from the fumes of the guy on the other side. I didn't have to worry about talking to the politician. He did all the talking while he squeezed my knee and poured me more wine. So, I survived the first course. The second course was rock Cornish game hens, glazed Belgian carrots, and Indonesian rice pilaf. A veritable United Nations of nourishment. I had never eaten such a small bird before and really got nervous when one of the other wives referred to it as pigeon. From what I had seen going on in Central Park, those filthy, bedraggled birds looked about as appetizing as my hardy crew of roaches. After checking out how the other folks at the table were handling their birdies, I stuck my fork into what I thought might be the breast and picked up my knife and began to cut, when suddenly the slippery little bastard did a 180 and skidded off the plate right into the lap of the horny politician, whose head was turned in the other direction. When my hand dived for his crotch he completely misunderstood my intentions. I don't remember much about dessert, but as far as the other people at the table were concerned, it wasn't nearly as interesting as the entrée.

Our social lives were not ruined by this slip of the bird, however. People in the firm were quite curious about the new associate's wife who goosed the guy at the fancy dinner. After that we were invited to lots of dinner parties — in the Dakota, on Park Avenue, and all over Westchester. I did such a good job behaving myself that, after the first rush, the invitations sort of dried up.

"Now it's our turn to invite them," says my husband, who doesn't even know if the fork goes on the right or left of the plate.

"You want me to cook for those people? Are you crazy? They give us smoked salmon and beef Wellington. I should maybe make fish cakes Brody [that's burned on the outside, frozen on the inside, served with lumpy Velveeta sauce]?"

"Hey, how about all those fondue pots we got for wedding presents? Fondue is easy, and we could have a practice dinner before the real one."

Okay. Okay. I agreed. We invited our friends who didn't cross water (they made an exception if it involved food they didn't have to cook) and I got out my trusty *Joy of Cooking*. It did seem to indicate that any fool who could read and stir at the same time could whip up a batch of boeuf fondue. I planned my menu very carefully because I was still at the stage where I could never get the components of a meal to come out ready to eat at the same time. David would have finished his scrambled eggs and half the Sunday *New York Times* before I could give him his toast. I decided we would do away with a first course, and I made my mother's friend Doris's hot crabmeat dip and served it with Ritz Crackers and drinks (this was before the "now" generation discovered pâté, Kir, and white wine spritzers) in the living room (which was actually an annex of the dining room, which was actually an annex of the kitchen). I brought the cookbook with me to the butcher and he sold me gorgeous chunks of sirloin for the fondue. I made Minute Rice and spinach salad with sliced mushrooms, which was the big "in" thing that year. David had requested a dessert that we had eaten once in a Hungarian restaurant on the Upper West Side. It was called Mont Blanc au Chocolat, and the waiter who gave me the recipe said it was very easy to make.

"You know chestnut puree?"

"Sure," I said. Liar. I didn't have the vaguest idea what puree was, and chestnuts were something I threw at my brother on the way to school in the fall.

"Well, this is easy." He kept saying in his heavy Hungarian accent how easy this recipe was. "You get the chestnut puree, you put it in the nicest dish you have. You pour chocolate sauce over. You put whipped cream on top. No problem."

To my great relief my local supermarket sold chestnut puree in cans. I could handle opening a can, and I knew how to make chocolate sauce.

The night of the practice dinner came. Our friends crossed the water. The hot crabmeat dip was a big success, except for when David asked everybody if they wanted more and we didn't have more. Carefully following the directions I set the fondue pot half full of hot oil on the dining room table, which was set with my best tablecloth and brand-new china and silverware. The guests sat down and we each skewered a piece of raw meat with a fondue fork. As we plunged our forks into the pot we watched as the hot oil sizzled and bubbled around the cubes of meat. We sat and watched in fascination as the hot oil bubbled higher and higher in the pot, closer and closer to the top. We pushed our chairs away from the table and let go of the fondue forks as the hot oil bubbled right up over the rim of the pot and cascaded over the sides, spilling onto my new tablecloth, over the edge of the table, and onto the floor.

"Gee, I don't think this is the way it's supposed to work," says our host, the master of understatement.

I gingerly retrieved the forks, mopped up the oil, and we ate the now over-cooked meat. No matter how much oil I removed from that pot it still managed to bubble up over the sides when we put our forks in. Immediately after dinner the pot was retired from service. It is now a planter.

It is almost impossible to ruin Minute Rice, so that was okay, but I didn't realize that when the package says "washed spinach," that means it's not quite as dirty as when it came from the garden but not clean enough to eat. We had a spinach, mushroom, and sand salad.

The company was good-natured and took these disasters in their stride. I went into the kitchen to prepare dessert, which I was certain would be a no-hitch surefire hit. As instructed, I opened the can of chestnut puree. It looked like very firm, beige mashed potatoes. Instead of scooping the contents of the can onto a dish I ran my can opener around the bottom lid and pushed it through the can, which meant I now had a perfect, smooth, firm, squat beige cylinder sitting on my best china serving plate. I poured my mother's famous chocolate sauce over the thing and then (forgive me) squirted giant rosettes of Reddi wip all over it. It sure didn't look like the Mont Blanc au Chocolat we had in the restaurant, but it was the only dessert I had available at the moment. Everyone at the table was pretty quiet while I served. They were even quieter when they took their first taste. Have you ever tasted unsweetened chestnut puree? Not only does it look like and have the texture of firm mashed potatoes, it also tastes like firm mashed pota-toes, only worse. Three of us sort of pushed the dessert around on our plates until an appropriate length of time had passed and I could start to collect the dishes. David, bless his heart, finished his whole plate and asked for more. Thank God there wasn't any more.

While I have never ever made boeuf fondue again, I have put several of those pots to use making a fantastic Toblerone Milk Chocolate Fondue.* I have learned to wash spinach and make real rice, and I did learn how to make a fantastic and innovative version of Mont Blanc au Chocolate (Coupe Glacé Mont Blanc au Chocolat*). The day after the practice dinner fiasco one of my friends (whom I could now probably never get to cross water again) sent me a copy of Craig Claiborne's The New York Times Cookbook. Inside the cover she inscribed, "You have the makings of a great cook, let Craig teach you the fine points." I sat down and read it from cover to cover before ever taking it into the kitchen. I was more than encouraged; I was inspired and I felt confident. Craig Claiborne and his marvelous book taught me how to cook. I started with simple dishes and very quickly worked my way up to things with many ingredients that involved cooking procedures that transcended boiling. Then I bought Julia Child's magnificent Mastering the Art of French Cooking. I learned to make crêpes, how to roast beef, poach fish, and whip up omelets. I soon felt ready to feed the most discerning of David's associates.

Even though it was more than fifteen years ago I still remember the menu of our first real dinner party. I made a cheese soufflé for an appetizer and chicken à la Kiev for the entrée. Both these recipes were from The New York Times Cookbook. I served a salad of watercress, oranges, and walnuts with Gorgonzola dressing (lifted from the Ritz Hotel dining room in Boston), and for dessert, I made Julia's Reine da Saba. Imagine yours truly eating cheese with blue mold on it. How far I had come.

That evening kicked off many years of great dinner parties. I learned a lot about how to create a memorable evening and how to avoid a dud. The first and most important thing to remember (especially in this age of insane and overly intense focus on food) is that the guests and making them feel welcome and comfortable are far more important than what you give them to eat. Yes, you did bust your ass planning and shopping and cleaning and cooking. Yes, your menu is brilliant and your cooking sublime. So, why should your guests feel guilty? Why should every conversation be directed toward what goes in their mouths? How many times have you heard the following conversation:

"God, Harriet, this lamb is incredible. And the sauce is divine. Am I wrong, or is it enhanced with catsup?"

"What a great garnish. Leave it to clever old you to think of pine cones to go with the pine nuts in the acorn squash soufflé. Or is it sweet potato mousse?"

"Did you really go all the way to that health food store in Hoboken for these dear little geranium sprouts?"

"I think you are so brave to serve Coquilles St. Jacques when Mimi said just last Wednesday that it's passé."

A simple "this is delicious" should suffice. If the guests carry on too much the hostess gets sucked into expecting hours of discussion about and praise for her food and might get depressed if she doesn't get it at subsequent dinners. So, give her a break.

Even worse are the wine bores. Wine should be opened away from the table, poured, and enjoyed. Instead we get:

"Rodney, you son of a gun, I thought all the '34 Château Phydeaux was gone. Where did you manage to pick that up?"

"What a great nose on this baby. Really assertive and flowery. No tannin here, lively and forward. Love to find a gal as good as this wine."

"This is a new one to me. Could you have the little lady soak the label off and carefully dry it between two paper towels? That's the girl."

Maybe this kind of bologna is okay if you've invited the members of an international wine society to dinner, but for us lay folks a simple um um good should suffice.

I have several rules of thumb as far as planning the menu goes. I try to serve one kind of food (besides bread) that has to be eaten with the hands because there seems to be some kind of gentle challenge involved in getting the food into your mouth that tends to liven up the crowd. Roasted chestnuts, tiny blini with sour cream and caviar (you put out the components and the guests have to assemble them), a bowl of steak tartare surrounded by melba toast, capers and chopped onion, and bagna caôda scooped up with bits of French bread are great to serve before dinner. Artichokes, either stuffed or with mustard vinaigrette, will have your guests rolling up their sleeves and plunging right in. Spicy Chinese chicken served with lettuce leaves invites each person to make his own savory little package. The most natural choice for a dessert eaten with the hands is Chocolate-Dipped Fruit.*

Don't serve anything weird to people you don't know well unless you don't mind eating it cold yourself the next few days. Avoid most organs (the one exception is liver, if it's in the form of pâté — by now, everybody has learned to eat pâté). You may think sweetbreads are the cat's pajamas, but I would drop dead if someone served them to me. Avoid really spicy dishes, unless you know your guests are used to it; everything made with tofu; and things with unexpected ingredients that you feel compelled to blab out while your company has a mouthful of it. The best example I can think of is the woman who served us a rather strange-textured chocolate layer cake. "Bet you can't guess what's in this," says she. Right then I knew I didn't want to know. "Sauerkraut!" Oh my God, if David hadn't dug his nails into my arm I would have let my mouthful fly right across the table.

Always do as much advance preparation as you possibly can, and always make more than you think you'll need. If I'm having eight guests I always make enough for ten. Get your husband or your kids to clean the house, or hire someone. Save your energy for the cooking. Don't bother having them clean the upstairs — in a pinch you can take all the junk from downstairs and put it upstairs — just remember to close the doors of the uncleaned rooms. Just accept the fact that you and your spouse will have a fight the day of the dinner party, and by 4:00 in the afternoon you will realize that your guests are probably playing tennis, making love, or reading the new P. D. James mystery you meant to get to this weekend. You will hate their guts and hope they all cancel. Save time to take a hot bath and have a drink before they come, and don't get aggravated when they're late. I do tend to remember the people who are more than 30 minutes late and tend (with very few exceptions) not to invite them again. I also remember the people whose baby-sitters have to be home by 10:30. They don't get asked back either.

Don't bite off more than you can chew. If you're broke or if you don't have any dining-room chairs, don't plan a ten-course sit-down dinner for twelve. Make a pot of great chili, some corn bread, a salad, get some Carta Blanca or Dos Equis (two terrific Mexican beers) and invite your friends to sit on cushions on the floor. End dinner with frozen Spiced Chocolate Dacquoise* and your guests will think they dined in a palace. If your cooking skills are at the novice level, pick a simple menu and have a practice dinner. If you're feeling confident, add your own touches. Remember that people love to have someone else cook for them and clean up afterwards; the food is secondary to being waited on. Let someone else throw the monster New Year's Eve buffets until you have live-in help and a six-figure income. If you feel you absolutely must entertain during the holidays, keep it intimate and easy, because if you don't, everyone else's holiday will be joyous and you'll be a basket case. A simple meal of caviar or foie gras, rack of lamb, and Individual Chocolate Croquembouches* might break the bank, but will leave you some energy to enjoy yourself. If you don't feel up to a dinner party there are loads of other wonderful alternatives: Sunday brunch — yes, before those trendy little glassed-in sidewalk restaurants that have Bloody Marys coming out of the water tap, people did do brunch at home. This is my very favorite brunch menu: champagne and orange juice, eggs scrambled with lox and sautéed onions, brioche, assorted cheeses and fresh fruit, and of course for dessert, Chocolate Hazelnut Cheesecake.* What could be more fun than a champagne and dessert party? A champagne and chocolate dessert party! If you're a confirmed chocolate lover the latter will appeal to you. If you're not, try the first idea and see a good psychiatrist. You can organize it two ways: do it all yourself and get exhausted, or invite each of your pals to bring either a bottle of their favorite champagne or their favorite dessert. Just remember to keep a written list of who brings what so you don't tell Rachel that Beverly made the divine Vienna Squares* when Adele really did.

As you can see, of all the important tips for successful entertaining that I've learned, the most important thing is SERVE A CHOCOLATE DESSERT.

Coupe Glacé Mont Blanc au Chocolat

While this dessert is not the traditional Mont Blanc, I think it is just as delicious, and probably more appealing to people who still think of chestnuts as things used to stuff a turkey. Here, a scoop of creamy, rich chestnut/rum ice cream sits atop a meringue nest. The dessert is topped with a bittersweet chocolate sauce, whipped cream, and candied chestnuts. All the components of this dessert can be made the day before.

SERVES 10–12

For the ice cream:

1 cup heavy cream
1 cup milk
6 extra-large egg yolks
1½ cups dark brown sugar, firmly
  packed
15 ounces unsweetened canned
  chestnut puree (If you can find only
  sweetened chestnut puree, reduce the
  brown sugar to 1 cup.)

¼ cup rum
1 tablespoon vanilla extract
¾ cup candied chestnut pieces with
  syrup (available at specialty shops)

Scald the heavy cream and milk together in a 1½-quart, heavy-bottom saucepan. In the bowl of an electric mixer, beat the egg yolks and brown sugar until the mixture is thick and forms a ribbon when the beater is lifted from the bowl. With the mixer on low speed, pour the hot cream/milk mixture into the eggs and beat until mixed. Add the chestnut puree and beat until mixed. Return the mixture to the pan and cook over low heat, stirring constantly with a rubber scraper until the mixture thickens slightly and coats the back of the scraper. Do not allow the mixture to boil. Strain into a metal bowl and stir in the rum, vanilla, candied chestnut pieces, and syrup. Refrigerate until completely cold, then freeze in an ice cream machine.

For the meringue nests:

6 extra-large egg whites at room
  temperature

1 cup sugar

Preheat the oven to 200 degrees with the racks as near the center of the oven as possible. Line two heavy-duty baking sheets with foil or parchment. Beat the egg whites either by hand or in the bowl of an electric mixer, then add the sugar gradually. Continue to beat until the meringue is very shiny and stiff. Place the meringue in a large pastry tube fitted with a number 5 star tip and pipe twelve 3½-inch rings, then pipe another ring on top of each ring, making them approximately 1½ inches tall. Pipe any leftover meringue into little rosettes for use as decoration. Bake 30 minutes, then let the meringues sit in the turned-off oven with the door closed for one hour. If the meringues start to brown before the 30 minutes is up, reduce the oven temperature. If they are still sticky at the end of the hour, bake them 15–20 minutes more at the lowest possible temperature, then let them sit again in the turned-off oven until they are dry. My meringues will brown occasionally, but I like the way they taste. If you're a purist, try cooking them at the lowest possible temperature at which your oven will bake. When they are dry, let them sit unrefrigerated until you are ready to assemble the dessert.

For the sauce:

⅓ cup honey
1 cup heavy cream
4 ounces unsweetened chocolate,
  chopped

6 ounces semisweet chocolate, chopped
2 tablespoons sweet (unsalted) butter
  at room temperature
¼ cup dark rum

Combine the honey and cream in a medium-sized saucepan set over moderate heat. Cook until the mixture comes to a boil. Off the heat, add the chocolates and stir until they melt. Repeat with the butter. Stir in the rum. This sauce should be refrigerated until ready to use. If it becomes too thick to pour, heat it in a saucepan over very low heat, stirring to prevent burning.

To assemble:

1 cup heavy cream, whipped with 3
  tablespoons confectioners' sugar and
  1 tablespoon vanilla extract

Candied (glacéed) chestnuts, cut into
  large pieces
Meringue rosettes

Place a meringue nest on a plate and top it with a scoop of ice cream. Pour the chocolate sauce over the ice cream and pipe or spoon some whipped cream on top. Sprinkle with the candied chestnuts and top with a meringue rosette.

Vienna Squares

Here's another great recipe combining chestnuts and chocolate. These elegant squares have a chocolate marzipan crust, a rum chestnut filling, and a bittersweet chocolate glaze. This dessert can be made in a food processor.

MAKES 48–54 SQUARES

For the crust:

1 box chocolate wafers

7 ounces almond paste or marzipan

4 tablespoons (2 ounces) sweet
(unsalted) butter, melted

Preheat the oven to 350 degrees with the rack in the center position. Generously coat with butter an 8½ x 13-inch baking dish with 2-inch-high sides. Place the wafers, marzipan, and butter in the bowl of a food processor and process until well blended. Distribute the crumbs evenly on the bottom of the prepared pan and press gently to form a crust.

For the filling:

14 ounces (1¼ cups) condensed milk

15 ounces (1⅓ cups approximately)
unsweetened chestnut puree (If you
can find only sweetened chestnut
puree, reduce the sugar to ⅔ cup.)

1 cup dark brown sugar, firmly packed

⅓ cup dark rum

1 tablespoon vanilla extract

2 extra-large eggs

1 egg yolk

Place all the above ingredients in the bowl of a food processor and process until blended and very smooth. Pour over the crust. Bake 30 minutes. While the cake is baking prepare the bittersweet glaze.

For the glaze:

½ cup heavy cream

2 tablespoons instant espresso

8 ounces bittersweet chocolate (I use

Tobler Extra-Bittersweet), cut into
small pieces

1 tablespoon sweet (unsalted) butter

In a small saucepan, scald the cream with the instant espresso, stirring until the coffee dissolves. On low heat add the chocolate and stir until smooth. Off the heat, add the butter and stir only until the butter melts.

Remove the cake from the oven and let it cool for 15 minutes. Pour the glaze over the cake, smooth it with a long metal spatula and let it cool completely before cutting it into small squares.

Toblerone Milk Chocolate Fondue

Toblerone is a brand of fine Swiss milk chocolate that contains tiny bits of honey nougat and crushed almonds. It lends itself to a delicious and easily made fondue.

SERVES 4

3 bars milk chocolate Toblerone
(9 ounces in all)

½ cup heavy cream

¼ cup cognac (optional)

Chop the chocolate into small pieces.

Scald the cream in a small, heavy-bottomed saucepan.

Off the heat, add the chocolate and stir until it is completely melted. If the milk solids in the chocolate separate, process the mixture for a few seconds in a food processor or blender.

Add the optional liquor and stir to combine.

Serve in a fondue pot or set the saucepan on a hot plate or warming tray.

On a platter have ready any of the following to dip:

Banana slices	Pear slices
Seedless grapes	Candied ginger
Apple pieces	Prunes
Peach slices	Dried apricots
Tangerine sections	Macaroons
Orange sections	Ladyfingers
Strawberries	Pound cake
Mango slices	Marshmallows (tacky, but I love them)

Using long wooden picks or fondue forks, dip a piece of fruit or cake into the chocolate and enjoy.

White Chocolate Fondue and Sauce

SERVES 8–10

1 cup heavy cream
9 ounces Tobler Narcisse, cut into
  small pieces

⅓–½ cup Drambuie

Scald the cream; off the heat, add the chocolate. If milk solids do not dissolve, process for a few seconds in a food processor or blender. Add the Drambuie to taste. (I like it strong.)

To serve as fondue, follow the directions for the Toblerone Milk Chocolate Fondue. For sauce, cool slightly to thicken and serve with ice cream or over fresh fruit such as strawberries, raspberries, poached pears, or baked apples.

Chocolate-Dipped Fruit

Making chocolate-dipped fruit is easy, and the end product will be beautiful if you are very careful about how you prepare the fruit and melt the chocolate. If you are dipping strawberries, it is important to buy clean fruit. Strawberries do not do well when they have to be washed to remove sand. They retain moisture, which can ruin your chocolate coating. If you must wash them, do so briefly and then pat them dry with paper towels. If you are dipping orange sections, use navel oranges, and peel them carefully so that the membranes are intact. Remove as much of the white part as possible.

1 pound bittersweet or semisweet chocolate	**3 pints strawberries and/or orange** sections

To melt the chocolate:

In order for the chocolate to be shiny and set correctly, it must be tempered (melted correctly) so that the cocoa butter is stabilized and won't rise to the surface of the chocolate, causing the unattractive gray streaks called "bloom." The following is a method of tempering that will work if you are careful to watch the temperature when you melt the chocolate. Use a mercury thermometer.

Grate or chop one pound bittersweet or semisweet chocolate. It must be in *very small* pieces. Place two-thirds of it in a metal mixing bowl. Using a pot into which the bowl of chocolate will fit, fill the pot with water (up to a level that will touch the bottom of the bowl) and heat the water until the thermometer reads 120 degrees. Turn off the heat and place the bowl of chocolate into the pan of water. Stir gently until the chocolate melts and is smooth. Remove from the heat and stir in the remaining chocolate. Continue stirring until the additional chocolate has melted and the entire mixture is smooth. Wipe the water from your thermometer and check the temperature of the chocolate. It should be between 85 and 88 degrees before you begin to dip.

An alternative method is to melt 1 pound of chocolate with 4 tablespoons sweet (unsalted) butter in a bowl set over gently simmering water. If you use this method, you won't need to temper the chocolate.

Once the chocolate is melted, it is important to work fast before it cools down too much. Dip the fruit and place it onto wax paper–lined baking sheets to dry. It can be refrigerated until serving time. Two pints of strawberries or 3–4 large navel oranges will serve approximately 4–6 people.

Individual Chocolate Croquembouche

A traditional croquembouche is a towering structure of little cream puffs all held together by caramelized sugar. Beautiful to look at, a challenge to make, and potential dental murder. This version, while not as majestic to behold, is just as delicious and much easier to make. It consists of a small pile of chocolate cream puffs sitting in chocolate cups, filled with chocolate cream, covered with chocolate sauce. Now, is that enough chocolate for you?

For the pastry:

1 cup all-purpose flour
¼ cup unsweetened cocoa
¾ cup water
¼ cup milk
1 stick (4 ounces) butter — it doesn't
  have to be unsalted, cut in pieces

2 tablespoons sugar
4 *large* eggs or ¾ cup plus 1
  tablespoon whites and yolks

Preheat the oven to 425 degrees with the rack in the center position of the oven. Cover a heavy cookie sheet or jelly-roll pan with aluminum foil and place this pan on top of another one — the double pans prevent burning.

Sift the cocoa and flour together into a small bowl. In a small, heavy-bottomed saucepan cook the water, milk, butter, and sugar until the mixture comes to a rolling boil. Add the flour/cocoa all at once, and over a medium flame stir vigorously with a wooden spoon until the dough dries out a bit and doesn't stick to the sides of the pan — approximately 2 minutes. Be careful not to scorch the mixture — it burns easily because of the cocoa.

Place the dough in the large bowl of an electric mixer. Place the mixer on medium speed and beat the dough for a minute to cool it slightly before adding the eggs. (See note.) Add the eggs one at a time, beating well after each addition. Make sure each egg is incorporated before adding the next. After all the eggs are added, place the machine on high speed and beat an additional minute.

Using a large pastry tube and a number 8 round tip, pipe the cream puffs at least 3 inches apart on the double pan. Hold the pastry bag perpendicular to and 2 inches above the cookie sheet. Squeeze a 1-inch mound of dough and cut it from the metal tip with a small sharp knife. Unless you have two ovens, you will have to repeat this procedure. Refrigerate the remaining dough covered with a thin film of butter to prevent a skin. Bake the puffs in the preheated oven for 15 minutes. At the end of this time turn the oven down to 350 degrees and bake an additional 5–7 minutes. Reach into the oven and, using a long sharp knife, make a small slit in each puff to release the air. Bake one more minute. Remove the pans from the oven and, using a small sharp knife, immediately scoop out the bottoms and any raw dough inside. Repeat with remaining dough. Remember to reset the oven back to 425 degrees. After the puffs are thoroughly cooled, they may be frozen in plastic bags. They can be filled while frozen. Makes 36–48 puffs.

For the filling:

2 cups heavy cream
2 tablespoons instant coffee (optional)

20 ounces bittersweet chocolate, cut
  into very small pieces

Scald the cream in a heavy-bottomed medium-sized saucepan. If you like a mocha taste, add the coffee and stir until it dissolves. Off the heat, add the chocolate and stir gently until it melts and the mixture is smooth. Pour two-thirds of the mixture into the large metal bowl of an electric mixer and refrigerate until it is very cold and almost solid. Save the remaining third in a small pitcher at room temperature.

When the refrigerated mixture is cold, beat it at high speed with the wire whip attachment of an electric mixer until it is light and fluffy — like whipped cream. Place the filling in a pastry tube fitted with a number 2 plain tip and fill the puffs. This should be done no more than 2 hours before serving so the puffs won't get soggy.

To assemble and serve:

I serve this dessert in store-bought individual chocolate cups. They are shallow and measure about 3 inches across. You may, however, simply serve this dessert on a plate. Either way, pile 4 or 5 puffs in a mound in a chocolate cup or on the plate. Pour the reserved sauce over them.

For an optional presentation, make the white chocolate Drambuie sauce on page 82. Pour some of the white sauce into the chocolate cup or onto the plate before placing the puffs. Pour the dark chocolate sauce on top.

Note: *Always make it a practice to break eggs to be added to a moving mixer or food processor into a small bowl or measuring cup first. You won't run the risk of having to fish tiny pieces of eggshell out of your batter.*

Chocolate Gâteau Paris-Brest

This is a chocolate version of the classic French cake made with the same chocolate cream-puff pastry and filling as the individual croquembouche. It is made in one large ring that is split and filled with chocolate whipped cream. The addition of toasted hazelnuts makes it a sublime treat. (To skin hazelnuts see note at end of recipe.)

MAKES ONE 9-INCH CAKE

For the pastry:

1 cup flour
¼ cup unsweetened cocoa
¾ cup water
¼ cup milk
1 stick (4 ounces) butter — it doesn't
  have to be unsalted, cut in pieces

2 tablespoons sugar
4 large eggs or ¾ cup plus one
  tablespoon whites and yolks

Preheat the oven to 425 degrees with the rack in the center position. Cover a heavy cookie sheet or jelly-roll pan with aluminum foil and place this pan on top of another one — the double pans prevent burning. With a felt-tip pen trace a 9-inch circle on the foil.

Sift the cocoa and flour together into a small bowl.

In a small, heavy-bottomed saucepan cook the water, milk, butter, and sugar until the mixture comes to a rolling boil. Add the flour/cocoa all at once, and over a medium flame stir vigorously with a wooden spoon until the dough dries out a bit and doesn't stick to the sides of the pan — approximately 2 minutes. Be careful not to scorch the mixture — it burns easily because of the cocoa.

Place the dough in the large bowl of an electric mixer. Place the mixer on medium speed and beat the dough for a minute to cool it slightly before adding the eggs. Add the eggs one at a time, beating well after each addition. Make sure each egg is incorporated before adding the next. After all the eggs are added, place the machine on high speed and beat an additional minute. Prepare the egg wash and the topping before baking.

For the egg wash:

1 egg beaten with ⅓ cup heavy cream

For the topping:

⅔ cup lightly toasted ground hazelnuts

Place the dough in a large pastry tube and, using a large (number 8) plain tip, pipe a 2-inch ring of dough inside the marked line. Pipe another circle inside and touching the first, and pipe the third on top of the other two. Brush the top of the cake with the egg wash, taking care not to drip any down the sides and onto the pan. This will hamper the rising. Sprinkle with the hazelnut topping and more egg wash.

Bake on the double pan at 425 degrees for 15 minutes. Lower the oven to 350 and bake for 20 more minutes. Reach into the oven and with a long thin knife make several slits in the cake. This will allow the steam inside to come out, which prevents the cake from getting soggy. If during the baking time the top becomes too brown, cover the areas with pieces of foil.

At the end of the baking time, open and turn off the oven. Let the cake sit in the oven to cool with the oven door ajar (approximately 30 minutes).

When the cake has cooled completely, slit it in two with a long serrated knife and prepare the filling.

For the filling:

1 cup heavy cream
10 ounces bittersweet chocolate, cut
  into small pieces

¼ cup Frangelico (hazelnut liqueur),
  optional

Scald the cream, and off the heat add the chocolate, stirring until it has melted and the mixture is smooth. Add the optional liqueur. Chill until the mixture is very cold — not quite solid. Then, using the whip attachment of an electric mixer, beat until light and fluffy.

To assemble and serve:

Place the bottom cake layer on a cake plate or serving platter. Spread the filling on it, and top with the other layer. Cut with a serrated knife.

Note: *Although it is preferable to work with blanched skinned hazelnuts, which are available in some gourmet food shops and health food stores or by mail from H. Roth and Sons (see address page 3a), it may be necessary to buy unskinned nuts. To get rid of the skin, preheat the oven to 400 degrees. Place the shelled nuts on a heavy-duty baking sheet and place them in the oven for 5–10 minutes; shake the pan and bake them another few minutes. Continue shaking the pan every few minutes after that to make sure the nuts don't burn. As soon as they turn golden brown, remove them from the oven and place a bath towel over them. Rub the towel vigorously over the nuts while they cool. As soon as you can handle them, rub the remaining shells off with your fingers. It is best to use the palest (least toasted) nuts for the top of the Paris-Brest, as they will get darker during the baking.*

Spiced Chocolate Dacquoise

This cake consists of four spiced chocolate-meringue layers with a ricotta and chocolate filling. The filling makes the meringue turn soft and the dessert has a mousselike consistency.

SERVES 10

For the meringue layers:

⅓ cup confectioners' sugar
4 rounded tablespoons unsweetened
  cocoa
½ teaspoon cinnamon
¼ teaspoon nutmeg

¼ teaspoon cloves
6 extra-large egg whites at room
  temperature
⅓ cup granulated sugar

Preheat the oven to 300 degrees, spacing the racks on the two lower levels.

Cover two jelly-roll pans or heavy cookie sheets with parchment. Using a ruler and pencil draw two 10 x 4-inch rectangles on each sheet of parchment.

Sift the confectioners' sugar, cocoa, and spices. Set aside.

Beat the egg whites until foamy, add the ⅓ cup granulated sugar, and continue to beat until the egg whites are firm and shiny.

Using a rubber spatula, fold the dry ingredients into the egg whites. The whites will deflate somewhat — try not to overwork the mixture, but make sure all the dry ingredients are combined.

Using a large pastry bag and a number 8 (the largest) plain tip, pipe an outline of meringue into the rectangles on the parchment. Then fill in the space by piping concentric circles until you have a solid meringue rectangle. Don't worry too much about making even edges — they will be trimmed later.

Place both cookie sheets or jelly-roll pans in the oven and set the timer for 15 minutes. At the end of this time reverse the positions of the pans, then set the timer for another 10 minutes. Reverse the pans again — back to front (this is to make sure that they brown evenly and don't burn). Cook 5 more minutes. Total cooking time is 30 minutes. The tops should be soft but not sticky.

Invert the parchment onto another piece of parchment and immediately peel off the top piece. If the paper sticks, wet a dish towel and gently moisten the parchment. It will come right off. Trim the edges of the rectangles with a pair of scissors so that the sides are straight. Cool these layers, uncovered.

For the filling:

4 ounces bittersweet chocolate, chopped into small pieces	1 teaspoon cinnamon
2 cups whole milk ricotta cheese	½ teaspoon nutmeg
¾ cup sugar	½ teaspoon cloves
1 teaspoon almond or bitter almond extract	1 cup heavy cream
	Cocoa for decoration

Melt the chocolate in a metal bowl placed over hot water. Cool slightly.

Beat the ricotta with the sugar, extract, and spices just until smooth.

In a separate bowl, whip the cream until it is firm. Fold the cream into the ricotta mixture.

Stir one-third of the cheese mixture into the chocolate. The chocolate will seize and become stiff, and the mixture may look grainy. That's okay. Just make sure it is well mixed.

To assemble:

Place one meringue layer on a cake plate. Using one-third of the remaining cheese filling, cover this layer. It is not necessary to use all the filling. It is better to have a thinner, even coating than a thicker one that may run down the sides of the cake. Place another layer on top, and using all the chocolate mixture, cover it. Place the third layer on top, spread this with half of the remaining cheese filling. Place the final layer on top of this and carefully spread a thin layer of the remaining cheese filling on it.

Place wax paper on the cake plate to keep it clean. Sift enough cocoa on the top of the cake that you can no longer see the cheese topping. This cake should mellow in the refrigerator for a couple of hours before serving. Cut it with a serrated knife.

Chocolate Hazelnut Cheesecake

When Craig Claiborne published his recipe for hazelnut cheesecake in *The New York Times Magazine* it was an instant hit. The fabulous flavor and texture of the smooth cheese and the toasted hazelnuts knocked socks off from coast to coast. There was no way this dessert could be improved . . . except maybe with the addition of a little chocolate.

This cheesecake is made in an 8-inch-wide by 3-inch-high round cake pan — *not* a springform. Don't be tempted to substitute another pan — the results will be a disaster. Most department stores and cookware shops stock these pans. Before you begin to bake, see the notes on cream cheese and ground toasted hazelnuts at the end of the recipe.

SERVES 12–15

For the crust:

1 generous cup crushed chocolate wafers (I use Nabisco Famous brand and grind them in the food processor)	6 tablespoons sweet (unsalted) butter, melted and cooled slightly
	½ cup ground toasted hazelnuts

Butter an 8 x 3-inch cake pan and line the bottom with a circle of parchment. Butter the parchment. Combine the above ingredients and toss them with your hands or a fork. Press the mixture into the bottom and halfway up the sides of the prepared pan. Don't worry about making the edges even — it looks better if they're not.

For the filling:

2 pounds best-quality cream cheese at room temperature	1¾ cups sugar
½ cup heavy cream	1½ teaspoon vanilla extract
4 extra-large eggs	1½ cups ground toasted hazelnuts

Preheat the oven to 300 degrees with the rack in the lower third, but not the bottom position, of the oven. Place the cream cheese, cream, eggs, sugar, and vanilla in the bowl of a food processor or mixer. If you use a food processor, blend until the mixture is very smooth. If you use a mixer, beat on low speed until the mixture is smooth. Do not beat on high speed. Add the nuts and process or mix until just blended.

Pour into the prepared pan and shake gently to level. Slam the pan once or twice on the counter to get rid of any air bubbles. Set the cake pan into a slightly wider pan and pour hot water into the larger pan to the depth of about 1 inch. Make sure the pans' edges do not touch. Place the pans in the oven and bake two hours. At the end of that time, turn off the oven and let the cake sit in the oven one more hour. Lift the cake out of its water bath and let it sit on the counter for another hour or until it is cool. Do not refrigerate the cake to cool — you won't be able to remove it from the pan.

To unmold: place a piece of plastic wrap over the top of the cake. Place a cookie sheet on top of the plastic. Invert the cake; you may have to give it a slam on the counter to release it. Remove the pan and the parchment. Place a cake plate on the top (really the bottom) and flip it over. Remove the plastic. Cut with a long sharp knife that has been dipped in hot water. (This cheesecake freezes beautifully.)

Note: *I get the best results with this cake when I use cream cheese that has sat at room temperature for several hours. Also I recommend using the food processor — if you have one — rather than the electric mixer, which tends to aerate the cake, causing it to rise in the oven and then fall when cooling, leaving an unsightly crack on the top. If you must make it in a mixer use it on low speed and take care not to overbeat.*

Note: *Occasionally, you can find blanched (skinned) hazelnuts in gourmet or health food stores. To toast these, simply place them on a baking sheet or in a shallow roasting pan in a 400-degree oven, shaking the pan every minute or so, until they are golden. If your hazelnuts still have the thin skin on them, proceed the same way as with the blanched nuts, but when you remove the pan from the oven, immediately cover it completely with a bath towel. Vigorously rub the towel over the nuts to remove the skins. As soon as the nuts are cool enough, rub the rest of the skin off with your fingers. Don't worry if some of the skin sticks to the nuts. You can use them anyway. When they are cool, chop them in the food processor or blender. Take care not to make hazelnut butter. You want some coarse pieces and some fine ones, too. I find it's much easier to toast three or four times the amount of nuts I need for this recipe. I freeze the rest and then don't have to go through this process next time I want to make this dessert.*

The Chocolate Baby

Fried eggs, Bickford's rare hamburger on white toast with lettuce, mayonnaise, and a slice of raw onion, Wise potato chips and a chocolate milk shake with coffee ice cream, or rare roast beef sandwich on a soft onion, poppy-seed roll, lettuce, extra mayo, hold the onion slice, and a Coke float, or three large slices of Ebinger's Blackout Cake.

I know this sounds like the Weight Watchers "No No" list, but it's really the food that nourished the heir to the Brody name while he was gestating. I get a real kick out of the mother-to-be of the eighties. She denies herself almost everything that I survived on during my pregnancies. When I had my last baby in 1981 I took a look at the diet my doctor recommended, then I took a look at my very normal and perfectly healthy ten- and twelve-year-old sons and ate whatever I wanted. I only regretted this three times: after each birth I had forty pounds to lose.

In 1968, when I became pregnant with my first child, all my friends were busy getting their Ph.D.'s, writing the great American novel, and rising through the ranks of their corporations. Most of them were still agonizing about whether or not to get involved in a serious relationship, never mind get married and have a kid. They didn't know what to make of me. I didn't have a whole lot of companionship and support with the first baby, and having my husband and most of my friends rushing off to glamorous jobs in Manhattan didn't help the matter much. I kept busy by writing freelance direct-mail advertising brochures for a large publishing house, and sticking to the above diet was pretty time-consuming in itself. Everything was status quo until my mother came to visit. We went to the city to shop for three-month-size undershirts for the baby and size sixteen maternity dresses for me. I took her to David's office and then the two of us went to

Serendipity for lunch, where I had two of my all-time favorite thing: Frozen Hot Chocolate* (Granite de Chocolat Amer).

"Do all the associates have to share their offices?" asks Mom.

"No, I don't think so. Why?"

"Well, I think it's great that you don't mind having David share his office with that attractive young woman," says Mom, never one to beat around the bush.

The truth is that, until she mentioned it, I didn't mind.

"Do you think she's so attractive?" I asked.

"Well, her dress was so short I noticed her legs first. It took me awhile to get to her face. I hope David has the decency to close his eyes when she bends over. Is she there all those nights when he works so late?"

"Mother, I have never even given it a thought. Anyway she's got a boyfriend, I think. Do you want the rest of your quiche?"

"Dear, if you're not careful you'll never get into that size sixteen dress."

This was March; only seven months before, I had weighed 106 pounds and worn a size four. Now I was a blimp wearing a tent that could house a platoon. Not only that, my husband was sharing his tiny office with a gorgeous, thin female lawyer. I knew I could trust her. It was him I worried about. I had to wait up past midnight to ask him about it.

"Forget it. I'm not her type," he assured me. I think I was supposed to be comforted.

Perhaps to convey her honorable intentions in this matter, Jenny, the tall thin lawyer, invited us to her apartment for dinner. I was reluctant to go for several reasons: I felt less than attractive and would have rather holed up in our apartment until the birth when I could reclaim my own body, and I had, because of my pregnant state, such strong aversions to the smells of several foods that I could not remain in the room where they were.

"Are you sure you told her that I can't eat lamb?" Eat lamb? The mere suggestion of it made me retch; the smell would kill me. The other problem was mushrooms. Something about the idea of mushrooms made me almost as nauseous as the idea of that dastardly lamb.

"I believe I mentioned it."

"Was she in the room at the time you mentioned it?"

Do you sense the makings of a fight here? One good thing about riding from Brooklyn to Manhattan on the IRT is that you can yell and carry on as loud as you want and no one pays any attention since that's considered normal behavior by 90 percent of the people who use the transit system. By the time we reached Astor Place we were friends again. Jenny's apartment was in the West (Greenwich) Village, as opposed to the grungy hippy East Village, on a beautiful tree-lined street. It had snowed most of the night before and big flakes were still coming down, so the stoops and sills of the brownstones were frosted with thick puffs of sparkling white snow. The noises of the city were muffled and everything looked clean and bright. All was right with the world while we crunched our way toward Jenny's house carrying the dessert I had offered to bring.

According to the directory she lived in the penthouse. Isn't it amazing how far a young associate's salary can go if it doesn't have to be used for frivolous expenses like obstetrician's bills? Her apartment was fabulous. It had a balcony that wrapped around three sides with fantastic views of the city. I had never been in the apartment of someone our age who could afford to have wallpaper on the walls, and this wasn't Con-Tact paper either. There were oriental carpets on the floor, the drapes and the sofas were decorated with Schumacher fabric, and the chrome and glass coffee table looked like something from the Museum of Modern Art. There wasn't a Marimekko wall hanging in sight. The table was set for three with beautiful china and crystal. There was a bowl of purple irises in the center. I thought I was at the home of one of my parents' friends. Jenny came to the door in her fur coat. She invited us in and excused herself. It seems she was barbecuing on the balcony. We sat down on the couch, drank some wine, and munched some string cheese (the "in" appetizer that year).

"Isn't this fabulous?"

"I smell lamb."

"You don't smell lamb. It's roast beef."

"Even I know you don't barbecue roast beef. Why would anyone barbecue anything outside in the middle of a snowstorm?"

"Maybe there's no oven in this apartment."

"I doubt it. I know I smell lamb."

"Please shut up about lamb."

If he hadn't said "please" I would have slugged him.

Jenny came back in with a big platter filled with long metal skewers. I recognized the mushrooms right off the bat.

"Isn't it great to have shish kebab in the middle of winter? I've had this lamb marinating for a week."

I went into the bedroom to lie down. David and Jenny, who spend all week in a tiny office together, got to have a lovely dinner together.

I managed to save face when the time came for dessert. Her shish kebab was no match for my Mocha Velvet* (coffee/chocolate ricotta cheesecake). She was beaten and she knew it. Even David knew he had made the right choice.

My due date was May fourteenth. By the end of May, I was sure the baby had grown too big to ever get out, or he was taking no chances with the draft board and had plans to stay there till he was too old for induction. I made my dear friend Kitty Boles go with me to ride the carousel in Central Park, thinking that might stimulate labor. What it did stimulate was the anxiety of the man who ran the thing. He made me get off after only five rides.

The Chocolate Baby

The weather turned hot (in New York, spring lasts one afternoon). I tried to keep my summer maternity wardrobe expenditures limited. I didn't want this baby thinking I was willing to go along with the waiting game much longer. I bought one light cotton dress (size 18) and wore it constantly. After a while it made me more ill than the lamb. Growing tired of the constant obnoxious phone calls — "Are you still there?" — I took the phone off the hook. I holed up in bed with several four-hundred-page books and a large box of Oreos. Now that's lying-in.

The acid test of a dedicated chocolate lover is that she asks for Baskin Robbins Mandarin Chocolate sherbet before she lets her husband call the doctor to say she's in labor.

"The doctor said not to eat anything if you think you're in labor."

"Well, Mrs. Bing and Marjorie Karmel both say to eat. I need some Mandarin Chocolate sherbet."

"Can't you eat the chocolate chip ice cream that's in the freezer?"

"The baby needs Mandarin Chocolate sherbet."

My obstetrician, Sheldon Cherry, said Mrs. Bing wasn't delivering this baby, and I was to not eat anything, including sherbet, and to get to the hospital. So, we got to the hospital and waited. We were never bored while we waited. The hospital had all sorts of fun activities to amuse me. First, there was the game of trying to escape the sadistic nurse with the razor and the enema bag. I tried to convince her these items were not necessary for or had in fact anything to do with the delivery of a healthy human baby. Then, there was what we subsequently referred to as the "First-Year Intern Challenge," which involved a still-wet-be-hind-the-ears preppy-looking postadolescent who thought he was going to give an internal examination to a very anxious first mother only slightly older than himself:

"What do you think you're doing?" (He's greasing up his rubber glove.)

"Just a little examination to see if you've dilated."

"I think a doctor should do that."

(Self-righteous indignation.) "I am a doctor."

"You look like the male equivalent of a candy striper to me. I'm paying Dr. Cherry a bloody fortune, and I don't mind waiting until he comes for this examination."

(He's getting hostile.) "Dr. Cherry won't come until I call him, and I won't call him until after I examine you, so why don't you start to cooperate, Lora?"

"Sure enough, Gerald." Two can play the first-name game and it's made especially easy for the patient since the doctor wears it on a name tag. Most patients don't have the guts to use the first name.

"Well, Gerald," I say, wiping away tears of pain after the prerequisite exam, "I sure hope you're going to make thousands of women happy by not going into gynecology. You have the sensitivity and lightness of touch of a six-car pileup."

We waited several hours longer until Dr. Cherry showed up to tell us nothing much was happening in the way of labor. I could have told him that. I asked if we could send out for Mandarin Chocolate sherbet. He offered me ice chips. David and I played poker for several hours. Dr. Cherry left, David went to sleep, and I sat shaved, emptied, and hitched up to an I.V. that contained nothing more interesting than sugar water. Boring. Dawn rolled around, and everything in the hospital began to pick up except my labor. David woke up (and ate breakfast) and I began to complain, loudly. Dr. Cherry returned with a hypodermic needle full of stuff that he injected into my I.V. "This should get things rolling."

Did it ever. The labor took off like an express train with no scheduled stops between Earth and Mars. Even my hours with Mrs. Bing had not prepared me for this. White-coated experts came and went, feeling my belly, listening to the baby, mumbling and conferring — all outside of earshot. After an eternity, it was agreed that while I was big, the baby was bigger and in a breech position. They regretted to inform me that a Caesarian section was in order. Well, I was never such a believer in natural childbirth anyway. They could pull the baby out of my nose if they thought it would end this agony.

It took a while for the effects of the anesthesia to wear off. The first thing I remember is Dr. Cherry telling me that we had a nine-and-a-half-pound son, and then I remember David standing by my bedside with a big grin, holding a large carton of Baskin Robbins Mandarin Chocolate sherbet and a spoon. What I really wanted was a meatball sub. What I got were more ice chips and a shot of Demerol. It took almost two days to convince the nurse that chocolate sherbet fell into the category of clear fluids.

Once I had a baby to care for it didn't take long at all to lose the weight. I learned how to navigate the subway system with infant and stroller in tow and soon had the pleasure of introducing the new Brody to smells and tastes that were almost as new to his mother. I vowed this kid would grow up eating things that I, as a child, had considered life-threatening. As soon as he learned to gum things down, we shared knishes, sour pickles, and goat cheese. Those new teeth chewed on spinach lasagne and egg rolls. For his first birthday I initiated him into the world of chocolate with a three-layer sour cream fudge cake that we called the Chocolate Initiation Cake* in his honor. It made him an instant convert. Don't wait until you have a one-year-old to make it.

Chocolate Initiation Cake

What a way to start your child on the chocolate diet! A moist and tender sour cream chocolate chip layer cake with creamy rich milk chocolate filling that is also used to frost the cake. This recipe calls for milk chocolate chips in the layers, but you can substitute semisweet chips if you prefer.

SERVES 12

For the layers:

2½ cups all-purpose flour, sifted before measuring
2½ teaspoons baking powder
1 teaspoon baking soda
½ teaspoon salt
1½ sticks (6 ounces) sweet (unsalted) butter at room temperature

1⅓ cups sugar
4 extra-large eggs, separated
1 teaspoon vanilla extract
1½ cups sour cream
1 cup milk
12 ounces milk chocolate chips (mini size, if available)

Preheat the oven to 350 degrees with the two racks positioned in the upper and lower thirds of the oven. Grease three 9-inch cake pans, line the bottoms with parchment, grease the parchment, and dust the pans with flour. Knock out the excess flour.

Sift together the flour, baking powder, baking soda, and salt. In the large bowl of an electric mixer cream the butter and 1 cup of the sugar. Add the egg yolks, one at a time, beating well after each addition. Mix in the vanilla, and on the lowest speed, the sour cream and milk. Add the sifted dry ingredients and mix only until incorporated. Stir in the chocolate chips. Be very careful not to overmix — this will cause the texture of the cake to be rough.

In a clean bowl, with clean beaters, beat the egg whites with the ⅓ cup sugar until they are stiff but not dry. Fold the whites into the batter. Divide the batter among the three pans and level it with a long metal spatula. Position the cakes on the two oven racks and bake 30–40 minutes, reversing the position of the pans (rack to rack) once, halfway through the baking. The cakes are done when they are golden in color and the sides have pulled away from the pans. Unmold the layers onto racks for cooling. Prepare the milk chocolate filling/frosting.

For the filling/frosting:

2 cups heavy cream
12 ounces (2 cups) milk chocolate or milk chocolate chips

2 tablespoons sweet (unsalted) butter, cut in small pieces

In a medium-sized saucepan over moderate heat bring the cream to a simmer. It boils over easily, so watch it. Lower the heat and continue to simmer until the cream is reduced by approximately one-half. On the lowest heat, stir in the chocolate chips. Continue stirring until they melt and the mixture is smooth. Off the heat, stir in the butter, bit by bit, stirring until it is incorporated. Cool in the refrigerator until it is cold, but do not let it solidify. Whip until it is fluffy and light in color. (If it remains in the refrigerator too long to whip, stir it over a low flame until part of it starts to melt and the rest is solid. Break up the solid pieces and whip.)

To assemble:

Place one cake layer on a cake plate with four long pieces of wax paper tucked under the edges. Spread a thin layer of the frosting on this layer and repeat with the next layer, spreading it with frosting. Top with the third layer. Spread the frosting on the sides, then the top of the cake. Pull out the wax paper strips. You can use additional chocolate chips to decorate the top of the cake, or to spell out happy birthday.

Granite de Chocolat Amer

While this isn't the real frozen hot chocolate, it's a more than acceptable substitute. This unusual and wonderfully delicious chocolate dessert is the creation of my cousin and dear friend, Betsy Bisberg, who is a talented and inventive pastry chef. The confection is a grainy bittersweet sherbet that will please the most sophisticated palate. You will need an ice cream maker for this recipe.

SERVES 6–8

8 ounces unsweetened chocolate (I use Ghirardelli Eagle Brand baking chocolate.)

2 cups cold water
1¼ cups (17 ounces) sugar

Chop the chocolate into small pieces and set it aside. In a medium-sized saucepan combine the water and the sugar and cook, stirring, until the sugar dissolves and the syrup is clear. Cool the syrup to room temperature.

In a small bowl set over gently simmering water, melt the chocolate. Combine the chocolate and syrup and whisk until smooth. Strain through a fine strainer or through cheesecloth. Cool to room temperature and process in an ice cream machine.

The granite should not be served rock hard, so you might want to mash it a bit with a fork before you scoop it for serving.

Mocha Velvet

This is a large, beautiful, delicious refrigerator cake (the filling is not baked) with an unusually mellow and exotic flavor that comes from a combination of ricotta cheese, coffee, and chocolate.

It is best to make this a day ahead. You will need a 10-inch springform pan. Amaretti (Italian macaroons) are available in gourmet shops and Italian specialty shops. This dessert, like all desserts stabilized with gelatin, cannot be frozen.

MAKES 12–14 PORTIONS

For the crust:

8 ounces Amaretti
½ cup graham-cracker crumbs

¼ pound (1 stick) sweet butter, melted

Adjust rack one-third up from the bottom of the oven and preheat oven to 400 degrees. Butter the sides only (not the bottom) of a 10 x 3-inch springform pan.

The Amaretti must be ground into fine crumbs. Grind them in a food processor fitted with the steel blade, or in two or three batches in a blender, or place them in a heavy plastic bag and pound them with a rolling pin. You will have 2 cups of crumbs. Set aside and reserve ½ cup. Place the remaining 1½ cups in a mixing bowl. Stir in the graham-cracker crumbs and then add the melted butter and mix well.

Turn the crumb mixture into the pan. With your fingertips press some of the crumbs against the sides of the pan, but leave a rim of uncrumbed pan about 1½ inches wide around the top of the pan. The crust should be 1½ inches high. Don't worry about the top edge of the crumbs being in a perfectly straight line. Press the remaining crumbs firmly against the bottom of the pan. (Try not to concentrate the crumbs too heavily where the sides and the bottom of the pan meet.)

Bake the crust for 5 minutes, then let it cool completely.

For the filling:

1 tablespoon plus 1½ teaspoons (1½ packages) unflavored gelatin
3 tablespoons plus 1 teaspoon cold water
8 ounces semisweet or sweet chocolate
⅓ cup dry instant espresso or other dry instant coffee

1 cup boiling water
½ cup granulated sugar
32 ounces (2 pounds) whole-milk ricotta cheese
1 teaspoon vanilla extract
1 cup heavy cream

Sprinkle the gelatin over the cold water in a small cup and set aside to soften.
Break up the chocolate and place it in a heavy 2- to 3-quart saucepan.

Dissolve the espresso in the boiling water and pour it over the chocolate. Place over low heat and stir frequently until the chocolate is melted. Then stir with a wire whisk until smooth. Add the softened gelatin and the sugar and stir over low heat for a few minutes to dissolve. Do not let the mixture boil. Remove from the heat and set aside, stirring occasionally, until cool.

In the large bowl of an electric mixer beat the ricotta cheese well. Add the vanilla and the chocolate mixture and beat until thoroughly mixed. Remove from the mixer.

Whip the cream until it holds a shape but not until it is stiff. Fold into the chocolate mixture.

Pour about half of the filling into the cooled crumb crust. Sprinkle the reserved ½ cup of ground Amaretti evenly over the filling. Cover with the remaining filling. Spread the top smoothly, or form a design with the back of a spoon (I make parallel ridges).

Cover with aluminum foil and refrigerate overnight.

Several hours before serving, remove the sides of the pan as follows: Insert a sharp, heavy knife between the crust and the pan. Pressing firmly against the pan cut all the way around the crust, then release and remove the sides.

The cake may be removed from the bottom of the pan if you wish. If so, it should be done now. Use a firm (not flexible) metal spatula (either a wide one or a long, narrow one). Insert it gently and carefully under the bottom crust and ease it around to release the cake completely. Use two wide metal spatulas, or a small, flat cookie sheet, or the removable bottom of a quiche pan or layer-cake pan to transfer the cake to a platter.

For the topping:

1 cup heavy cream
1 tablespoon granulated or
  confectioners' sugar
½ teaspoon vanilla extract
About ¼ cup toasted almonds,
blanched or unblanched, and thinly
sliced (toast by baking in a 350-
degree oven for 10 to 15 minutes until
lightly browned)

In a small, chilled bowl, with chilled beaters, whip the cream with the sugar and vanilla until it holds a shape and is firm enough to be used with a pastry bag.

Fit a pastry bag with a star-shaped tube, place the cream in the bag, and form a decorative border around the rim of the cake. Or place it by spoonfuls around the rim.

Crumble the toasted almonds slightly and sprinkle them over the whipped cream.

Refrigerate.

Welcome to Boston

*T*he divorce rate in David's fancy Wall Street law office seemed to rise in direct proportion to the lawyers' desire to "make it" there. It was easy to understand why. The associates knew that in order to become partners (a carrot held in front of their noses for so long that when they finally got to eat it, it was fossilized) they were expected not only to work the usual daytime hours, but most evenings and every weekend too. It was hard to complain about the salary, which was generous, but living in an apartment in New York City with one toddler, one infant, and a husband who was never home was the pits. When he did come home, he was so jazzed up from working with the giants of the legal world and rubbing elbows with famous clients that he didn't have to bother opening the door to our apartment — he just flew in through the mail slot. After he buzzed around the living room a few times jabbering about this motion and that injunction, my hostility thinned the air so much that he fell to earth with a thud. While he was worrying about proving the innocence of his white-collar criminals (or at least getting them off the hook), my days were spent pulling the baby away from the lead paint–covered sills he liked to gnaw on, and digging cat excrement out of the sandbox in the playground so my kids wouldn't get some fatal disease. He wore $300 suits from Saks and I wore jeans and banana-stained work shirts. It was hard to find a restaurant where we could both look presentable in our work clothes. It was also hard to go to those dinner parties with the other associates. My world was babies and colic and diapers, pounds gained and first words spoken. They were into bonuses and evaluations, office politics, and case loads. We were the only parents in the group, and the one time we tried to do something that could involve the children, our two-year-old threw up on an associate who already had mixed feelings about kids. We watched our friends' marriages grow strained and dissolve under the stress of the work and the life-style that went with it.

Leaving New York replaced David's mother as the topic most likely to be fought over. As much as he loved his job, my husband couldn't help but agree that there had to be more to life than work, no matter how glamorous. When he tried to give notice, the firm countered with a proposal that was impossible to turn down: a big case that David had worked on since he started at the firm needed someone to be in Europe for four weeks. How would we like to go to France, Switzerland, and England for a month? Do ants love a picnic?

Even though this was a business trip we somehow managed to have lots of fun. The European lawyers treated us like royalty; we stayed in hotels fancy as palaces and we ate like kings. David had to meet with people in Lyons, so we were there for almost a week. I was on my own for much of the time and my French was nonexistent, so I spent a lot of time wandering around the old city stopping at pâtisseries and chocolate shops to look at all the beautiful culinary works of art to be found there. When I found something I wanted to buy, I pointed a finger and held out a bunch of bills in my hand so the clerk could help herself to the right amount. Everything tasted as beautiful as it looked, and since it was Easter time, there was the added attraction of items that were prepared just for that holiday. The shop windows were filled with gigantic bunnies made out of the most elegant dark, milk, and white chocolate; there were magnificently decorated chocolate Easter eggs tied with yards of pink-and-gold satin ribbon; and baskets made from pulled sugar filled with tiny chocolate eggs and marzipan carrots. There were marzipan ducks and chicks peeping out of chocolate nests, and lambs made out of génoise and frosted with white-and-pink royal icing grazing on marzipan grass. In one shop there was a display of dark chocolate oysters with the shells half opened displaying the white chocolate pearls nestled inside. Even the stores that sold things as mundane as meat were a treat to visit. The butcher displayed his yet-to-be cooked paschal lamb on a garden of parsley garnished with perfect tiny carrots and miniature eggplants. Everywhere I looked there was beautiful food to awaken and inspire the budding cook in me. What most inspired me was one meal we ate during our stay in Lyons.

I had been invited to join David and the team of French lawyers and their clients for lunch at what was promised to be an extraordinary restaurant. I met them at the lawyers' office and walked to a very unassuming building located across a busy intersection from the railroad station. The restaurant was plain but nice. There were white walls with low ceilings. Here and there was a touch of wood that reminded me of the blond maple furniture my parents used to have. There was nothing to indicate that we were in a temple of haute cuisine. It looked like a nice businessman's lunch place. We were met at the door by a tall, very handsome bearded man who greeted the French lawyers and their clients very warmly and then showed us to a private dining room. When we were seated (another dinner where I didn't get to sit next to David — I was surrounded by people who didn't speak English — all I could do in French was ask for the bathroom), the bearded man, dressed in white, proceeded to discuss the menu with the French lawyers. Every time someone asked me something I just grinned and nodded my head very enthusiastically. Meanwhile, a young man in a long white apron passed around a crock of pâté made out of tiny birds called thrushes. Live and learn. I thought thrush was a mouth infection babies get. It had the color, texture, and consistency of the richest, creamiest chocolate ice cream. The bearded man, who turned out to be the chef, went into the kitchen and returned almost immediately accompanied by another, shorter and jolly-looking man who turned out to be his brother — the other chef. I was glad they came back so soon because I was getting tired of grinning and nodding. One brother carried a metal grill and a bunch of dried fennel twigs, and the other brother carried a platter with a big shiny blue-gray fish on it. They set the grill on a cart by our table, set the twigs on fire, and proceeded to cook the fish right in front of us. Every once in a while one of the chefs would give the fish a squirt of anisette from a bottle and the flames would dance up around the fish and the fennel would crackle, throwing tiny sparks in the air. In my whole life I had never smelled anything as delicious as that fish. My eyes were tearing and my mouth was watering. I watched in amazement at the effortless skill with which the chef-brothers quickly skinned and filleted the sea bass and served it to the twelve hungry diners. I took a bite, closed my eyes, and thought I had died and gone to heaven. The fish was so moist and tender that it required no chewing; it just slipped right down my throat. What didn't slip all the way right down, however, was a tiny bone that lodged right in the middle of my throat. I quietly cleared my throat. Still there. I coughed discreetly. Getting worse. I was beginning to panic. The Frenchman on my right was wondering why I wasn't eating my fish. Didn't I like it? he wanted to know. Not only could I not say in French, "I'm choking on a goddamned fish bone," I couldn't speak at all.

"Please God," I prayed, "if You remove this bone I'll promise to eat Velveeta sandwiches on Wonder Bread every day for lunch for the rest of my life." God took me up on my offer.

The rest of the meal was just as delicious but, fortunately, far less eventful. We had lamb (Imagine *me* eating rare lamb!) with garlic and roasted eggplant. For dessert there was raspberry sorbet garnished with fresh raspberries.

Years later David and I returned to Lyons and the restaurant of the brothers Troisgros. We were just regular tourists then, and the place had been redecorated by someone who must have worked for Bloomingdale's. Although the food was still delicious, we missed the personal touches we had enjoyed during our first visit. One personal touch was not lacking, however. As we went into the dining room a still, small voice whispered in my ear, "You owe me 13,489 Velveeta sandwiches."

It was a great trip and we were grateful to the firm for giving us the opportunity to go, but New York was becoming more and more a nice place to visit, but . . .

So we moved to Boston. I guess I had led a pretty sheltered life in Hartford because I really had never been exposed to any kind of racial or religious bias there. In New York you were judged on how much money you made — no one cared if your parents spoke English, never mind left you a trust fund. A certain amount of importance was placed on how smart you were, but those smarts could have been cultivated at East Podunk U. or Princeton, it really didn't matter. Because we have what can be construed as an Irish last name and we don't look particularly Semitic, our neighbors assumed the obvious — until Christmas rolled around. It took about thirty seconds for the entire neighborhood to be alerted to the fact that something was amiss with the new neighbors. The next day I was invited to my first coffee klatch. We sat around and drank instant coffee out of mugs sporting sayings like "Have You Hugged Your Child Today?" and nibbled on sticky buns from the A & P. While our children threw Legos at each other and whined for juice, cookies, and attention in general, the women asked me the strangest questions about chicken soup and Kosher salt. Finally one of them said, "You know, I feel like I'm asking a black person (only she didn't say "black") about soul food, but we've never met a Jew before." These are the parents of the children my children were going to school with? I told her that she could relax, not everyone in my family was Jewish. My brother-in-law, the Hare Krishna, was planning a long visit to our house soon and was bringing the three hundred members of his ashram. The kids and I left without even finishing our sticky buns.

When I look back on that incident now, I can laugh, both at my neighbors' ignorance and my overreaction to it. You have to understand that for me and my family that kind of thing had never been an issue. You were who you were, period. My initial reaction was to become incredibly defensive and paranoid. Never before had it been so important to me to be visibly Jewish. We joined a Conservative synagogue, and I did a weekly carpool of what I jokingly called "The Future Rabbis of America." My sons did not find that funny. For a long time I was afraid that if I didn't speak up right away and let people know we were Jewish, they would say something anti-Semitic, and I would then be in the position of having to clue them in. I almost got into a fist fight with the secretary who was registering one of my children for kindergarten:

"Child's name?" she asked.

"Max Brody," I answered.

"Is that spelled M-A-C-K-S?"

"No, M-A-X."

"Is it short for Maximilian?"

"No, it's long for M."

"We once had a boxer named Max."

I know, I know. That's not necessarily an anti-Semitic slur, but because I was so paranoid, that's how I heard it.

David's new law firm was, in many ways, very different from the New York firm. The atmosphere was more relaxed, and people tended not to kill themselves working unless they were on trial or in the middle of a crisis. While there was a mix of people, there was one group that, at first, in a perverse way, fascinated David and me. These were the young Etonians, as David called them, who had been registered at Harvard the day before they were conceived. All they ever talked about was THE Law School (Now, we had always thought that THE Law School was N.Y.U.) and THE Law Review. And they did sports with a fervor we had never seen. They played tennis, squash, and golf. They went white-water canoeing, trout fishing, and, of course, downhill and cross-country skiing. They sounded like David and me before we had sex. They drove BMWs and had recreational vehicles as second cars. They owned ski houses and sailboats and didn't worry about money because of trust funds. We were definitely out of our element socially, educationally, and financially. To my knowledge our parents thought a trust fund was something we should be creating now to support them in their old age.

As I said, there were other people in the firm, people more like us, who made us feel welcome, but there was always that other segment that awakened a powerful hostility in me. Except for the Prom Queen and her court in high school, no one had ever said to me, "You don't belong." Of course, it was much more subtle than that, but the message was clear, and I didn't like it. The chip on my shoulder was enormous, and, in some instances, my vision was warped, but our first two social functions with the firm didn't help my perception.

The first firm party we were invited to was on a Sunday afternoon at a client's home in a suburb that must have had ten-acre zoning. If you wanted to borrow a cup of sugar from your neighbor, you'd have to use your car. We drove around in circles for an hour looking for this guy's house because it was stuck so far back in the woods it was hard to see. I had never been to a house with two tennis courts before — that's what the landscaping was, woods and tennis courts. The house looked very expensive, and I'm sure it cost a fortune. Even so, the walls and doors were so thin that it almost seemed that someone could hear you going to the bathroom two rooms away. So, here were all these people from the firm dressed in tennis outfits — little white skirts (or shorts), white jerseys, white tennis shoes and little white socks, little terry cloth wristbands, and lots of sweat. It seems that some of us were invited to play tennis and some of us were invited to watch the first group sweat. I had never seen such a group of healthy, good-looking people. They were all tall, so well groomed (even though they were sweating), and so attractive. Beautiful teeth, straight, un-Semitic noses, clear skin. I sought out our host and introduced myself.

"Gee whiz, you certainly seem to like to play tennis." (What a great intro.)

"Yes, we play every day."

I once managed to sprain my ankle walking onto a tennis court, but I don't share this piece of information.

"What happens in the winter? Do you have someone snowblow the courts?" Easy, kid, don't get fresh.

"Oh, no. We play inside, at the tennis club."

"Oh. Is it nice there?" What can you ask about a tennis club? — "Do you like the color of the ceiling? How's the Coke machine?"

"That crowd from Newton is ruining it."

Hmm, I thought, could he mean "our crowd"? Time to go home. I wanted to start looking for a house in Newton.

Shortly after that, we were invited to a dinner party on Beacon Hill. This is certainly some of the highest-priced real estate in all of metropolitan Boston. In order to get one of the magnificent town houses in this area, someone in your family has to own one and then die and leave it to you.

The dinner party was in one of these very houses. I couldn't get over the fact that the young lawyer and his wife who owned this showcase were younger than we. We had six rooms and one-third of an acre in a middle-class suburb. Every single cent we owned had gone into buying that house (which we couldn't wait to sell). These people not only owned this fantastic house and another house on some island where the temperature never dipped below eighty-seven degrees, but they owned things my parents were still saving for, like pieces of art that were valuable enough to be insured. I was the only wife not wearing a Marimekko print dress and matching espadrilles. I hoped they could overlook my not coming in uniform. The men drank Chivas Regal and the women had sherry on the rocks. We nibbled on Triscuits and cheddar cheese. The men talked and the women listened with rapt attention to their stories of Harvard days. We didn't have any Harvard stories so I was beginning to feel a little out of place. At dinner I was seated (once again) between two people not related to me. I didn't have to worry about making conversation because the men did all the talking. When it got to the point where I was sick and tired of hearing about The law school and The good old days, I turned to the woman next to me and asked what she did. She replied that she was a dancer. My, that's interesting. I pressed her for more information about her career, but she motioned for us to remain silent because her husband was speaking. I turned to the pregnant woman on the other side of me and asked,

"What do you do." She said, "November." I gave up. The hostess brought in a magnificent china casserole and set it on the table. For the first time the women spoke — in unison: "Oh, you've made Julia's Jambon Braise Morvandelle from Volume One."

Now, wait just one minute. Every man at the table knew by heart the scores of every Harvard-Yale homecoming game since 1803 and every woman could correctly identify each recipe ever written by Julia Child. What kind of place was this?

So we didn't fit in. Several years passed before David found another, more compatible law firm. While I never did learn to love tennis or white-water canoeing, the Brodys became respectable hockey players and passable Red Sox fans. I developed quite a reputation in the firm, both for my ideas on entertaining (when we invited those Beacon Hill folks to our house I served a Moroccan dinner that had to be eaten completely with your hands and Chocolate Angel Pie* for dessert) and my big mouth.

I am delighted to report that I have mellowed quite a bit. I desperately needed to carve out my own niche and establish my own Boston identity. The disappearance of my hostility was directly proportional to the success of my catering business.

Chocolate Angel Pie

This dessert is a spectacular-looking delectable combination of silky smooth chocolate filling with a two-layered topping. A chocolate cookie crust and the garnish of chocolate-covered strawberries make it a real showstopper.

SERVES 8

For the crust:

1 8-ounce package (36 wafers) chocolate wafers, crushed into fine crumbs	6 tablespoons sweet (unsalted) butter, melted ¼ teaspoon cinnamon

Preheat the oven to 450 degrees. Place the rack in the center position. Grease a 9-inch pie plate with either butter or vegetable shortening.

Combine the crushed wafers and cinnamon, reserving ¼ cup of the mixture. Mix the butter into the rest. Press the mixture into the bottom and sides of the prepared pie plate.

Bake the crust for 5 minutes.

Reduce the oven temperature to 325 degrees.

For the filling:

4 ounces bittersweet chocolate, cut into little pieces	1 pound good-quality cream cheese
⅓ cup heavy cream	2 extra-large eggs
3 tablespoons dry instant coffee	¾ cup sugar
	1 teaspoon almond extract

Place the chocolate in a small bowl set over a pan of gently simmering water. Stir occasionally until the chocolate melts and then remove it from the heat.

Scald the cream and dissolve the instant coffee in it.

Place the cream cheese, eggs, sugar, and extract in either the bowl of an electric mixer or a food processor. Mix until very smooth. Add the cream/coffee mixture and then the melted chocolate.

Pour this mixture into the pie plate and bake for 35–40 minutes or until the top is dry to the touch and slightly firm.

Allow to cool completely.

For the toppings:

4 ounces cream cheese at room temperature	Reserved chocolate wafer crumbs
½ cup confectioners' sugar, sifted	½ cup heavy cream
1 teaspoon vanilla extract	6 ounces bittersweet chocolate, chopped
1½ cups heavy cream	1 tablespoon light corn syrup
	8 large, perfect strawberries

Beat the cream cheese together with the sugar and vanilla. Add the heavy cream and continue beating until the mixture is stiff enough to spread. Reserve one-third of the mixture in the refrigerator and spread the rest over the cooled pie. Refrigerate one hour or until cold.

Sprinkle the reserved crumbs in a 2-inch band around the edge of the pie. Use the reserved topping to pipe 8 rosettes at equal intervals on top of the band of crumbs around the edge of the pie.

Scald the heavy cream, and off the heat, add the chocolate, stirring until it has melted. Add the corn syrup and stir gently until the mixture is very smooth. Dip the strawberries halfway into the chocolate and set them on top of the rosettes.

Pour the remaining chocolate onto the middle of the pie and, using a short-handled cake spatula, carefully spread the glaze smoothly over the top of the pie — up to the rosettes.

Chill briefly before serving.

Catering

My catering career started almost by accident. I was agonizing about whether or not I should pursue a career in genetics, a long-time interest. It meant I would have to go to medical school (no easy feat for someone with two little kids) or try to get some clinical training while working as a researcher in a lab. The lab job I did get didn't pay enough to cover my baby-sitting costs, so I found another part-time job at night teaching yoga at a health club. The only baking I was doing were the meringue mushrooms I made for Bloomingdale's.

One evening I brought in some meringue mushrooms as a birthday present for one of my yoga ladies. The rest of the class went nuts. They all wanted to buy the mushrooms directly from me because the Bloomingdale's markup was so prohibitive. Several said they had tried to find out from Bloomies who made the mushrooms, but that information was a closely kept secret. The ladies didn't waste any time spreading the word, so soon I had to give up both part-time jobs and go into full-time mushroom production. So much for genetics. It was not long after that that people asked if I made other food items. Could they buy a cake? Could I make some frozen appetizers, how about a casserole or two? That is, quite simply, how it started. I really had no idea what I was getting myself into. I had no business experience, my operation was highly illegal (as are most home cooking businesses, unless the zoning is right), my only assistants were two elementary school children and a husband who could only give me ten hours a week because he had, as he kept reminding me, another job.

I was still in the drop-off stage — they call, I cook, I drop off, they heat up — when I got a telephone call from a woman to whom I had been delivering chocolate cake for about six months. I had never met the woman because I would leave the cakes on her enclosed porch and she would send me a check.

"Hello," she said, "this is Dotty Sternburg. Do you do dinner parties?"

"You mean do I cater them?"

"That's right. I'm having a party for one hundred people. Can you do it?"

All I could think of were the bills for my sons' summer camp and orthodonture work sitting, on David's desk, six weeks overdue. The threat of my beautiful sons sitting home all summer with crooked teeth prompted me to say, "Oh, yes. That's no problem. I'd love to do your party."

"Are you sure you've done things this big before? My husband and I are celebrating our twenty-fifth wedding anniversary and we want our party to be elegant and the food delicious."

"Oh sure, I can handle it." I could be a Boston politician for all my honesty.

We set up a time to meet and I stopped sleeping at night. I pored through volumes of *Gourmet* magazine and studied recipes from old Sunday *New York Times Magazines*. I created menus, agonized about prices, tried to figure out food costs and serving help. When I arrived at Mrs. Sternburg's house for our preliminary meeting, I felt better prepared to fix peanut butter and jelly sandwiches for my boys than create an "elegant and delicious" meal for a hundred people.

As I rang the doorbell I remembered that someone in my yoga class had told me a little bit about this family. I vaguely recalled her saying that Mr. Sternburg was ill. I loved Mrs. Sternburg the moment I met her. A beautiful woman, sparkling with energy and overflowing with vitality and tremendous enthusiasm, she made me feel so happy to be there, and her excitement about her party was so contagious, that I knew I could not only do the job, I could surpass her expectations.

As well prepared as I now felt to tackle the dinner, no one and nothing could have prepared me for meeting Mr. Sternburg. I followed Mrs. Sternburg into a large wood-paneled room whose walls were decorated with abstract paintings and colorful lithographs. There were several pieces of sculpture on tables and a whole wall of books and records. There were warm colors everywhere — the curtains, the rugs, and the fabric on the couch and chairs. All of those things were in the room, but I didn't notice any of them until much later. The thing my eyes locked onto when I walked into that room was a bed sitting atop a complex metal frame connected to a whirling motor that pushed and pulled the mattress part of the bed up and down in a head-to-foot rocking motion. Strapped onto this rocking bed lay a man who couldn't move anything but his head and the fingers of one hand. He was talking to me and I couldn't hear what he was saying, partially because of the noise of the motor that was moving the bed, and partially out of shock at what I was seeing. My instant feeling, after shock, was anger that no one had warned me, and because no one had warned me, I felt vulnerable and embarrassed. I moved close to the bed to hear what he was saying. At first I couldn't understand him because he spoke softly and coordinated his speech with the movement of the bed, which enabled him to breathe, but after a few minutes the difficulty passed and I could understand him without straining. He asked me all about myself in a way that was more than just making conversation. He seemed genuinely interested in me, who I was and what I did. He wanted to know all about David and the children, too. While he was asking me, I had a million questions myself. What horrible thing had happened that this man (whom I was beginning to find absolutely fascinating) had to be strapped into this bed that moved back and forth, back and forth. He anticipated my questions and told me in a very straightforward way (with quite a bit of wry humor thrown in) his story. Polio, in 1955, when he was thirty and I was ten, was the horrible thing that had happened. That summer my mother kept me close to home — away from public swimming pools and crowded beaches. I had been lucky.

He was married, with a two-year-old son and a six-week-old daughter, when he walked into a hospital feeling achy and feverish. He never walked again or took a breath without the aid of an iron lung or the special rocking bed. Most of the children and adults that contracted this most severe type of polio died. The few who lived did it, in part, because of luck, skilled treatment, and, most important, sheer will and determination, combined with incredible love and support from husbands, wives, parents, children, and friends. Twenty-nine years ago when Louis Sternburg got sick he was a successful businessman, an ace athlete, and a loving, involved husband and parent. He had to learn to get his athletic thrills vicariously by watching others. In the business world he has, along with his amazing wife, Dotty, continued his success and found time to get a Ph.D. in psychology from Brandeis University and write an inspiring book. As far as the husband and parent part goes — I hope to be half the parent to my children that Lou and Dotty have been to theirs. Their love and support of each other continues to be an inspiration to David and me in our marriage. They became my mentors and our extended family, and the godparents of our third child. (But this wasn't until after the party.)

Here I was on my first big catering job and I met a couple who would in many ways change my life and the kind of person I was. I wanted to stay and talk to them longer, but knew I had better get home and start cooking — I was determined that this party would be the best they ever had.

We had decided on a fairly involved menu: spinach roulade (rolled spinach soufflé) filled with poached salmon, served with ginger/lemon sauce; cold rice salad with pineapple, water chestnuts, and toasted almonds with a soy/honey/ mustard dressing; watercress and orange salad; and for dessert, a Chocolate Hazelnut Torte* served with fresh strawberries. I made spanakopetes and marinated shrimp to pass around first.

The party was on Saturday night. Months before, I had made a commitment to a friend of mine to model on TV for our local educational television fund-raising auction. My time slot was late Friday night. Most of the cooking was under control and I had all of Saturday to finish, so I had no qualms about going. I hung around the studio until almost 1 A.M. until I was finally called. I was wearing every bit of makeup I owned and modeling a full-length fake fur–lined leather coat. I felt like a hooker in a sauna. I did my thing for public TV and then rushed back to the dressing room to get the gop off my face. A call had come for me while I was on the air. The message read:

"Lora, Mrs. Sternburg called. She was really bummed out [that's TV talk for furious]. She said to tell her caterer that she has no business being on television the night before her party. She wants to know why you aren't home cooking."

Dotty was only half kidding, so we were both delighted and relieved that the party was a huge success. I catered many wonderful parties for them after that. My all-time favorite was the Just Desserts party Dotty gave when Lou got his Master's degree from Brandeis. I made tortes and layer cakes and mousses and frozen soufflés. There were cookies and bars and chocolate-dipped fruit, not to mention three different kinds of Chocolate Truffles.* We had ice cream with four kinds of toppings and fruit platters and dessert cheeses. What Dotty and I didn't figure on were her diet-crazed friends who didn't eat any of this glorious stuff. Next time, we decided, we'd serve Perrier and lime.

So, my career was born. The girl who gagged at the sight of moldy cheese and was revolted by the smell of lamb cooking was whipping out cold roast lamb salad with Stilton sauce for 350 people. Because at first I never had the nerve to charge enough, I had more business than I could handle. I was drowning in orders for stuffed grape leaves and strawberry tarts, when God sent Marie to help out. She made puppets for a living, but really wanted to cook. She was calm where I was always on the verge of hysteria. She was organized where I was out of control. I flunked math and she knew how to add, subtract, and could do the books. She could make fabulous Italian dishes and bake like a pro. Best of all, she was happy to let me be the boss and make the decisions. She was the perfect person for me to work with and she never once let me down. I know that God sent Marie because He knew I couldn't handle cooking dinner for Julia Child alone.

I got a call from Ruth Lockwood, who worked for public television as the producer of "The French Chef." Ruth and her husband, Arthur, entertained frequently and liked to try new caterers. She was calling to hire me to cater a small dinner party for her. I was thrilled to be asked. Up until this time I had only had customers in the western suburbs and Brookline. I viewed this as a chance to branch out into what was, at least for me, virgin territory. I also sensed it would be a treat to work for Ruth Lockwood, a gracious hostess and a lively, interesting woman who had a tremendous knowledge and great love of good food. I was thrilled indeed until she told me who her guests would be: Julia and Paul Child.

Now, I am sure that every cook, professional or otherwise, fantasizes about cooking dinner for Julia Child, James Beard, and Craig Claiborne. I myself had this fantasy. Let me assure you, while the fantasy is terrific, contemplating the reality is a nightmare. Ruth said she liked to introduce Julia and Paul to the new cooks in Boston and I shouldn't be nervous because they were both lovely, nonjudgmental people and I would find them delightful and easy to be with. I started mainlining Valium right away. I also lost my appetite and five pounds on The Fear of Julia's Dinner Diet. Marie and I immediately planned a series of Julia rehearsal dinners at which we tried out different menus on our friends, who were so wildly impressed by what we had been asked to do and so thrilled that they were involved (even if it was by proxy) that they indiscriminately pronounced everything delicious. Some help. We settled on the following menu, which Ruth Lockwood graciously approved:

Pirogen (tiny meat-filled flaky pastry turnovers — my mother's recipe); double consomme of leeks and beets garnished with ginger root julienne; chicken Ballotine stuffed with sausage, apricots, and prunes (the sauce was divine — it was a reduction made with stock, port, and apple cider); baked stuffed tomatoes; watercress, water chestnut, and endive salad; and for dessert, a JuliaTorte.*

The "JuliaTorte," created by yours truly just for the occasion, consisted of rectangles of hazelnut meringue layers with three fillings: bittersweet chocolate, raspberry, and mocha. It was covered with a dark chocolate glaze and decorated with pieces of meringue.

As nervous as I was (Marie had to walk me around the block several times before I could go in to start the final preparations in Ruth's apartment), the dinner, or what I remember of it, went extremely well. Julia and Paul were indeed easy to talk to and as unpretentious and straightforward as could be. They seemed delighted at my efforts and Julia encouraged me to "keep up the good work." I will be forever grateful to Ruth. She provided me two valuable things: her friendship, and the chance to prove that I could pull off a dinner for Julia Child.

After that, Marie and I settled into a rigorous schedule of dinner and cocktail parties, receptions, weddings, and Bar Mitzvahs. We cooked all week long and then worked at the functions every weekend. Since we were too compulsive to delegate, one or both of us were at every job. This compulsiveness paid off because in the many years we ran the business, we never had a real disaster. I must say, however, that we did have some near catastrophes. When caterers get together they love to share their horror stories. Here are my favorites:

We were hired to cater a fund-raising cocktail party at the home of a couple with a fabulous art collection. The house was very modern. Actually, it looked like it was designed just to house the many priceless etchings, lithographs, and pieces of sculpture that lined the walls. Even the swimming pool, with its adjacent deck, was surrounded with abstract statues and massive pieces of carved stone. The hostess was willing to give us a free hand with the menu, which included individual blue cheese quiches, smoked salmon rolls, and a stunning caviar mold, but there was one other dish that she wanted served: chicken livers and onions in a Marsala sauce. This wasn't something on our menu, but she had a recipe and she wanted us to make it. She also wanted us to serve it in a chafing dish that had been designed by a famous artist. I tried to explain to her that chicken livers and onions in Marsala sauce does not exactly lend itself to a visually outstanding presentation, but she insisted. She explained that the chafing dish was known to be a bit temperamental and we were to take special care when lighting the Sterno that went underneath it. The afternoon of the party we set up the chafing dish and its contents (I used as much chopped parsley as I could justify to try to break up the great lumpy brown expanse of the concoction) on the dining-room table. We very carefully set a match to the Sterno and made sure the lid was in place. About an hour into the party, Marie and I were passing through the dining room picking up dirty glasses and used napkins. To our horror we saw that some of the Sterno had leaked out of the container. As we stood frozen, the flames leaped out from underneath the chafing dish and quickly engulfed the entire thing. Most of the guests were oblivious — it's amazing what good wine can do — and the others were as horrified as we were. Marie and I exchanged a panicked look, each mentally picturing the Picassos and Andy Warhols going up in flames and taking our fledgling business and our families' entire life savings with them. We each wrapped our aprons around a handle and as calmly as could be, we picked the flaming dish up and started for the kitchen. Unfortunately, our way was completely blocked by people attacking the marinated shrimp. We shifted gears, swung around, and headed out toward the deck. Our eyebrows were beginning to singe and our hands blister so we did the only thing we could. We dropped the dish, chicken livers and all, into the swimming pool. I hear that the chafing dish went the way of my fondue pot and is now a planter.

A very special thing resulted from that job. I had lots of blue cheese and smoked salmon left over, and I also had a quantity of cream cheese that had been destined for cheesecakes that somehow never got made. These ingredients were about to go round the bend so I decided to use them to create something unconventional: savory cheesecakes. They were divine! Inspired, I went on to make a Ginger Cheesecake* with a chocolate crumb crust. Heaven! I sent the recipes to Maida Heatter to see what she thought of them. She suggested that I send them to Craig Claiborne, who published them in the *New York Times Magazine*. Not only was I legitimatized as a cook and caterer, but I got letters and calls from friends and relatives I hadn't heard from in years. It was great.

I still get palpitations when I think of the next incident. We were hired to cater a wedding for a couple who were both getting married for the second time. They were so happy and excited and put so much thought and energy into their wedding plans that they were a joy to work with. The wedding date was Sunday afternoon, May twelfth. At that time, besides making chocolate wedding cakes, I was making a dessert called a WindTorte. It is an enormous round container made out of very hard meringue, decorated with piped meringue whirls and swirls accented with hundreds of candied roses and violets. Just before serving, it is filled with gallons of cognac-flavored whipped cream mixed with raspberries, strawberries, blueberries, and cherries. Then, a hard meringue lid with more swirls and roses is placed on top. It looks like a rococo hatbox. To serve, some of the inside filling is spooned onto a plate and then a piece of the meringue is chipped off and placed on top. It is truly a sensational-looking (and tasting) dessert. It is incredibly time-consuming to make; if I am really efficient I can whip one out in three days. It takes this long because it is made in many sections, each of which has to bake for twenty-four hours at a very low temperature. As each section is added to the base of the cake, it has to undergo yet another long baking process. I usually use two ovens. This is what my happy couple chose as their wedding cake.

The Monday before the wedding I woke up in the middle of the night to what I thought were rifle shots. To my amazement there was over two feet of wet snow on the ground and more coming down. The noise I heard was the weight of the heavy snow snapping the leaf-covered tree limbs. A blizzard in May! It was most bizarre. Our power was gone for three days — no heat, no lights, no phone, and no oven. Now, I am convinced that any other caterer would, in a situation like this, say, "Okay, no oven, no WindTorte." Not me. I just couldn't bring myself to let this couple down. I paced and wrung my hands and worried until Thursday, when we got our power back. Thank God Marie got hers back two days before — she made the rest of the meal (but didn't know how to make the damn cake). I knew I had to rush the process, so I turned the oven up a bit higher and didn't bake the layers quite as long. I knew the meringue would be a bit sticky but figured what the hell, why should anyone be putting their fingers on it anyway? I pulled it out of the oven for the last time just two hours before the ceremony. It looked find to me.

I felt so sorry for the bride. She had intended to be married in her garden, which was her pride and joy. Instead of watching the couple exchange their vows amid daffodils and tulips in the warm spring air, the guests tramped into the house from the freezing cold and looked for a place to stow their wet galoshes and down coats. This crowd loved champagne. The groom kept telling me to hold off serving dinner because the guests wanted more time to drink. We finally served at 10:30. I'm sure that the next morning none of them could remember what they had eaten the night before. As I whipped the four quarts of filling for the WindTorte, I began to relax, thinking that I was home free. I folded in the berries and put the lid on. Marie grabbed a stack of dessert dishes and followed me to the living room, where the cake-cutting ceremony was to take place. All the guests gasped and applauded when we raised the cake's lid. The bride took the knife and chipped out a little piece of meringue, which she fed to the groom. The groom chipped out a bigger piece and fed it to the bride. Then the cake fell apart. All I could think of was Mount Vesuvius as the sides began to crack and topple over, sending great rivers of berry-dotted whipped cream cascading onto the table. In my rushing to complete the cake on time I had burned one of the sections and it had weakened the entire structure. I was paralyzed, but quick-thinking Marie put both her arms around the cake and held it together while she motioned me to pick up the platter. In this fashion (like Siamese twins joined at the cake) we started to walk back to the kitchen. I was really close to tears until I realized that the bride and groom and all their guests were clapping. Someone yelled, "It's a piñata!" I realized that this well-inebriated crowd thought that that was the way the cake was supposed to act. Who was I to argue? Marie and I had several glasses of champagne ourselves as we served the rest of the cake from the kitchen.

The next two stories are about the kind of people I rarely worked for. Because Dotty and Lou Sternburg were generous about giving my name to their friends, I could be sure of being treated well — that is, not like "help." I never had to worry about being paid, or getting undeserved complaints when I worked for their friends. More often than not, I was treated more like a friend than an employee, and to this day, I am still very close to many of the people I once cooked for. Once in a while, though, someone got my name and passed it along to someone else outside this circle.

I got a call from a woman who was having a party to honor her husband, who had just been made a full professor at Harvard. She lived in a beautifully renovated Victorian mansion. We sat in her kitchen, which looked like something out of *Architectural Digest*. Whoever had done the renovation had created a masterpiece. I complimented her on her stunning kitchen, and she said, "Don't think for one minute we could have done this on Benson's salary. It was the trust fund, of course."

Right. I should have known.

We went on to discuss the meal. She seemed pretty happy with the things I suggested, but had one cautionary note: "Under no circumstances are you to use pimentos. I don't want the food to look too Jewish."

Now, if she had said, "Don't use matzoh balls," I could have understood, but what did pimentos have to do with food looking Jewish? Anyway, it was an outrageous thing for her to say to me. I knew I had two choices. I could tell her to stuff her party and leave, or I could double the price and put pimentos in everything. I did the latter.

The last catering job I did I got conned into. The woman, a South American banker's wife, called in desperation. They had just moved here, and her husband had invited ten people to a buffet dinner party. Could I just make a four-course meal for twelve and drop it off? It sounded pretty straightforward. We agreed on a menu and the price. I gave her the name of the agency through which I got my waitresses and bartenders and told her to hire one of each. I arrived at her home at the agreed-upon time and found her in tears in the kitchen. The oven was broken. The repairman promised he would come but never showed up. I showed her how, if she was very careful, she could heat the main course up on top of the stove. I could tell she wasn't catching on. I glanced into her dining room and saw with great surprise that her table was set for sixteen. "Wait a minute," I said, "you told me that this was a buffet dinner for twelve people." She said that her husband objected to people eating while standing, so they had to sit at the table. He had also just phoned to say that he was bringing four more guests home. "But you've ordered food for twelve." She said that she and her husband wouldn't eat. "What about the other two people?" She said she'd serve small portions. "What do you mean you'll serve small portions? Where's the waitress?" Her husband had objected to a uniformed waitress. He said he wanted her to find a college girl to help, but she hadn't been able to find one. She was crying harder now. This was absolutely unbelievable. She begged me to stay and help cook. She said she would do all the serving herself. I didn't really feel like I had much choice.

Her husband came home with the guests. They milled around the living room waiting for someone to serve drinks.

"I think someone should serve drinks," I said to the hostess.

"Who?" she said.

"Well, how about your husband?" I suggested.

"He wouldn't know how. The servants always did it."

Guess who served the drinks? The host and hostess stood around helplessly while I went out in my denim skirt and sneakers and served the damn drinks. While I was playing barmaid, I realized that one of the guests was a woman who for years had bought meringue mushrooms from Bloomingdale's and had tried to reach me to buy other chocolate things. Bloomies had never given her my name and only referred to her by this ridiculous nickname when they called me with her orders. So, here was the famous lady. How could I introduce myself?

The first course was cold soup, so while the guests were polishing off their drinks, I ladled out the soup and put the bowls on the table. I had to thin it out considerably with the light cream the hostess had bought for the coffee. What the hell. I figured that by the time coffee was served, I would be long gone. While I set the bowls on the table I was mentally upping my bill.

The guests sat down at the table, and I went out to pick up the dirty glasses so I could really justify all the money I was planning to charge her. I overheard her guests exclaiming over the cream of carrot soup.

The Chocolate Diet
———

"Rita, this is marvelous soup!" I began to pat myself on the back.

"Thank you, it was my mother's recipe."

That bitch! She not only was taking credit for my recipe, but for making it as well. Here I was in her kitchen reheating in a jerry-rigged stovetop oven her fancy "drop-off" dinner while she was out there taking credit for it. I should have just walked out the door, but the professional (masochistic) side of me wouldn't allow that. Also, I didn't want to pass up the opportunity to meet the Bloomingdale's lady.

I waited in the kitchen for her to bring the soup bowls from the table. I waited and waited — damned if I was going to wait on her table. I could hear her husband growling about the "quality of help available in this country." Finally, she came in (empty-handed) and beseeched me to clear the table. "You can charge anything you want," she promised. I thought of plane tickets to Paris for four and did it.

So, in that manner, the meal was served and the dishes cleared. When it came time for dessert I knew it was now or never for meeting the Bloomingdale's lady. I cut pieces of Chocolate Mousse Cake.* There was no way I was going to allow her to pass off this original recipe of mine as hers. As I put a plate down in front of each guest they stopped talking and just sat there salivating. I got to the Bloomies' lady. When she saw the cake she said, "Rita, did you . . ."

"No!" I interrupted. "I did, and it's my recipe." There was silence at the table. The Bloomingdale's lady looked right through me and said, "Get me more coffee." Who would want to cook for her, anyway? I walked right out of the dining room and kept going. Sure hoped they could figure out how to wash dishes and scour pots, because I had left one hell of a mess. I sent them an enormous bill that, of course, they never paid. David tried to sue them, but they had moved back to South America, where they had diplomatic immunity.

It was quite a farewell to the catering business.

So you want to be a caterer. Even after hearing all this? You'd better have a strong, healthy back. Even if it's strong and healthy it will still ache a lot. Your feet will hurt, too. I used to have fairly nice legs. Now the backs of them look like a relief map of Bulgaria. You have to be compulsive, organized, very fast, and be able to punt. That's if you want to be successful and make money. You'll have to learn to read people right away — that goes for employers and employees.

You have to be prepared to work days, nights, weekends. You have to be prepared to not work at all in February, March, and August.

You can't ever forget quality, even though you're working with so much quantity you'll want to throw up.

Buy two medium garbage cans with tight lids to use for fifty pounds each of flour and sugar. Store them in a dry cool place. You'll probably need extra freezer and refrigerator space (I didn't say this would be cheap).

Even if you hate math and numbers you have to keep books. If you can't make yourself do it, hire someone.

Work out the legality of your cooking premises before you get involved. Most city apartments and suburban homes are not zoned as cottage industries, and the local health departments tend to frown on entrepreneurial activities.

Try to work with a partner. Even though you've already had mumps and chicken pox, there are other nasty viruses out there to lay you up.

Sit down and write up a menu — not of things you think you would like to make, but of things you already make, and make well. Add items to this list only after you have tested them several times in your own kitchen. The list doesn't have to be excessively long. I had nine appetizers, seven main courses, five salads and vegetables, six breads and rolls, and fourteen desserts. Have your menu and price list typed or hand done in calligraphy and then printed — and get business cards. This makes you look like a professional. When a customer calls and you're in the middle of cooking or changing diapers — call that customer back. Don't talk business unless your full attention is devoted to what is being transacted. And write everything down — in a notebook, not on pieces of scrap paper. Even if you think you won't forget — you will! I used to keep a date book and then copy the information onto a special form I had created that I hung up on my kitchen cabinet. The paper remained there until the job was over. That made it easy to check off items that I had already cooked for that particular party. The form contained a standard list of pots, pans, and utensils that I might need for the job. I checked these off and added things like an oven thermometer (I don't trust the dial), portable mixer, depending on what the hostess's kitchen had. I also had a space on the paper for rental items required, waitresses, and bartenders, etc. I also made it a habit to write down how many ovens (and what size), burners, etc., the hostess's kitchen had. (See what I mean about being compulsive and organized?)

Scour your yellow pages for food wholesalers. Some of them won't sell to you and some will. You just have to ask. If you want to make something with caviar and you can't get it wholesale, your hostess will probably be a little upset at your price — unless you're happy not to make a profit. You might want to bag the caviar idea.

There are several rules of thumb for prices and charging. The standard formula for the retail price (what you charge the customer) is three times the price of the ingredients. But if the ingredients for something are wildly expensive and the item is not labor intensive, then you should charge less — if you want to sell the product. If the ingredients are not at all expensive, but the item is very labor intensive, you can charge more. If you are selling something no one else makes and so have a monopoly, so to speak, you can get away with charging more than the formula. The perfect example is the meringue mushrooms. They cost about two and a half cents each to make, were moderately labor intensive, and tied up a whole oven for twenty-four hours. The formula says I should charge seven and a half cents apiece, but I sold them for twelve dollars a dozen. Another way of figuring out how to charge is to see what other people are charging. I think it's perfectly alright to call up another caterer and ask what they would charge to make stuffed mushrooms for five hundred people. You're not asking for a secret recipe — just a price.

Okay, now you know what to do, all you need is some publicity to get those customers rolling in. Here are several suggestions:

Pick a charity or two. Call them up and offer to donate one of your specialties for a function — pick your functions carefully, you don't want to donate a $40 drop-dead cake to a children's Christmas party — I'm sure the kids would love it, but how many would empty their piggy banks to buy a $40 cake? Go for the black tie galas. Make sure you have a stunning (not cutesy) business card to paste on the plate the cake or whatever goes on. Make sure you get credit as a caterer in the program book.

Volunteer to assist at cooking demonstrations — if you see that Jacques Pepin is coming to town, call the place where he's doing his thing and offer to assist. Chances are they already have ten people for the job, but you never know — those ten people might all drink too much the night before and Jacques will call you to fill in.

Approach a gourmet shop or the food section of a department store and convince them to sell your specialty under your name (good luck). Be prepared for most of the department stores to ask for a hundred-percent markup, which means you get zilch. The bigger the store, the worse they treat your product.

Do a mailing. Send a beautiful flyer about what you're doing to all your friends, the parents of your childrens' friends, the local paper. Put your flyer up at church (where you should have already volunteered to cook for something).

This suggestion may appeal to you, or it may not: try a different angle with your menu. Specialize in a certain area. Do just breakfast or brunch (I know a woman who created a fantastic business of delivering breakfast on Sunday mornings), clambakes (very seasonal, and you need an ocean), Tex-Mex dinners (I would order some of that), Chinese banquets, vegetarian feasts. I could go on forever. If your idea is good (and feasible) your business will take right off.

Most important of all — don't be shy. Tell people about your new business. They will tell their friends. It may take a while, but I promise, if you make good food that's presented beautifully, if you work hard and are dependable and conscientious, obsessive and compulsive, you'll soon have more business than you know what to do with.

There is just one more thing: when you become successful, try to remember how insecure you felt when you were just starting out. Remember all the questions you had and the logistics you had to figure out. Remember the people who helped you out. Remember all this when some young man or woman calls you and says that he or she is interested in getting into the catering business.

Chocolate Hazelnut Torte

This incredibly dense, moist torte combines my three favorite ingredients: chocolate, hazelnuts, and raspberries.

To make this cake you will need 1½ cups toasted, ground hazelnuts. Follow the directions for toasting hazelnuts in the recipe for chocolate hazelnut cheesecake on page 89.

SERVES 10–12

For the cake:

8 ounces bittersweet or semisweet chocolate, cut into small pieces
6 ounces (1½ sticks) sweet (unsalted) butter
¾ cup sugar

6 extra-large eggs at room temperature, separated
9 ounces (1½ cups) ground, toasted hazelnuts
⅓ cup seedless raspberry preserves

Preheat the oven to 350 degrees and place the rack in the lower third — but not the very bottom — of the oven. Grease a 9-inch-diameter by 3-inch-high cake pan or springform and line the bottom with a circle of parchment; grease the parchment and then dust the pan with flour. Knock out the excess flour.

Melt the chocolate in a small metal bowl placed over gently simmering water. Stir, and set it aside to cool slightly.

In the large bowl of an electric mixer cream the butter and sugar until the mixture is very light and fluffy. Mix in the egg yolks one at a time and beat until they are well incorporated.

Add the chocolate and nuts, mixing just until they are incorporated.

In a clean bowl, with clean beaters, beat the egg whites until they hold a soft shape — do not overbeat them. Mix a large spoonful of whites into the chocolate mixture to lighten it, and then pour the remaining whites on top of the chocolate mixture and fold them in thoroughly. The batter will deflate considerably. Pour the mixture into the prepared pan and level it off with a rubber scraper. Bake for 50–60 minutes. It is essential not to overbake this cake. The baking time depends on your particular oven — I know the cake is done when I can smell it. It is hard to tell exactly when it's done, but it's better to err on the side of underdone. The top will be puffed and crusty and the cake will feel firm when you press it. If the top of the cake is browning and 50 minutes is up—take it out!

Let it cool in the pan for 15 minutes and then turn it out onto a wire rack to cool completely. Remove the parchment and let the cake cool right-side up.

When ready to assemble the cake, place the preserves in a small saucepan and heat them until they come to a boil. Place the cake flat (bottom) side up on a flat plate with four strips of wax paper underneath. Pour the preserves on top and smooth with a cake spatula. Use only enough to cover the top of the cake. Try not to let the preserves run down the sides, but don't worry if they do. Let the preserves set a bit while you prepare the chocolate glaze.

For the glaze:

3 tablespoons water
3 tablespoons light corn syrup
2 tablespoons butter
6 ounces bittersweet or semisweet
  chocolate, cut in small pieces

2 ounces unsweetened chocolate, cut in
  small pieces
Fresh raspberries (optional)

Place the water, corn syrup, and butter in a small saucepan and bring the mixture to a boil, stirring occasionally. Remove from heat and add the chocolates. Stir gently with a wire whisk, then set aside to cool.

When the glaze begins to thicken slightly, pour over the cake and smooth over top and sides with a cake spatula. Remove the wax paper. Garnish with the fresh berries or serve with a bowl of unsweetened whipped cream.

Carol Pollak's Chocolate Truffles

As practically every living person knows, there are two kinds of truffles: real and real chocolate. The first kind, associated with oak trees and trained pigs with snouts of gold, cost upwards of $400 a pound and enhance such dishes as Beef Wellington and fancy pâtés. Black olives have been known to impersonate this kind of truffle. The other kind are associated with a quick trip to heaven and cost only the price of the ingredients. While they can be used to enhance tortes and garnish mousses, I think straight down the old hatch is the best way to deal with them. No one would confuse a chocolate truffle for an olive.

This recipe was created by my friend Carol Pollak, who owns the fabulous Savoy French Bakery in Brookline, Massachusetts. The following recipes are my variations on her chocolate theme. No matter which truffles you make, please don't make them the size of ostrich eggs. They should be delicate, one-bite little morsels.

1 cup heavy cream

10 ounces sweet, semisweet, or
bittersweet chocolate, coarsely
chopped

3 tablespoons sweet (unsalted) butter,
cut into four pieces

¼ cup amaretto

⅛ teaspoon almond extract

Approximately 1 cup unsweetened
cocoa powder, sifted onto wax paper

Place the cream in a one-quart saucepan and heat it until small bubbles form around the edge. Add the chocolate and stir over very low heat until the chocolate begins to melt. Off the heat, continue to stir until the chocolate is completely melted. Add the butter a piece at a time, stirring until the butter melts and is incorporated. Scrape down the sides of the pan and let the mixture cool to room temperature. Stir in the amaretto and almond extract and cover the pan with plastic wrap. Refrigerate the mixture overnight, until the mixture is firm.

Line two baking sheets with wax paper. Use two teaspoons to drop the mixture into 36 rough balls onto the paper. Place the sheets in the freezer for one hour or until the balls are quite firm.

One by one drop the balls in the cocoa and roll them gently and quickly with your fingers to cover them completely with cocoa. Return the truffles to the baking sheets and refrigerate until serving.

Chocolate truffles freeze beautifully. Place them on a cookie sheet uncovered until they are frozen solid, then wrap them in several layers of plastic wrap and finally in a layer of foil. Be sure to defrost them in the wrapping.

Hazelnut Gianduja Truffles

Gianduja is milk chocolate that contains finely ground hazelnuts or almonds. It has a silky smooth texture, and a fabulous taste. It is not always easy to find. Perugina makes a gianduja candy bar, which is sold in fine candy stores and gourmet food shops. Carma (listed at the end of the book) also makes a very fine gianduja. Frangelico, a delicious hazelnut liqueur, is available in most fine wine shops.

MAKES 36 TRUFFLES

½ cup heavy cream

10 ounces hazelnut gianduja, chopped

2 tablespoons sweet (unsalted) butter
at room temperature, cut into pieces

3 tablespoons Frangelico liqueur

½ cup finely chopped toasted hazelnuts
or ½ cup Dutch process cocoa for
covering the truffles

Scald the cream in a heavy-bottomed, medium-sized pan. When tiny bubbles form around the edge of the pan, turn the heat down to low and stir in the chocolate. Stir gently for a minute until the chocolate melts. Remove the pan from the heat and stir in the butter, piece by piece. Stir until the butter melts. Add the liqueur to taste. Pour the mixture into a small metal mixing bowl and place this bowl over a slightly larger bowl filled with ice water. Mix gently and continuously with a wire whisk until the mixture gets cold and firm. Place the mixture into a pastry tube fitted with a number 5 round piping tube. Pipe small mounds onto a baking sheet covered with wax paper. Use a small sharp knife to separate chocolate from the metal tip. Refrigerate for 30 minutes.

To coat the truffles:

Place either the chopped hazelnuts or cocoa in a small shallow dish or saucer. Drop the mounds, one at a time, into the dish and roll them around in the coating. You may want to use your fingers to press the coating firmly onto the truffle. Refrigerate until serving time, or freeze.

Champagne Truffles

Follow the above directions substituting 10 ounces milk or dark chocolate for the gianduja and ¼ cup Marc de Champagne (champagne brandy) for the Frangelico. If you have trouble with the solids in the milk chocolate separating in the hot cream, blend in a food processor or blender until smooth. Coat in cocoa.

Raspberry Truffles

Use 10 ounces milk or dark chocolate, 3–4 tablespoons Framboise or Raspberry Eau-de-Vie. Coat in cocoa.

Hazelnut Gianduja Sauce

Gianduja is milk chocolate containing finely ground hazelnuts or almonds. It has a silky smooth texture, and a fabulous taste. It is not always easy to find. Perugina sells a gianduja candy bar, and Lindt, Carma, and Callebaut sell gianduja couvertures (2-kilo bars of coating chocolate). They can be ordered from Madam Chocolate. (See address on page 3.) Or they can be ordered directly from the companies. (See address list at the end of the book.) The other slightly obscure ingredient in this recipe is Frangelico, which is a delicious hazelnut liqueur. It is available in most fine wine shops.

MAKES 2⅓ CUPS
1 cup heavy cream
10 ounces hazelnut gianduja, chopped
2 tablespoons sweet (unsalted) butter
  at room temperature, cut into pieces
¼ cup Frangelico liqueur

Scald the cream in a heavy-bottomed, medium-sized pan. When tiny bubbles form around the edge of the pan, turn the heat down to low and stir in the chocolate. Stir gently for a minute until the chocolate melts. Remove the pan from the heat and stir in the butter, piece by piece. Stir until the butter melts. Add the liqueur. Cool slightly and serve over ice cream.

JuliaTorte

This three-layer meringue cake has a chocolate and raspberry mousse filling. While it is a bit time-consuming to make, the elegant and delicious results are well worth it. A heavy-duty electric mixer with a large bowl is essential. You will also need a large pastry bag with a number 7 round tip.

MAKES ONE 10-INCH THREE-LAYER CAKE TO SERVE 12–14

For the meringue layers:

½ cup Dutch process cocoa
1 cup confectioners' sugar

10 extra-large egg whites
1 cup granulated sugar

Preheat the oven to 300 degrees. To make the three layers of this cake at one time you need either an oven with three racks or two ovens. If you have neither of these things you can bake two layers, keeping the third covered with a large roasting pan on the counter, then bake the third one when the others are finished. Do not bake a layer on the lowest rack position.

Line three cookie sheets or jelly-roll pans with parchment or foil (wax paper will not work). Using a 10-inch cake pan as a guide, trace one circle on each sheet.

Sift the cocoa and confectioners' sugar together into a small bowl and set aside.

Start beating the egg whites on medium speed. When they get frothy start adding the granulated sugar slowly. When the sugar is all added, set the mixer on high speed and continue to beat until the meringue is very shiny and has tripled in volume.

Remove the bowl from the mixer and, using a large rubber spatula, fold in the cocoa/sugar mixture. Be thorough but gentle.

Fill the pastry bag with meringue and, starting at the inside edge of the drawn guide, pipe the meringue in a spiraling inward circle until you have a solid layer. Repeat with the other layers.

Pipe the remaining meringue in strips along the edge of but not touching the layers. These strips will be broken into pieces to be used as decorations for the top of the cake.

Place the layers and strips in the oven and set the timer for 20 minutes. At the end of this time alternate their rack positions as well as turning them back to front. This is to ensure even baking.

The total baking time is 30–40 minutes. The layers will be dry, but soft to the touch, and the edges will have started to brown. If the strips brown faster than the layers remove them to a cake rack with a metal spatula and let the layers cook a little longer.

At the end of the baking time remove the pans from the oven one at a time. It is important to remove the meringues from the parchment while they are still very hot. If you have not already done so, remove the strips with a metal spatula and then flip the parchment over onto a cool cookie sheet or cake rack and peel the paper off the layer. Allow to cool completely.

Break the strips into 1½-inch pieces and set aside. Prepare the chocolate glaze.

For the glaze:

½ cup heavy cream
6 ounces bittersweet chocolate, cut
  into small pieces

2 tablespoons sweet (unsalted) butter,
  cut into small pieces

In a small saucepan scald the cream. Add the chocolate and butter and stir until smooth. Pour one-third of the glaze onto each layer and spread it with a long flexible metal spatula. The glaze will be fairly thin. Don't worry if spots show through on the layers. Allow to cool and set. Prepare the raspberry filling.

For the filling:

12 ounces or 1½ cups fresh or frozen
  raspberries, drained of their juice
½ cup confectioners' sugar

⅓ cup raspberry liqueur or Framboise
1 tablespoon gelatin
1½ cups heavy cream

Puree the raspberries and set them aside. If you dislike seeds, strain the puree.
  Sift the sugar.

Heat the raspberry liqueur or Framboise in a small saucepan or in the micro-wave oven in a small glass dish. Sprinkle the gelatin over it and stir to dissolve completely. Cool slightly.

Whip the cream, add the sugar, and gradually add the liqueur. Beat until the cream is firm. Fold in the raspberry puree.

To assemble:

Place the bottom layer on a large cake plate. Spread one half of the raspberry filling on it. Cover with another layer. Spread the rest of the filling on it. Add the top layer. Refrigerate briefly while preparing the chocolate cream topping.

For the topping:

¼ cup confectioners' sugar
2 tablespoons cocoa

1 cup heavy cream

Sift the sugar and cocoa together. Whip the cream until it is stiff, then fold in the sugar/cocoa mixture.

Spread the chocolate cream over the top of the cake. Scatter the pieces of meringue on top. Allow to mellow in the refrigerator for at least 2 hours. Cut with a serrated knife.

Ginger Cheesecake

This is an unbelievably and sublimely delicious combination of flavors and textures. I like to put lots of fresh ginger in because I love the taste. It is one of the most sophisticated desserts I have ever eaten and when I want to end a very special dinner party with an unforgettable dessert, I serve this one. It's easy to make and freezes beautifully.

This recipe calls for a cheesecake pan. This is *not* a springform. It is 8 inches in diameter and 3 inches high. Cheesecake pans are sold in most cookware shops.

This cheesecake is best when made in a food processor. An electric mixer incorporates too much air, which makes the cake soufflé up when it's cooked, then fall and crack when it cools. If you must use a mixer, it is essential to have the cream cheese at room temperature so beating is kept to a minimum.

The gingers should be chopped by hand using a chef's knife. The candied ginger gums up in the food processor and the small quantity of fresh ginger makes using the processor impractical.

SERVES 12–14

1–2 tablespoons softened butter for greasing the pan	½ cup heavy cream
½ cup crushed gingersnaps	4 extra-large eggs
½ cup crushed chocolate wafers	1½ cups sugar
⅓ cup sweet (unsalted) butter, melted	1 teaspoon vanilla extract
2 pounds best-quality cream cheese at room temperature	2 tablespoons finely grated fresh ginger
	1 cup finely chopped candied ginger

Preheat the oven to 300 degrees and place the rack in the center position.

Butter the sides and bottom of an 8 x 3-inch cheesecake pan and line the bottom with parchment. Butter the parchment.

Combine the crushed gingersnaps, chocolate wafers, and melted butter. Press the crumbs into the bottom and halfway up the sides of the pan. Don't worry about getting the edge even. It looks prettier when it's not.

Place the cream cheese, heavy cream, eggs, sugar, vanilla, and grated ginger in the bowl of a food processor. Process until thoroughly blended and very smooth.

Add the chopped candied ginger and process for 10 seconds more—just to distribute the last ingredient.

Pour the batter into the prepared pan and shake gently to level.

Set the pan in a slightly larger pan and pour boiling water into the outer pan up to a depth of 2 inches. Do not let the edges of the pans touch. A roasting pan is good for this.

Bake the cake 1 hour and 45 minutes. At the end of that time, turn off the oven and let the cake remain in the oven with the heat off and the door closed for one more hour.

Lift the cake pan out of the water bath and let it rest on the counter one additional hour, or until it is completely cool. Do *not* refrigerate; this will make it very difficult to get the cake out of the pan. (See note.)

To unmold, place a piece of plastic wrap over the pan. Cover the wrap with a cookie sheet. Invert. Remove the parchment. Place a cake plate on the bottom of the cake (which is now the side facing you) and invert it once again.

Note: *If by accident the cake gets refrigerated or gets so cold it's hard to unmold, spin the bottom of the pan for a few seconds on the burner of your stove turned on "high." The heat will melt the butter used to grease the pan and the cake will release. This trick works for most cakes. Just be careful not to burn the bottom.*

Chocolate Mousse Cake

If you love the combination of bittersweet chocolate and coffee, then this dessert is for you. If you don't love the above combination, leave out the coffee.

SERVES 10–12

For the cake:

6 extra-large eggs at room temperature, separated	3 tablespoons instant powdered espresso
¾ cup sugar	¼ cup flour
	¼ cup Dutch process cocoa

Preheat the oven to 350 degrees with the rack in the center position. Line a 17 x 11-inch heavy-duty jelly-roll pan with a piece of parchment.

In the large bowl of an electric mixer, beat the eggs and half of the sugar until they are thick and light-colored and form a ribbon when the beater is lifted. Add the instant coffee and beat until it is incorporated. On low speed mix in the flour and cocoa. In a clean bowl, with clean beaters, whip the egg whites with the remaining sugar until they are stiff but not dry. Fold the whites into the yolk mixture and spread evenly on the prepared pan. Bake 12–15 minutes, reversing the pan once, front to back, during the baking time. Cool 5 minutes in the pan.

Place another piece of parchment on top of the cake, then place a cookie sheet on top of that. Flip the cake over and unmold it onto the cookie sheet. Peel off the top parchment.

Oil a 7-cup loaf pan. (The one I use measures 12½ x 4 inches and is 2½ inches deep.) Line the inside of the pan with plastic wrap, allowing the wrap to extend outside of the pan. Lay the pan, right-side up, on top of the cake and, using a small sharp knife, trace the outline of the bottom. Then lay the pan on its side and trace two long side pieces. Repeat for the two short side pieces. Cut the pieces out and use them to line the inside of the pan. The remaining scraps will be used to cover the top. Prepare the mousse.

For the mousse:

3 cups heavy cream
3 tablespoons instant espresso
10 ounces bittersweet chocolate, chopped
2 ounces unsweetened chocolate, chopped
1 stick (4 ounces) sweet (unsalted) butter at room temperature, cut into small pieces

3 extra-large eggs at room temperature, separated
½ cup sugar
1 cup heavy cream, whipped (garnish)
Chocolate coffee beans (optional garnish)

Bring the cream to a simmer in a 2-quart saucepan and let it simmer until it reduces by one-third (2 cups will remain). This will take about 30 minutes. Add the instant espresso and stir until dissolved. On lowest heat add the chopped chocolate. Pour this mixture into the bowl of a food processor, and with the machine on, add the butter, bit by bit, and then the three egg yolks. Process until smooth. Beat the egg whites with the sugar until they are stiff but not dry. Pour the chocolate mixture into the whites and fold together. Pour the mousse into the prepared loaf pan and lay the remaining pieces of cake, patched together, to form a top. Cover with plastic wrap, place a light (1 pound) weight on top and refrigerate until firm. To serve, remove the cake from the pan, remove the plastic wrap, and cut with a sharp knife that has been dipped into hot water. Garnish each piece with unsweetened whipped cream and chocolate coffee beans.

King Kong Conquers Fear of the Marketplace

When I was a child my mother used to do most of the grocery shopping. She would buy the mundane things like onions, paper towels, and ground chuck. On Sundays, however, my father, who always got up very early every day, would leave the house at 8 A.M. for his weekly pilgrimage to the Crown Market. On the rare weekends that I did not stay at my aunts' house, I would hustle myself out of bed so I could go with him. When I was very young, the Crown Market, which closed on Saturday but opened on Sunday to cater to the religious Jews who wouldn't shop on the Sabbath (and people of all religions who found it more convenient to shop on Sunday), was located only one block away from my aunts' house on Magnolia Street.

There were three things I loved about the Crown Market: the deli, the bakery, and the fact that my father said yes to anything I suggested buying. We would load up our cart with pounds of sliced Kosher bologna (which I would roll up into cylinders and pretend were cigars before I ate them), pastrami, and spiced beef. He bought whitefish, sable (both of which I came to appreciate only later in life — when I had to pay for them), and salty lox. Since this was the time before the advent of those repulsive gourmet cream cheeses, we mercifully had our choices limited to with or without chives. We bought without. For my mother we got a couple of slices of pickled tongue (yuck). We never bought herring salad here because my mother's homemade was the best in the world.

On the way to the bakery department my father habitually made a pilgrimage down what we called the "jelly aisle." He loaded our cart with heavy glass jars of all shapes and sizes full of seedless raspberry and Oregon blackberry jams, greengage plum and lemon/lime jelly, ginger conserve and Seville orange marmalade. He also bought several boxes of crackers to go along. My favorite were the Milk Crackers, which I loved to slather with sweet butter and raspberry jam. My mother usually hit the ceiling when she saw what he had bought because she maintained an entire cabinet full of jams and jellies from his previous forays to the Crown.

No million-dollar lottery winner could have been happier than this kid at the bakery at the Crown Market. First of all, you didn't have to rush to make up your mind. There was always such a big crowd waiting to buy breads and pastries that you had to take a number and wait a long time for your turn. While my father stood with our loaded cart I inched my way to the case to check out the goods. We always bought the cinnamon babka and sliced pumpernickel bread. Bagels and bialys were also on the list of required buying. The agony came in trying to decide about what my mother called "that hazarai," which is Yiddish for "all that junk." Should I choose cupcakes with chocolate fudge frosting, or a brownie with grated nuts on top? How about a gingerbread man decorated with blue icing and silver balls? I loved the cream-filled chocolate cupcakes with mocha icing and colored dots on top. But it was so hard to decide. Finally when our number was called and the prerequisite stuff out of the way, I would start to negotiate with my father. Thanks to the pressure from the people with the numbers after ours, more often than not I could get two sugar-filled treats. I loved food shopping in those days.

When the problem first began I could still, somehow, manage to go food shopping alone. Later on I had to bring one of the kids with me. It was when the catering business was winding down and I was looking around for something else to do that things really began to get out of hand. I didn't have to shop very often, and I put it off as long as possible until there was no toilet paper (or Kleenex to use instead), and the boys pointed out that they had eaten pizza three nights in a row. At first the anxiety didn't start until I was halfway through the last aisle, and I could make it through the checkout line if I concentrated very hard on the latest issue of *People* magazine. Then it moved up to the cereal aisle and all the boxes began to look the same. I grabbed what was closest and sped on, clipping the backs of several elderly ladies' legs in the process. The kids protested that now we had six boxes of Raisin Bran, and they hated Raisin Bran. The fussy eater who would only allow Hellmann's and Bumble Bee to pass through her lips now grabbed any old thing off the shelf in her frenzy to get the ordeal over with. Very soon I could feel it in the pit of my stomach as I pulled into the parking lot. Most of the time, although I was in extreme agony, I managed to get through it; only once did I leave a half-full cart and bolt. What had happened to the kid who used to love to go grocery shopping, not to mention the woman who had to do it as part of her living?

Sigmund Freud and I waltzed together a long time when I lived in New York.

When our Blue Cross ran out the dance was over. I learned enough about myself in therapy to know that the anxiety attacks I was experiencing in the supermarket probably stemmed from some deep-seated neurosis acquired in my early childhood. Only additional treatment could root out the cause. The hell with that! I didn't care about the cause, I just wanted to be able to buy groceries without feeling like I was having a heart attack. I have a wonderful friend who was into alternative therapy. Most of the ways she treated people were so off the wall that the patient was either cured or had to be committed. This was her suggestion to me: "You don't feel in control of the situation when you're in the market. You have to do something that changes that. Do something to make yourself feel in charge, that will make you feel bigger and more powerful than the market itself." Okay. I know that you're not going to believe what I did to make myself feel more powerful than the market. I swear to God the following story is true (you can even ask Fran in the produce department).

On Halloween day I rented a gorilla costume. At three o'clock in the afternoon, my friend Kathleen Ehrlich picked me up in her VW bus. Kathleen, who is the most gorgeous six-foot-tall knockout blond you ever saw, came dressed in a very conservative skirt and tweed blazer. She was my straight lady. As I was getting into the bus, the neighborhood children were climbing up the hill by our house on their way home from school.

"Hey, look. There's a gorilla at your house, Max."

"Oh, yeah. It's my mom."

The kids climbed in the bus and off we went to the supermarket.

Once we were inside I made straightaway for the produce department, where I grabbed several huge bunches of bananas. Next to the candy aisle for several giant bags of M & M's. I raced around through the store flinging bananas here and there, thumping my chest and making (at least what I thought sounded like) ape noises. There were several reactions to these goings on: some people just totally ignored me (This is the stupidest thing I've ever seen, thought they. They must have been from Beacon Hill); then there were the people who laughed so hard they cried; and finally, there were the people from the senior citizen van who were absolutely terrified. Kathleen kept cluck clucking her naughty beast and finally encouraged me to go to the cashier, where we could pay for the bananas I hadn't yet thrown around the store and get the hell out of there before someone called the cops. The clerk insisted (convulsed with laughter) that she had to take the bananas from me so she could weigh them. I went ape. I jumped up on top of the checkout counter (thank goodness she had turned the roller off) and pounded my chest and shrieked. As the whole store stopped and watched with amazement, I could feel all my anxiety draining away forever. The manager was making his way over, so we grabbed the kids and the bananas and hotfooted it out of there.

King Kong Conquers Fear

Outside the supermarket (since it was very close to election day) were a bunch of politicians handing out leaflets and shaking hands. For a while I stood with them, shaking hands and handing out bananas. Next we went to the bank. As we walked in, there was complete silence. The tellers' hands hovered over the alarm buttons. Kathleen approached the branch manager and said she wanted some information about the safe deposit boxes. Were they climate controlled, how much space was available? She said her gorilla was interested in finding a safe place for the bananas. Meanwhile, I tiptoed over to the safe-deposit area. It was behind a wall of iron bars. Sitting with his back to me, filling out a form, was the man who lived several houses down from us who always let his nasty yipping dogs out too early in the morning and too late at night. I put my hands on the bars and crouched down low. I made a low grumbling noise and he turned around. I screeched and jumped up and down causing the poor old devil to age twenty years. Then we left. That evening Max and I went trick-or-treating together. He wore a cut-down refrigerator box on which he had carefully drawn hundreds of tiny windows. I wore my costume and carried a Barbie doll. We were King Kong and the Empire State Building.

After that, whenever I went to the supermarket I never had a bit of trouble. On occasion, I took great delight in leaning over the American cheese slices and packages of Crinkle Cut Frozen French Fries to break the somber reverie of the checkout clerk and say:

"Psst. Were you here when the gorilla came?"

Her face would break into a big smile. "Yeah, what a scream. Hey, do you know who it was?"

Then I would grin and raise my eyebrows à la Groucho Marx and jab my thumb into my chest. "I'm on a diet now, because next year I'm coming as Lady Godiva."

I created the following recipe to celebrate the return of my mental health (and at what a bargain price — $25 to rent the gorilla suit — you couldn't even get fifteen minutes of therapy for that kind of money).

Caramel Baked Bananas with Chocolate Rum Sauce

This easy-to-prepare dessert is a delicious combination of flavors and textures. I serve it in large wine goblets. The chocolate sauce should be made before the rest of the recipe. It will keep, under refrigeration, for two weeks, or it can be frozen. Soften it in the microwave or in a double boiler before serving.

SERVES 6

For the chocolate sauce:

¾ cup heavy cream
10 ounces bittersweet chocolate, cut
  into pieces

2 tablespoons dark rum

Scald the cream in a small saucepan. Add the chocolate and stir until it melts. Mix in the rum.

For the banana sauce:

4 slightly underripe medium-sized
  bananas
⅓ cup brown sugar
1½ cups heavy cream

3 tablespoons dark rum
1½ pints best-quality vanilla ice cream
Unsweetened whipped cream
2 tablespoons candied ginger, chopped

Slice the bananas in half the long way and then cut them into 2-inch slices. In a large, heavy skillet combine the brown sugar, heavy cream, and rum. Bring to a simmer over high heat and add the bananas. Cook for 5 minutes over moderate heat. It is better to shake the pan rather than stir the bananas. This will help retain their shape. Turn off the heat and let the bananas sit in the reduced sauce.

To assemble:

Place a scoop of ice cream into each goblet. Spoon some of the banana and rum/cream sauce over the ice cream. Spoon some chocolate sauce on top and garnish with a rosette of whipped cream and a sprinkling of the candied ginger.

King Kong Conquers Fear

The Executive Dining Room

While I was waiting for fate to hand me a new food career I kept money coming in the door by making desserts to order. One day fate stepped in in the form of Stephen Elmont, president of Creative Gourmets Ltd. He told me that he was bidding on a contract to operate the executive dining room of one of Boston's major banks. He wanted to know if I might be interested in the job of chef. I told him that I was certainly most interested and that, in fact, I had a good friend who worked at that bank.

"I don't think you understand, Lora," he replied. "This is the executive dining room, where the executives eat, not the employees' cafeteria."

I replied that, in fact, my friend was an executive, a vice-president.

"What's his name?" Stephen asked.

I told him what HER name was and then Stephen was quiet for a long time.

"What's the matter?" I asked

"That's the executive I'm negotiating the contract with."

"Well," I said, "that's what's known as the old-girl network."

Stephen, God bless him, took a real flier when he hired me for this job and I'll always be grateful to him that he did. I was to prepare a three-course lunch for anywhere between two and thirty people every day. The hours were such that I could be home before my children got out of school (no sitter costs), I was blessed with a gorgeous, brand-new, ultramodern kitchen in which to work, a generous food budget, and a benevolent boss who was willing to give me responsibility, listen to my ideas, and, for the most part, give me a free hand in the kitchen.

Everything about the job was ideal with one major exception. I was not exactly qualified. I mean I could cook, but I had never learned to cook to order. Making Beef Wellington for one hundred for a catering job, where you can cook several days in advance and everyone eats the same menu, is far different from cooking for a group of six who arrive at noon, wanting soup, two steaks, three duck breasts, and one omelet, then having eight more people arrive and want eight different things when you're struggling to get the first group's food out. I was hugely relieved when Stephen promised that he would send someone over to help me out for the first two weeks.

I arrived at 7 A.M. my first day of work. Considering lunch was at 1 and I was only feeding four people you might say I was a bit overanxious. I got into my chef's black-and-white checked pants and white jacket and paraded around in front of the mirror trying to feel like I was really what I looked like, and then got to work. The menu was Caesar salad, tomato bisque, and a choice of sirloin steak with béarnaise sauce or salmon fillet with herbs beurre blanc, green beans, scalloped potatoes, and crème brûlée for dessert. I started by washing lettuce and cutting up the vegetables. Since I was used to making food for large numbers of people I used two heads of lettuce and several pounds of beans. I took out the salmon to prepare the fillets, and then remembered that the crème brûlée needed time to cook and set, so I left the salmon and got out the eggs. I glanced up at the clock. It was almost 11. Where had the time gone? And where was my "assistant"? Everything was in a half-done stage and I was beginning to feel a little panicky. "What the hell is this mess?" I jumped and almost removed my thumb with the chef's knife I was using to open a box of brown sugar. "Don't use a good knife for that! Jesus, this place is a disaster — you cook like a housewife." Welcome Ann Sullivan, my "assistant." I prickled for a second at being told I cooked like a housewife and then heaved a huge sigh of relief as this tall, curly-headed young blonde woman, with the warm grin and aura of self-assurance, began to establish some order in the chaos I had created. As she did this she threw out pointers and advice:

Do one thing at a time. Do it from start to finish. Then wash the dishes and utensils and put them away. Wipe down your work area before you start the next project.

Work in one area. Don't spread out all over the kitchen. It wastes time and energy and is an inefficient way to operate.

Don't make more than you need. (She pointed out that I had made enough Caesar salad and green beans to prevent scurvy in six third-world countries for four generations.)

Organize the refrigerator so that you'll know instantly where everything is. Cover everything well and label it clearly. Don't save little bits of things.

These are just some of the things that Ann taught me. In the two weeks she spent with me she showed me how to fillet a fish, how to make sauces using the cooking juices in the pan, how to broil a steak and how to tell when it was rare, medium, or well-done. How to carve a duck and how to resurrect a curdled soup. She helped me organize not only the kitchen but the way I worked in it, so that every step counted and I didn't waste time doing unnecessary jobs. She showed me how to place orders and how to deal with the purveyors — especially when they sent things that weren't up to the high quality Stephen demanded for his operation (with Ann directing me I once told a fish wholesaler that the scallops he had just sent smelled like a hundred-year-old whore). Making a plate look beautiful was extremely important to Stephen. Ann showed me how to place the food on the plate and how to garnish it so that it looked like a work of art. She taught me how to time the preparation of the food and the cooking, how to sauté with one hand and finish-off vegetables in butter with the other. I learned how to make a perfect omelet, roast a standing rib, and make the best shrimp cocktail sauce you ever tasted.

In the two weeks that Ann Sullivan spent with me I learned more than I could have in a year at the Paris Cordon Bleu. Ann, who had trained with Madeleine Kamman and had run a series of restaurants before going to work for Stephen Elmont, shared with me not only her knowledge of the kitchen and food — she showed me what it meant to be a professional cook. When people ask me if I am a "trained" cook, I look back on what I learned from Ann Sullivan and answer, "Yes, I am."

I loved everything about this job. I worked right in the financial district of Boston in a brand-new office building. I got to leave the suburbs behind for a part of each day and got to join in the hustle bustle of the city. I loved the beautiful dining room that served as a showcase for the meals I made, and I loved the executives and their guests for whom I cooked. They were so appreciative of my efforts in the kitchen. We had a curious relationship, the bankers and I. For the first few weeks I was an object of mild curiosity. I would show up for work wearing jeans, or my chef's uniform and heavy brown workshoes. In those days my hair was very short, and it was only after I overheard a remark in the elevator and realized that some of the men thought the new chef was a boy that I began to wear earrings to straighten them out. So, here I was, this unisex kid (turns out they thought I was nineteen — I was thirty-four) wearing a blue-collar uniform in a world of gray flannel suits and Mark Cross briefcases. Since they didn't know a whole lot about what I did and I certainly didn't know anything about what they did, and since it wasn't really encouraged, there wasn't a lot of verbal exchange — at first. It turned out that they all assumed I had gone to a vocational school instead of high school. This was without a doubt the most conservative environment in which I had ever worked. I was used to noise and tumult in the kitchen, but here, since the dining room was immediately adjacent to the kitchen, it was necessary to keep the noise level down to zero. The first week, there were several moments when we forgot. Our laughter and the clangs and bangs of dishes and pots caused the dining-room door to swing open, revealing a disapproving face with an index finger bisecting a pair of frowning lips in that universal "quiet" sign. This reduced us first to silence and then, as the door closed behind the reprimander, hysterical giggling. The other thing I found it difficult to get used to was the size of the portions. I was used to people wanting as much food for their money as they could get. Stephen and my friend from the bank who was in charge of the dining room insisted on small servings. In the first few weeks, no matter how small I made them, they weren't small enough. When I started to pretend that I was feeding twenty finicky eight-year-olds with food phobias I seemed to get just the right amount of food on the plate. It was also hard for me to get used to my kitchen being part of the bank, and therefore on display. It had to be kept neat and spotless at all times because you never knew who might walk through. This led to the conflict about what could be hung on the walls. My Miss Piggy poster had to go.

My bankers loved to eat. They never complained or sent things back. After a while they even began to stop into the kitchen to say thank you. The rule of thumb established by Stephen was to keep the food simple, elegant, and instantly identifiable. I started out with "safe" items like rack of lamb and mixed grill, broiled fish and chicken breasts. I made straightforward sauces to go with these dishes. After a while I began to experiment a little with these dishes and soon instead of roast duckling à l'orange I was serving rare duck breast with ginger and mango — the bankers thought it was flank steak, but didn't seem too unhappy when I told them it was duck. Clam chowder became oyster bisque and broccoli and cauliflower were replaced by Jerusalem artichokes and sugar snap peas. It was the beginning of the nouvelle craze in America and I was having a blast.

The president of the bank loved desserts and so did his cohorts. It was intensely gratifying to rack my brain to come up with new and different sweets and have my efforts so wildly and enthusiastically applauded. The list of favorites was long and featured not only some classic and traditional items, but variations and brand-new ideas as well. The all-time favorites were my special version of crème brûlée called Black and White Crème Brûlée,* a creamy rich chocolate- and vanilla-layered custard with a hard burnt-sugar topping, and strawberry shortcake made the right way with old-fashioned buttermilk biscuits, sweet native strawberries, and lots of softly whipped cream. The sliced berries would be sprinkled with sugar and left for an hour at room temperature so that their juices would seep out to form a delicious syrup. The ice cream and sorbet that I made almost every day came in all sorts of wild and unexpected flavors: blueberry/raspberry, kiwi (that was a failure), burnt almond macaroon, peach/ginger. I made fresh fruit sauces to go over the ice cream. These people shared my passion for chocolate, and I was delighted to indulge us all as often as I could. I was working on the Chocolate Cherry Torte* recipe then and made many versions of it, which were gobbled up quite happily by the bankers. I made an elegant chocolate cheesecake called Mozart Mousse Torte,* Chocolate Ginger Tart,* and Chocolate/Coffee Ice Cream Coupe.* I developed a special cookie for their afternoon meetings called the Chocolate Phantom* (What was in this cookie? Only the Phantom knew for sure). For breakfast meetings I made individual Chocolate-Filled Brioche.* The only grumbles I got were about the pounds people seemed to be accruing as a result of the daily ration of desserts. Funny thing, when I put fruit on the menu as an alternative, no one ordered it.

Chocolate-Filled Brioche

These buttery, chocolate-filled morsels are perfect for a fancy tea or brunch. A dozen packaged in a pretty basket make a lovely gift. They freeze well. They call for baker's sugar, which is coarse cut. It is available through some bakery supply shops and by mail from H. Roth and Sons in New York City. (See address on page 3.)

The recipe for this easy-to-make brioche-type dough is an adaptation of a recipe from James Beard's wonderful book *Beard on Bread*.

MAKES 12–15 BRIOCHE

1½ packages active dry yeast

2 tablespoons granulated sugar

½ cup warm water (approximately 100 degrees)

1 cup sweet (unsalted) butter, melted

1½ teaspoons salt

4 cups all-purpose flour

4 extra-large eggs

12–15 chunks of semisweet chocolate, each measuring approximately 1 to 1½ inches

1 egg yolk mixed with ¼ cup light cream

Combine the yeast, sugar, and warm water; mix well and allow to rest for several minutes until bubbles begin to form. This is called "proofing." Mix the melted butter and the salt. In a large bowl combine the flour, eggs, and the butter and yeast mixtures. Beat by hand until smooth. Place in a buttered bowl, cover with plastic wrap, and set in a warm, draft-free place to rise until light and doubled in bulk, about 1 to 1½ hours. Punch the dough down and refrigerate it for at least one hour.

Generously coat one dozen small brioche molds with butter. Roll the chilled dough to a thickness of ½ inch on a floured work surface and with a 3-inch round cutter cut out circles. Place a chunk of chocolate in the center of each circle and roll the dough up, around, and completely covering the chocolate. Place the dough in the prepared mold. Repeat the procedure for each circle of dough. If you want to be authentic, make little balls from the remaining dough and push them on top of the dough in the molds, to make top knots. Depending on the size of your molds and how large you make the brioche you may make as few as 10 or as many as 15. Place the molds on a heavy-duty baking sheet. Make sure they have a few inches between them. Let the dough rise, uncovered, in a warm, draft-free place until the brioche are double in volume.

When ready to bake, preheat the oven to 400 degrees with the rack in the center position. Gently paint each one with an egg wash made by mixing the egg yolk and the light cream. Take care not to get any wash down inside the pan — this will prevent the brioche from rising when baking in the oven. Sprinkle the tops with the baker's sugar. Bake for 15–20 minutes, or until the tops are golden brown. To make sure they are fully cooked, remove one brioche from the mold and tap the bottom — there should be a hollow sound. If the bottom is still soft, you can remove all the brioches from their molds and continue baking them an extra 5 minutes. These are best served right from the oven with raspberry jam, but they can easily be refreshed (even after freezing) by being warmed in a 350 degree oven for 10 minutes.

Black and White Crème Brûlée

We once went to a local restaurant that served this dessert. It was so delicious that we ordered two more, then two more after that. On our way out, my husband paused at the door, turned around, and said to the entire dining room, "We strongly recommend the crème brûlée." My family and friends are so wild about this dessert that I make very large portions. It is okay to use smaller custard cups and make more servings, however, you might want to reduce the cooking time by a few minutes.

MAKES 8–14 SERVINGS, DEPENDING ON THE SIZE OF THE CUSTARD CUPS USED

For the custard:

5½ cups heavy cream
½ cup sugar
6 ounces bittersweet chocolate, chopped

2 ounces unsweetened chocolate, chopped
8 extra-large egg yolks

Preheat the oven to 350 degrees and place the rack in the lower third (but not the lowest position) of the oven. Set eight 1-cup ovenproof custard cups or ramekins into a shallow roasting pan or jelly-roll pan with at least 1-inch sides. The cups should not touch.

In a large metal bowl set over gently simmering water combine the heavy cream and the sugar. Stir until the sugar dissolves. Pour 1⅓ cups of the mixture into a two-cup glass measure and set it aside. Add the chocolate to the remaining mixture and stir gently until it melts. Don't worry about the speckled appearance. Remove from heat.

Beat 6 egg yolks in the large bowl of an electric mixer until they are light and have doubled in volume. On the lowest speed, mix in the chocolate. Pour the mixture into the custard cups, filling each one three-quarters full. Pour ½-inch boiling water into the roasting pan. It's easier to do this after you have placed the pan in the oven. Bake 40 minutes or until custard is set but still soft in the middle. While the custard is baking, beat the other two egg yolks slightly and add the 1⅓ cups reserved cream/sugar mixture. When the baked custards are set use a soupspoon to carefully place a layer of the egg/cream/sugar mixture on top and return it to the oven for an additional 8–10 minutes, until it is set. Remove the custards from the water bath and cool slightly at room temperature, then refrigerate until cold.

For the topping:

2–3 tablespoons boiling water
1⅓ cups dark brown sugar, firmly
  packed

Make a thick paste with the water and brown sugar, and using the back of a teaspoon spread about 1½–2 tablespoons of the mixture on top of each custard. Set the cups on a cookie sheet and place them under the broiler, 3 inches away from the element, until the sugar bubbles and just begins to get very brown. An alternative method is to place them, two at a time, in a toaster oven set on Top Broil. Refrigerate until serving time.

Chocolate Phantoms

These were the bankers' favorite cookie. Since macadamia nuts are not exactly a bargain food it doesn't hurt to be a banker when you shop for the ingredients.

It is helpful to use two cookie sheets, one on top of the other, or a heavy-duty jelly-roll pan to bake these cookies on, so the bottoms don't burn.

MAKES APPROXIMATELY 48 COOKIES

8 ounces bittersweet chocolate (I use
  Tobler Extra-Bittersweet), cut into
  small pieces
2 tablespoons sweet (unsalted) butter
3 tablespoons flour, measured after
  sifting

¼ teaspoon baking powder
2 extra-large eggs
⅔ cup sugar
1 teaspoon vanilla extract
8 ounces semisweet chocolate chips
8 ounces whole macadamia nuts

Preheat the oven to 350 degrees with the rack in the center position. Line either
two cookie sheets (one on top of the other) or one heavy-duty jelly-roll pan with
parchment. If you don't have parchment use aluminum foil. Do not use wax
paper.

In a small bowl set over a pan of gently simmering water, melt the bittersweet
chocolate and the butter. Stir occasionally until melted. Remove from heat.

Sift the flour and baking powder onto a piece of wax paper. In the bowl of an
electric mixer, beat the eggs, sugar, and vanilla. On lowest speed add the melted
chocolate and butter and then the dry ingredients. Remove the bowl from the
mixer and fold in the chocolate chips and nuts with a rubber scraper.

Use two teaspoons to drop the batter onto the cookie sheet. Make the cookies
very small, no bigger than a teaspoonful, and mound each one as high as possible.
You can place them fairly close together on the baking sheet.

Bake 6 minutes, then reverse the position of the baking sheet. Bake 3 or 4
more minutes, until the tops are dry. It is much better to underbake these than
overbake them. They will be very soft when removed from the oven. Let them
cool on the baking sheet and then peel them off.

Chocolate/Coffee Ice Cream Coupe

This easy but divinely delicious ice cream preparation should be served in a large
wine goblet.

SERVES 6

1 pint best-quality coffee ice cream
1 cup chocolate coffee beans (These are
  chocolate candies with a strong coffee
  flavoring made in the shape of coffee
  beans. They can be purchased in
  many gourmet shops or fine candy
  stores.)

1 cups heavy cream
1½ cups Kahlúa or crème de cacao

Let the ice cream soften at room temperature and then place it in the bowl of an
electric mixer. Mix in the chocolate coffee beans and place the bowl into the
freezer until the ice cream is hard again.

To serve:

Whip the cream. Scoop the ice cream into 6 wine goblets. Pour ¼ cup of the liqueur over each serving. Garnish with a spoonful of the whipped cream.

Mozart Mousse Torte

This dessert is made with two unusual ingredients: gianduja — milk chocolate with an infusion of hazelnuts — which is available in some specialty food stores, and Mozart Liqueur, which can be purchased in fine wine shops or mail-ordered (see page 245 for information). You may substitute another cream chocolate liqueur, although I don't think the result is as good. (See page 87 for information on toasting hazelnuts.)

SERVES 10

For the crust:

4 ounces butter, melted	½ cup ground, toasted hazelnuts
1 8½-ounce package chocolate wafers (36 wafers), finely ground in food processor	

Preheat oven to 375 degrees.

Butter a 10-inch springform pan. Line the bottom with a circle of parchment and butter the parchment.

Place the melted butter, the ground crumbs, and the nuts in the processor. Blend for a few seconds. Place the mixture in the prepared pan. Smooth on bottom and up along sides of pan, pressing in with your fingers to form a crust. The crust doesn't have to be even around the top edge of the pan.

Bake for 5 minutes. Cool in refrigerator while you prepare the filling.

For the filling:

6 extra-large egg yolks	1 tablespoon unflavored gelatin
⅔ cup sugar	1 cup Mozart Liqueur
4 cups heavy cream	1 tablespoon vanilla extract
10 ounces gianduja, cut into small pieces	Toasted hazelnuts (optional garnish)

Beat the egg yolks and sugar until they are thick and form a ribbon when the beater is lifted from the bowl.

Scald 2 cups of the heavy cream, reserving the rest in the refrigerator.

Whisk the cream into the eggs and then return this mixture to the pan and cook over medium heat, stirring constantly, for 5 minutes or so, until the mixture coats the back of a spoon. Remove from the heat and add the chopped chocolate, stirring until it is melted, and then pass the whole mixture through a fine sieve. Cool.

Dissolve the gelatin in ½ cup Mozart Liqueur. Heat gently to dissolve completely, but do not allow it to come to a boil.

Add the gelatin mixture to the slightly cooled chocolate mixture and stir gently but well. Cool this mixture completely, but do not allow it to set.

Sprinkle the other half cup of Mozart Liqueur on the bottom crust.

Beat one cup of cream until it holds firm peaks. Fold it into the chocolate mixture.

Pour this into the prepared crust, cover with foil (taking care not to let the foil touch the filling), and chill at least 4 hours before serving.

To serve:

Whip the remaining cup of cream and add the vanilla. If you wish, you can flavor the whipped cream with ¼ cup Mozart Liqueur. Pipe the whipped cream around the edge of the dessert and garnish with the toasted hazelnuts.

Chocolate Ginger Tart

This tart has a sweet short crust and a custard filling accented with pieces of candied ginger and chunks of bittersweet chocolate. It's a lovely dessert to serve at an afternoon tea party.

SERVES 8

Sweet pastry for a 10- or 11-inch flan ring or quiche dish:

2 cups flour	**1 extra-large egg yolk**
⅓ cup sugar	**3 tablespoons ice water**
Pinch of salt	
¼ pound (one stick) sweet (unsalted)	
butter, very cold, cut into small pieces	

Place the flour, sugar, and salt in the bowl of an electric mixer or on a work board. Cut in the butter until it resembles coarse meal. Do not overwork or allow the butter to become soft. Mix the egg yolk with two tablespoons of the water. Blend into the dough. If it appears too dry, add the third tablespoon of water. Gently form the dough into a ball, trying not to work it too much, which will make it tough. Cover with plastic wrap and chill 30 minutes.

On a floured work surface roll the dough ⅛ inch thick. Line the flan ring or quiche dish, trim the excess, and prick the dough with a fork. Freeze 15 minutes. Heat the oven to 425 degrees.

Bake the shell for 15 minutes. If the pastry begins to rise during the baking, prick it with a fork. Remove from oven and prepare the filling.

For the filling:

1 cup heavy cream
¼ cup sugar
2 extra-large eggs
2 ounces (3 tablespoons) candied
 ginger, finely diced (It is better to do
 this by hand with a chef's knife than
 in a food processor.)

1 teaspoon vanilla extract
Grated rind of one orange
6 ounces bittersweet chocolate, broken
 into small irregular chunks

Mix the cream, sugar, and eggs. Stir in the ginger, vanilla, and orange rind. Pour into prebaked shell. Dot the top with the chocolate.

Bake 18–20 minutes, until the crust is brown and the custard is set.

Serve either hot from the oven or at room temperature.

The Guild

Cooking is a lonely job. Especially if you're a woman. If you work by yourself in a small kitchen, you have no one to talk to or compare notes with. After a while your waitress gets tired of trying your butter sauces and goes on a diet. If you're in a big kitchen, chances are you work with a bunch of men who hang out together and aren't too interested in chewing the fat with you. Obviously there are exceptions — kitchens run and staffed by women, kitchens where the karma is perfect and men and women work together, sharing information and support — but let me tell you, these kitchens are rare. Although trends are changing for the better, cooking is still pretty much a male-dominated profession. More often than not, men get the best jobs (jobs women wouldn't have even been considered for ten years ago) and the better pay. They are often promoted ahead of women who are better trained and have more on-the-job experience than they do. Women's asses still get pinched and their heads get patted by chefs who tell them they are doing a hell of a job, while the position of line cook is filled by some guy the chef knew from somewhere else. If you are a woman and want to make it in the food business, you have to work twice as hard as a man. You have to overcome bias about your skills, your speed, and your strength. You have to act tough both physically and mentally. You have to learn to curse instead of cry. While you're doing all this stuff you don't have much time for contacts with other women or other cooks. The other thing that happens is that because it has been so difficult for you to "make it," you tend to become reluctant to share your success secrets with other women — women who are as desperate to "make it" as you were. The industry was at one time perceived as having room for only a few good women — that's you, not her. Information, resources, and recipes become industrial secrets. Men, who have been traditionally secure in this profession, go off to meetings of chefs' organizations and share all kinds of resources while acquiring even more information from guest lecturers — and having a good time socializing. Women were not allowed this luxury; they had to work too hard. Besides, there was no organization for women cooks.

It would be great to be able to pat myself on the back and say I dreamed up the idea of the Women's Culinary Guild for the altruistic reason of elevating the status of the female cook. That's not exactly what I had in mind. The idea came to me during a reception that the Arthur and Elizabeth Schlesinger Library on the History of Women in America of Radcliffe College held in honor of Julia Child. Julia had done a series of three cooking demonstrations to raise money for the library and I was part of the committee that organized the affair. I was thrilled to be involved for several reasons. The first was that this was the closest contact I had ever had with Radcliffe. I was in the Ivy League by proxy. I loved it — maybe if I worked incredibly hard on this project they would award me an honorary degree. (Attending these meetings at Radcliffe opened up a whole new world of social intercourse for me. The rarefied atmosphere of the library seemed to magically turn all the committee members into excruciatingly polite gentlewomen who sat, ankles crossed, on priceless antique chairs, discussing how to get local merchants to cough up $200 for ads for the program book. No one ever interrupted anyone else.) Second, I relished the opportunity to work with Julia, and third, it was an opportunity to meet, in a social setting, some of the other women in the food industry in the New England area. The year before, Craig Claiborne and Pierre Franey had done the fund-raising demonstrations. At the receptions that followed these demonstrations the women cooks stood around in isolated little groups, staring with obvious curiosity at the other women in their little groups, but no one really made a move to talk to the others.

I talk to everybody. I can't help it, it's the way I am. I talk to people on buses, people on line in the movies. I am naturally curious and interested about people and I'm rarely disappointed because it seems that most of them like an opportunity to talk about themselves. I'd be a born hostess if I didn't have so much trouble remembering people's names. So, I'm standing in this room, full of women who are not talking to each other but getting stiff necks from craning around to see who's here and straining their eyes to figure out who's who by reading the tiny writing on the name tags. I say to the woman next to me, "This is weird. They'd like to socialize, but they're waiting for others to make the first move." She agreed that the level of paranoia was off the scale. We got through the buffet line and went to sit down. There were ten women at our table; each had a job or ran a business associated with food or wine. We talked about the social dynamics of the evening. Everyone agreed that in view of the push for equality for women in business, and the proliferation of women's support groups, there should be at least a dialogue between women in the food industry — that it should be possible for women to help each other, to share information and resources. This could only serve to strengthen women's positions in the industry. I was thinking about the support end more than anything else, thinking about how lonely I was and how much I craved the company and advice of other cooks, when I suggested that we form an organization of women who worked in the food business. I said that if we called all these women together with the purpose of forming a support network maybe the ice would be broken — maybe they were as lonely, professionally, as I was. The women at the table enthusiastically agreed. Unlike the usually staid meetings at Radcliffe, where each woman waited patiently until the others were through to speak, everyone spoke at once. We all had great ideas to share. It was as if everyone had this idea in the back of her mind and needed only my prodding to set it free. We decided to hold a meeting to which each woman would bring a list of names of the women she knew who worked in the food industry in the area. We would send the people on the lists an invitation to come to a charter meeting. We decided on a name, the Women's Culinary Guild, and a purpose, a networking organization for women who make their livings in the food industry. We would create a resource committee and a job bank. We would sponsor professional-level cooking demonstrations and business seminars. Most important, we would establish a comfortable setting where women could come together in a relaxed atmosphere to seek the support of other women in the industry, and, if they wished, exchange ideas and information. The ten women at the table became the steering committee: there was a food writer, two restaurateurs, a wine merchant, three cooks, a food consultant, a shop manager and teacher, and a producer of television cooking shows.

We sent out sixty-five invitations to the first meeting. Sixty women, one infant, and one husband showed up. We made sure the name tags had everyone's name in giant letters, and we made sure there was lots of wine to drink. The atmosphere was a little cool at first, but people warmed up both from wine and talk about the common interest that brought them to the meeting. I had to give a speech and I was terrified. What was the worst that could happen? All I had to do was read what I had written. The worst that happened was that one of the pages was out of order, and I had to stop speaking and shuffle around for quite a while looking for it. "Oh, well," I said, "now you can see why I'm a cook, and not a speechmaker." Everyone laughed. I talked about the purposes and aims of the organization and the programs we would offer. I talked about my own philosophy of sharing information, my need for support, and my curiosity about the other women in the room. Our next speaker was Nancy Korman, who heads her own Boston-based public relations firm. Nancy had formed a very successful businesswomen's network several years before. She spoke for several minutes about what a network is, and how it operates to assist and support its members. Both speeches were greeted with great enthusiasm, and the rest of the evening was dedicated to more wine and lots of lively conversation. Caterers chatted with other caterers, wine makers told restaurateurs about their new vintage, a line cook found a job, and food writers found material for hundreds of columns. I was in heaven. The camp counselor/social director part of me was enjoying ultimate fulfillment. Do you know the part in the movie A *Thousand Clowns* where Jason Robards gets up at the crack of dawn and goes careening around Brooklyn Heights yelling, "Okay, I want everybody up for volleyball!"? Well, that's me. I felt like I had pulled off the biggest volleyball game of the century. And I didn't think I would be lonely anymore.

Practically everybody who showed up for the first meeting joined the Guild. The steering committee met on Saturday mornings, first in closed meetings, and then, as other members expressed their desire to help, the meetings were open to all. Each member of the steering committee either headed a subcommittee or took on some aspect of running the organization itself. I became the chairwoman and took on, in addition to administrative responsibilities, the job of setting up educational and social programs (which could be suggested by any member of the Guild). I also made it a point to call each member once a month to fill her in on the Guild's activities, and just to stay in touch. This was before the inception of the newsletter, so I was on the telephone constantly. My children used to joke that if they removed the telephone from the side of my head, I wouldn't be able to talk. I learned how to wheel and deal, getting donations of space, reduced rates on printing, and other useful money savers. I began to learn how to work with the press. These experiences not only benefited the Guild, but made me a better, more secure businesswoman.

Each steering committee member contributed something much more important than time and energy to the Guild. In forging the basic philosophy and direction of the organization, each woman gave of her personality, experience, and background. We ranged in age from early twenties to mid-sixties. We were energetic and laid back, brash and abrasive, and classy and calming; we were Jewish American Princess and Earth Mother, cynical and refreshingly naive. We wore blue jeans and sweatshirts, and Celine pumps and cashmere sweater sets. We had manicures and grease burns. We were a collective genius: we could speak French and Spanish, run a great restaurant, type eighty words a minute with all the words spelled right, write cookbooks, teach courses, give a cooking demonstration, and film and edit it for TV. We could whip out meals for hundreds and still have the energy to make twenty phone calls. We could stand on our feet all day long in hot kitchens and busy food shops but be able to share the dirty joke the sous-chef told the guys — the one he thought you wouldn't get. We were all these wonderful things, ten women as different as could be, sitting around my dining room table on Saturday mornings, drinking endless cups of coffee, sharing a little gossip, lots of laughter, working hard toward our common goal. And we were friends.

This amazing ambience permeated the entire membership. The Guild meetings and events were warm and friendly gatherings of women who shared common interests and goals. It became a sisterhood of caring individuals who, in the right surroundings, felt secure enough to open up to other women. While some Guild events went more smoothly or were more successful than others, there was always an easy feeling of being with friends and having a good time while we learned from each other and the various guest speakers and demonstrators who appeared at our functions. The two most often heard comments were "This is unbelievable, I'm having such a good time." And, "It won't last."

Of all the affairs that the Guild sponsored when I was chairwoman, my favorite was the massive chocolate tasting run by Adrianne Marcus, author of *The Chocolate Bible*. I met Adrianne at the airport when she flew in from San Francisco. She was surrounded by boxes and bags of chocolate. As people walked by they sniffed the air and deviated from their original path to come closer for a better whiff. I could understand why. The lady smelled like a chocolate factory. Apparently, terrified at the thought of separation, she insisted on taking all the chocolate with her as carryon luggage for the flight East and had various passengers holding it on their laps. She almost caused a riot when she tried to get off without giving out samples. All week long before her arrival packages had arrived at our house addressed to her. There were ten-pound blocks of milk and dark coating chocolate from companies like Van Leer and Nestlé, cases of chocolate chips from Ghirardelli, and boxes of candies from a dozen shops around the country. To this we added the fifty pounds of stuff that Adrianne hand-carried on the plane.

If I thought I loved chocolate, Adrianne put my devotion to shame with her passion. We were still in our coats when she insisted that we try the hot fudge sauce from her favorite place in California. Then it was, "Here, try this, it's Sea Foam from See's." Crunchy aerated molasses center dipped in bittersweet chocolate. Fabulous. We manage to get out of our coats and Adrianne's tearing open the blocks of Van Leer chocolate. "This is the stuff that Colette used to make the Trianon." She loves Van Leer — and so do I. We send the kids to bed so we can get into the chocolate-covered cherries. "These are illegal in this country because of the kirsch — but I know a lady — she makes them up just for me." This woman has been in my home for under an hour and so far I have eaten more chocolate than I had all month. Boy, am I happy. David goes to lie down. I tell Adrianne that we have to cool it because the next evening is a chocolate dessert buffet in her honor. Members of the Guild are bringing their favorite chocolate desserts.

The party was a tremendous success. The magic combination of delicious chocolate desserts, nonstop champagne, and the excitement over Adrianne's visit made the occasion a warm and memorable event. Guild members pulled out all the stops making fabulous chocolate desserts for the buffet table.

The next evening one hundred and fifty Guild members, their friends and families, gathered for the chocolate tasting. A chocolate tasting is like a wine tasting, only much better. We sat at long tables in the basement of the Cambridge Electric Light Company and listened as Adrianne gave a brief but inclusive talk about the history of chocolate, the legends surrounding it, and its production and manufacturing process. Then she passed around huge metal trays filled with chunks of chocolate. We tasted five dark (bittersweet, semisweet, and sweet), four kinds of milk chocolate, and two white chocolates. This was a blind tasting, so the chocolates were unlabeled, and it wasn't until the end that people learned which brands of chocolate they had been eating. Several people didn't care what kind of chocolate they were eating and asked Adrianne to marry them. Many people who thought they could never get enough chocolate left (with smiles) carrying paper plates full of what they couldn't finish. Everyone was extremely happy. The event was a huge success.

As news of the Guild spread, several things began to happen: lots more people wanted to join, the press got interested, and the paperwork and telephone responsibilities became overwhelming. We had to hire a secretary. The second year there were close to one hundred members, and over one hundred and sixty the year after that. More and more members attended the board meetings and wanted a say in the running of the organization. The same competitive spirit that made them successful in business was driving them to take an active role in the Guild. It became clear that we had to establish some kind of organized procedure with which to conduct not only our meetings but the whole Guild (not to mention get a bigger coffee pot). It was clear that the days of our comfy rap sessions were nearing an end. For the first two years the governing board remained basically the same with a few additions to the steering committee. We made all the decisions without consulting the general membership. One of the most difficult things we had to decide about was who was qualified for membership. Because so many women wanted to join, it was necessary to institute some membership rules. Some of us thought that all women who worked in the food industry and were willing to pay the $30 dues should belong. Others thought that only "real professionals" should belong. What constitutes a "real professional" was the source of great and heated debate. I think that this issue was the first real divisive issue for the steering committee. I (the impractical idealist) thought it would be great if every woman cook could belong. Another member thought that allowing just any "prep cook" in would dilute the stature and importance of the organization. We arrived at a compromise that was, of course, immediately tested by one of the more combative members. Being the chairwoman, I took the heat.

This member had sponsored her catering assistant for membership. She had all the right credentials, but she was a high-school student. We hadn't put any age limits on membership. The board was divided about what to do. After a lengthy and agonized debate, we voted to turn the girl down — I don't remember how we worded our decision; hopefully, we said we screwed up in not putting age requirements in the membership rules, and please try again when you graduate. The sponsoring member was not buying that. Not only was she embarrassed in front of her assistant, but she was already planning her next career (as a law student) and was ready to litigate. The steering committee agreed to discuss the issue again and take another vote. The sponsoring member sent each one of us a many-paged memo detailing all the facts, the issues, and an impassioned plea on behalf of her client, I mean assistant. This whole episode spanned a four- or five-month period. When I received the memo I was several weeks away from the birth of my last child. I remember reading it and thinking that I'd get to it before the baby came. The final vote was the week of August fifteenth. I went into labor the morning of the twelfth. I was sitting in a rocking chair in our parlor telling my midwife and husband what an easy (ha!) delivery this one was going to be when the phone rang. My son answered it.

"Mom, it's for you. She says it's an emergency." Oy, they ran out of private rooms at the hospital and I'd have to have a home birth.

"Hello? (pant pant)," I said, bracing for the worst — my baby nurse deciding to take an early retirement.

"Hi, Lora. This is Sue Clarke. Did you get a chance to read my memo?"

"Gee (pant pant) Sue, I looked at it the other day, but haven't had time to make a decision yet."

"Well, I'd like to talk to you about it. Can I swing by your house?"

"I'm really (pant pant) tied up now."

"Did you get a dog?"

"Huh?"

"Someone is panting into the phone."

"That's me, Sue. I'm in labor."

"Oh, well, this will only take a minute. Look, we can do it over the phone. Do you have your copy of the memo handy?"

"Sue, did you hear what I said? I'm having a baby?"

"Lora, of course I know you're having a baby, why else would you wear all those enormous dresses with no belt."

"Now! Sue. Now! I'm having the baby now. I'm in labor. That's why I'm (ouch) panting. That's why your memo is the furthest thing from my mind. Can you understand that?"

"Look, the vote is tied. I need you to vote in my favor in order for my assistant to become a member."

The Guild

151

I'm thinking this is not happening. I'm thinking that when this woman is in labor I will hire a fifty-piece brass band to play loud music and throw pastrami sandwiches at her. I am thinking she will be a very successful lawyer. I am thinking I never want to be the chairwoman of anything else ever again.

"Okay, Sue. You have my (groan, pant) vote. Now please go away."

At the end of the second year, when I stepped down from the position of chairwoman, the vice-chairwoman took my place, and we held elections for several spots on the steering committee. It was the first time the rest of the members had a say in the running of the organization. During the third year the new board worked very hard to establish a set of bylaws and new membership rules. It was during this time that the Guild began its transition from a grass-roots networking organization to an establishment status association. It was, in many ways, an inevitable metamorphosis. As new members joined, and as the needs and focus of the charter members changed, the Guild had to adapt to meet the demands of the women who were now part of it. The Guild had seen me through a career change and supported me through what had to be a pretty earth-shaking occurrence for any soon-to-be-middle-aged professional woman — a new baby. I had extremely conflicting emotions about the direction the Guild was moving. I missed the old comfortable feeling, but rejoiced in the new energy and obvious success of the members. I hated the officiousness and pomposity (not to mention the bureaucracy) with which inquiries for membership were treated, but marveled at the level of talent the Guild attracted. It bothered me to see women flaunting membership as a status symbol, which was the result of an exclusive membership. I knew it was time to move on to other things after an exchange I had with a young woman at the third annual opening Guild meeting. She looked at my name tag and said, "So, you're Lora Brody."

I acknowledged that my name tag didn't lie.

She said, "Tell me, how did you (emphasis on you) get that recipe in the *New York Times?*"

I caught my breath, then I smiled my sweetest smile and said, "I slept with Craig Claiborne."

Beneath my smile I was seething. What did she mean asking me that unbelievably outrageous question? I had worked my ass off, standing over a hot oven, making that goddamn cake two hundred times, recording every detail, to create a fantastic dessert. That's how I did it. Too bad, sweetie. Eat your heart out. I did it because I'm a better cook than you. I worked harder. I deserved it. The last three items are out-and-out lies. I was lucky, that's all. I sent in a great recipe and it got published. Hundreds of great recipes get sent to the *New York Times* every week and only one or two are published. It's luck. That's all. But I'll tell you, that obnoxious girl and her question threw me for a loop. Wasn't this the Women's

Culinary Guild where everyone was friends? In answering her (and thinking my subsequent thoughts) I was no better than she was. I was just as nasty, just as paranoid. Suddenly the room took on the proportions of the supermarket before the King Kong cure. I couldn't wait to get out. Where were my coffee-drinking pals? Why were they all wearing silk dresses and nylons? Why was I? It was ironic; the Guild had helped to make me feel secure as a woman in the food industry. Now that I was secure I could go out and push for the success I wanted. I had learned how to compete for business and press. The people I was competing with were the very women I had helped bring together for the purpose of peaceful coexistence. How could I reconcile my conflict (and guilt) about competing with my friends, and how could I deal with their feelings about it? I wondered what a man would do. (I bet he wouldn't have agonized quite as long as I did — but how many men have such strong ties to other men in their professional circles?) In the end, I decided that it would be moving backwards to cool my career after I had worked so hard — besides, I was (conflict aside) having the time of my life — and making more money than I ever had before. I figured that my real friends would always be my real friends, as I would be theirs. I am delighted to say that I figured right.

Sue Small's Chocolate Peanut Butter Cake

This fabulous recipe is the creation of baker extraordinaire Sue Small, who with her husband, Joseph Stigliano, owns and operates the Peacock Restaurant in Cambridge, Massachusetts. It is my sons' all-time favorite birthday cake.

MAKES ONE 2-LAYER 10-INCH CAKE

For the cake:

4 ounces semisweet chocolate, cut into pieces
1¾ cups all-purpose flour
2 teaspoons baking powder
¼ cup peanut butter

½ cup (one stick) sweet (unsalted) butter
1½ cups sugar
4 extra-large eggs, separated
1 teaspoon vanilla extract
1 cup milk

Preheat the oven to 375 degrees. Place the rack in the center position of the oven. Grease a 10-inch springform pan. Line the bottom with parchment or wax paper, grease the paper, then dust the pan with flour. Knock out the excess flour. Melt the chocolate in a small bowl placed over a pan of gently simmering water. Stir occasionally, then, when completely melted, set aside to cool. Sift the flour with the baking powder. Beat the peanut butter and butter with ¾ cup of the sugar, until the mixture is smooth and creamy. Beat in the 4 yolks, one at a time, and then the vanilla. Stir in the flour and milk.

Beat the egg whites until they begin to stiffen, then sprinkle in the remaining sugar while continuing to beat until the whites are firm, but shiny.

Fold the whites into the cake mixture and then fold in the melted chocolate. Place the mixture in the prepared pan and bake for 45 minutes or until a cake tester inserted into the center of the cake comes out clean. Release springform and turn cake onto a rack to cool. When the cake is cool use a serrated knife to split it into two layers. Prepare the filling.

For the filling:

⅔ cup sugar	8 ounces (2 sticks) sweet (unsalted)
⅓ cup water	butter at room temperature
4 extra-large egg yolks	¼ cup peanut butter

Place the sugar and water in a small pan, and over high heat, stir only until the sugar dissolves. Continue to cook until the syrup registers 240 degrees on a candy thermometer.

Place the egg yolks in the bowl of an electric mixer and with the machine on high speed pour the syrup over the yolks in a steady stream. Continue to beat until the mixture is completely cool, then bit by bit, add the butter and finally the peanut butter.

Place one layer of the cake on a cake plate. Place strips of wax paper around the edge to keep the plate clean. Spread two-thirds of the filling on top of this layer. Reserve the rest for decoration. Place the other layer on top. Prepare the frosting.

For the frosting:

6 ounces semisweet chocolate	¼ cup sugar
¼ cup strong coffee, made by diluting	2 ounces (½ stick) sweet (unsalted)
2 tablespoons instant coffee in ¼ cup	butter
boiling water	4 extra-large egg yolks

Melt the chocolate with the coffee and sugar in the top of a double boiler. Stir until smooth. Keeping the mixture on the heat, add the egg yolks one at a time, stirring well after each addition. Remove from heat and beat in the butter, a little at a time. Cool slightly. When lukewarm, frost sides and top of cake. Place the remaining filling in a small pastry bag fitted with a star tube. Pipe rosettes around the top edge of the cake.

Carole Wald's Chocolate Pistachio Cake

Carole was trained by Madeline Kamman and is *the* Gourmet Kosher Caterer in Boston.

SERVES 10–12

For the cake:

9 ounces bittersweet chocolate, chopped
12 ounces (approximately 2 cups)
  pistachio nuts, ground
1 cup cake flour
1¾ cups sugar
½ teaspoon baking powder
8 ounces (2 sticks) sweet (unsalted)
  butter at room temperature, cut into
  pieces

8 extra-large egg yolks
1 teaspoon almond extract
9 extra-large egg whites at room
  temperature

Coat a 10-cup tube pan with butter and then dust it with flour. Knock out the excess flour. Melt the chocolate in a small bowl set over a pan of gently simmering water. Stir until smooth and then remove from heat to cool slightly. In the large bowl of an electric mixer set on low speed, combine the ground nuts, the flour, 1½ cups of the sugar, and the baking powder. Add the butter, bit by bit, mixing until it is incorporated. Add the egg yolks, one by one, mixing until each one is incorporated before adding the next. Mix in the chocolate and the almond extract.

In a clean bowl, using clean beaters, whip the egg whites with the remaining sugar until they are stiff but not dry. Stir a large spoonful of the whites into the chocolate mixture to lighten it, then pour the chocolate mixture on top of the whites and fold together.

Pour into the prepared pan and bake 50 minutes. Cool completely in pan, then unmold. While the cake is cooling, prepare the glaze.

For the glaze:

⅔ cup heavy cream
6 ounces semisweet chocolate, chopped
2 ounces unsweetened chocolate,
  chopped

2 tablespoons sweet (unsalted) butter,
  cut in pieces
½ cup chopped pistachios

Scald the cream in a small saucepan. Off the heat, stir in the chocolate, then the butter, bit by bit. Stir until smooth. Drizzle over the top of the cake.

Garnish with the chopped nuts.

Ellen Haiken's Chocolate Cake

This tender, rich chocolate cake, created by talented caterer/chef Ellen Haiken, has a satin-smooth glaze and is decorated with chopped nuts. I use pistachios, but walnuts, pecans, or toasted hazelnuts are delicious, too.

MAKES ONE 10-INCH CAKE TO SERVE 12 PEOPLE

For the cake:

10 ounces bittersweet chocolate, chopped

2 ounces unsweetened chocolate, chopped

⅓ cup strong coffee, made by diluting 2 tablespoons instant coffee in ⅓ cup boiling water

⅓ cup dark rum

6 extra-large eggs at room temperature, separated

1 cup sugar

1 cup heavy cream

1 scant cup all-purpose flour, measured after sifting

Preheat the oven to 325 degrees and set the rack in the center position. Grease a 10-inch cake pan (you can use a springform) and line the bottom with parchment. In a small bowl set over a pan of gently simmering water, melt the chocolates together with the coffee and rum. Stir together and set aside to cool slightly. In the large bowl of an electric mixer, beat the egg yolks and sugar until light and until the mixture has tripled in volume and forms a ribbon when the beater is lifted from the bowl. In a clean bowl, beat the heavy cream until it holds soft peaks, then set it aside in the refrigerator. In another clean bowl, beat the egg whites until stiff but not dry, and set aside.

Stir the cooled chocolate mixture into the beaten egg yolks. Fold in the sifted flour, and then the egg whites, then the heavy cream. The batter will deflate somewhat, but try to fold gently to deflate as little as possible. Pour the batter into the prepared cake pan and bake 50–60 minutes. The cake is done when the sides just start to come away from the pan and the top has formed a crust that yields with a light touch. Do not overbake.

Cool in the pan in the turned-off oven with the door half open for half an hour. Allow the cake to finish cooling in the pan on a rack out of the oven. Unmold onto a rack over a jelly-roll pan. Prepare the glaze.

For the glaze:

½ cup boiling water

8 ounces bittersweet chocolate, chopped

½ cup nuts, finely chopped

Whisk the water into the chocolate and cool until of spreading consistency. When slightly thickened, pour over the cake and smooth with a long metal spatula.

Cup the nuts in your hand and gently press the nuts into the sides of the cake. Sprinkle ½ teaspoon of nuts in the center of the cake. When the glaze has set, using two wide metal spatulas, transfer the cake to a serving plate.

Jane Lavine's Chocolate Cannoli

These elegant individual desserts are made by filling a crisp hazelnut lace cookie with a delicious milk chocolate hazelnut mousse made with gianduja, a hazelnut-infused milk chocolate. One brand, Perugina, is readily available in specialty shops. It may take a few tries to master the art of making these cookies, but the results are well worth the effort. Jane Lavine, an Italian cook extraordinaire, caters and teaches in Brookline, Massachusetts.

SERVES 6

For the cookies:

½ cup finely chopped toasted hazelnuts	½ cup sweet (unsalted) butter
½ cup flour	⅓ cup dark brown sugar
¼ cup dark corn syrup	Pinch of salt

Preheat the oven to 325 degrees with the rack in the center position. Spread the hazelnuts on a cookie sheet and toast until golden, turning them once or twice. If they are unskinned, remove the skin by covering them with a terry-cloth towel and rubbing vigorously. Chop the hazelnuts in a food processor.

Lightly oil 6 cannoli forms and set aside. Combine the flour and chopped hazelnuts. In a small saucepan, bring the corn syrup, butter, and brown sugar just to the boil, remove from the heat, and add the salt and the flour/hazelnut mixture and combine well. On a buttered cookie sheet, spoon out three 1-tablespoon circles of batter, leaving several inches between each circle. Bake 8–10 minutes. Cool slightly, but while still fairly hot, use a metal spatula to flip the cookies onto the oiled forms. Use your hands to roll the cookie around the form. When the cookies are completely cool, slip them off the forms and repeat, making three more cookies. There will be batter left over to account for any mishaps, as these cookies are extremely fragile. Store cooled cookies in a dry place (a tightly covered container is best) and do not refrigerate them.

For the mousse:

1 extra-large egg yolk	¼ cup sugar
4 ounces gianduja, coarsely chopped	¼ teaspoon instant espresso powder
2 ounces bittersweet chocolate,	Pinch of salt
coarsely chopped	½ cup milk, scalded
1 ounce Frangelico (hazelnut) liqueur	½ cup heavy cream

In a blender or food processor bowl fitted with the metal blade, process all of the above ingredients except the cream until no flecks of chocolate remain, or until thoroughly blended and the chocolate has melted completely. Pour the mixture into a shallow bowl to cool. Whip the cream to the shy side of the stiff-peak stage and fold it into the chocolate mixture. Whisk gently to break up lumps if necessary. Cover with plastic wrap and chill until set.

To assemble:

Just before serving fill a pastry bag fitted with a star tip with half the filling. Pipe some filling into each side of a cannoli. Repeat with the rest of the cannolis. Garnish with a rosette of whipped cream, a candied violet, and a mint leaf.

Peggy Glass's Chocolate Lasagna

You've no doubt seen Peggy's articles in *Bon Appétit*. Here she's created something new and different — dessert lasagna made with chocolate pasta and two fillings, sweetened ricotta cheese and chocolate. I've served it at brunch and at winter meetings when I've needed a substantial hot dish.

SERVES 10–12

For the pasta:

1¾ cups all-purpose flour (or 1 cup	Pinch of salt
all-purpose flour plus ¾ cup semolina	2 extra-large eggs
or pasta flour)	2 teaspoons vegetable oil
2 tablespoons unsweetened cocoa	
powder	

Combine the flour, cocoa, and salt in a bowl and make a well in the center. Add the eggs and oil in the center of the well and mix with a fork to form the dough. Knead the dough for 15 minutes until it is smooth and shiny, adding more flour if necessary to keep the dough from sticking. Wrap well with plastic wrap and let the dough rest for half an hour. Roll the pasta out by hand or with a machine and cut it into eight 4½ x 11-inch strips. Cook two strips at a time in boiling salted water. Cook just 20 seconds after the water returns to the boil. Plunge the noodles into cold water to stop the cooking. When cooled, place on towels in a single layer to drain.

For the fillings:

4 cups whole milk ricotta cheese	**1 tablespoon grated orange rind**
2 cups (one pint) heavy cream	**2 tablespoons Grand Marnier**
6 tablespoons sugar	**Pinch of salt**

Combine all the above ingredients and mix until smooth.

**12 ounces bittersweet chocolate,
  chopped**

To assemble:

Preheat the oven to 425 degrees with the rack in the upper third of the oven. Generously butter an 8 x 11 x 2-inch pan. Alternate layers of noodles, cheese filling, and chocolate, ending with a cheese layer. Bake for 20–25 minutes until the top is lightly colored. Let the lasagna stand for 10 minutes to solidify, then serve warm.

The Rites of Passage: Paying My Bill at the Temple of Haute Cuisine

How I cringe when some well-meaning person introduces me as a chef. I'm not a chef, at best I'm a cook. A chef is in charge of the total running of a kitchen: staff, ordering, menus, coordinating with the front of the house, etc. He/she is the head honcho — the person you want to praise when your culinary earth has moved, or the person you want to throttle when your $200 meal was a clunker. The closest I ever came to playing chef was when I ran an executive dining room for the officers of a bank in Boston. I did the ordering and part of the menu planning. Since there was only one, very able waitress, my dealing with the front of the house was limited to gossiping, over endless cups of coffee, with the waitress about the particular quirks of each diner. It was an ideal job, with only one thing missing. I was lonely for input from other cooks. I felt that making lunch for twenty or so distinguished and charming ladies and gentlemen was only playing at cook. I wanted to work in a real restaurant — so I could call myself a real cook.

The golden opportunity presented itself when a young couple, newly acquired friends, invited me to spend the summer working at their restaurant. At first I wouldn't take their offer seriously. I had no professional training, I had never cooked on the line (that means working with two or three other people at the stove, putting out dinners at the rate of six a minute, where you need the strength of Attila the Hun, the speed of Mario Andretti, and the grace and precision of a traffic cop at rush hour). Nothing in my professional experience as a cook made me feel that I was up to working in this very elegant restaurant that was known worldwide for its exquisite food. The couple insisted that it would be a great "learning experience." I would be treated with great patience and have an opportunity to share cooking expertise with my cohorts in the kitchen — after all, they promised, their kitchen was one big happy family and I would be welcomed by everyone. Mostly, they promised, we'd all have great fun. I still said no. In my heart of hearts I felt something was wrong. I was nervous about working for friends, I worried about how my family would cope with my long working hours, I worried about my inexperience, I worried that I wouldn't be good enough. My professional cronies told me I was crazy to turn down such a fantastic opportunity. What did I have to lose? Think of all I could learn. I'd be a "real cook" at last.

My first day I reported to the sous-chef and introduced myself. He turned away from the veal he was butchering, looked me up and down, and said, "Humph, we'll make you cry." It was clear that he wasn't joking. Welcome to the world of real cooks, kid. It was downhill from there. I worked at the cold station. My job was to turn out ten different cold appetizers daily, five of which changed every day. The restaurant was open seven days a week and served two seatings of sixty people every night. That meant that I was responsible for producing enough of each thing to feed all those people every day — even on my day off, which meant on the day before my day off I had to do double the work. I was handed a notebook of recipes with the warning that I was to come up with new and exciting things and not rely on the old standards in the book. A brief tour of the kitchen came next. A restaurant kitchen is a hot and noisy place. At seven o'clock in the morning the thermometer near the stove reads 130 degrees and the clatter of pots, the roar of the big dishwasher, the sound of voices trying to make themselves heard over the blaring rock music are constant company. I didn't remember where anything was after the first five minutes and was afraid to interrupt anyone to ask. My hands were shaking so much that I could hardly hold a knife. I grabbed the notebook and quickly flipped through it. Cucumber mousse appeared. That seemed fairly straightforward. I managed to assemble the ingredients and the utensils. It takes a long time to make cucumber mousse for fifty people (I just guessed at the number — I was too terrified to ask questions), but I somehow did it. I remember while I was making it that eighteen tablespoons of gelatin seemed like an awful lot — but that's what the book said. I let the mixture cool a bit and then started to spoon it into the individual molds. Something was terribly wrong. The pastel-green gop in the huge mixing bowl had turned into something incredibly solid — something approaching the consistency of a basketball. I couldn't even make a dent in it with a cleaver. It was married to the bowl. Just as I was thinking of tucking my nightmare under my arm and hotfooting it out the closest exit, the sous-chef sauntered by. He eyeballed the situation. First he laughed (just a little), and then he began to yell. Because of my overenthusiasm in the gelatin department (eighteen teaspoons, not eighteen tablespoons) I had not only made a fool out of myself, I had wasted time and ingredients — unforgivable sins in a busy kitchen. After that I was called the Jell-O Queen—when I wasn't called something worse.

I worked six days a week from seven A.M. to eleven P.M. on weekdays and one or two in the morning on weekends. My day off was Sunday and that was the only day I saw my family. My diet consisted of black coffee and gallons of lemonade during the day and Valium and double bourbons after work so I could sleep. I only took one break during the day—at three in the afternoon I would drive down the road to the soft ice cream stand and eat three double-dipped chocolate ice cream cones. I lost fifteen pounds that summer and any romantic notions I had about working in a restaurant. As the days passed I was able to get a handle on the work. My speed improved tremendously, and I began to be proud of most of the food I was turning out. The atmosphere was never friendly (we never did have all that fun I was promised), but I did begin to win the respect of the other people in the kitchen. The sous-chef (who now, by the way, is a good friend) begrudgingly admitted that some of my stuff "wasn't bad."

The two things that kept me going (Valium and bourbon aside) were David's willingness to listen to me tell my horror stories and hold me while I cried, and the fact that all my friends came to eat at the restaurant. I got to go out to the dining room to see them with my white chef's coat on—a uniform I felt I had earned a million times over. It was essential that they not know the awful truth. I would wash the sweat off my face, put on a big maniacal smile and breeze into the dining room to discuss the relative merits of fish mousse versus cold apricot soup. They usually gasped in horror when they saw me. I had exceeded the realm of thin—I was into gaunt. When I look at pictures taken during that time I realize it wasn't just the weight loss they reacted to. I was physically and emotionally exhausted. One friend told me that I looked like I had been running the kitchen at a concentration camp.

In the middle of the summer I got a call from a friend who worked for the *New York Times*. He told me that he had seen a table of contents for the magazine section, and my Chocolate Cherry Torte* was scheduled to be run on July twentieth. I dissolved into a frenzy of conflict. On the one hand, I was thrilled beyond words, and on the other, I was terrified about what the reception would be in the kitchen. I prayed that Craig Claiborne would mention the name of the restaurant. Maybe that would get me off the hook. On the morning of the twentieth, I raced down to the drugstore to pick up the twenty *Times*es that I had reserved. There was the recipe, there was my name, there was no mention of the restaurant. I slunk into work. I didn't feel joyous; I felt guilty. The restaurant's *Times* was sitting on the reservation table. I peeked to see if the magazine was missing. It was. Cold terror settled in. I walked into the kitchen and got right to work. No one said a thing—not even hello. The unspoken hostility was suffocat-

The Chocolate Diet

162

ing. The day dragged on. I wished someone would say something — anything — yell at me, throw a knife. Nothing. At five, the waiters and waitresses arrived to set up. Several came up and whispered "Congratulations!" That was better. As the evening wore on I began to mull over the fact that maybe I hadn't done anything wrong, and that maybe I should be just a little put out that the chef wouldn't give credit where credit was due. I began to wish that I had one of the cakes — to throw at him. I took gleeful satisfaction in learning my friends who came to dinner that night were requesting the cake.

You are probably wondering where the chocolate angle is in this story. During the summer the owners of the restaurant invited several chefs from Paris to come and do special dinners. These were called tasting dinners and consisted of eight or nine small courses with different wines with each course. The nights we had these dinners there was only one seating, usually of eighty people. All the people were served at once. Use your imagination — can you get your family of four or five their dinner all at once? You can? Good. Try doing it with nine courses for eighty people. The pressure was monstrous. Everyone in the kitchen had two or three jobs that had to be done perfectly and at once. No screwups were allowed. There wasn't even time for yelling. Toward the end of the summer a young chef came from France to do a tasting dinner. He spoke no English, but it was easy to tell he had a cocky manner and no tolerance for women cooks. I didn't care how obnoxious he was because he made one of the most interesting chocolate desserts I had ever seen. I had to watch him out of the corner of my eye because I had several million pounds of leeks to rinse and julienne. He was making what appeared to be chocolate quiche. A sweet pastry shell filled with an egg/chocolate/cream mixture. He floated different kinds of nuts and candied orange peel on top and then baked it. He must have made eight or so of these things. I wanted a piece so badly — they were cooling near the door — maybe if I grabbed one and ran I could eat it all before they could catch me. Could I be arrested for stealing a chocolate tart? I almost didn't care what the consequences would be. I hadn't eaten since the night before — it was now late in the evening. I was beginning to hallucinate about the tarts. Yet, piled in front of me were hundreds of huge purple grapes that had to be dipped in boiling hot sugar syrup. These frosted grapes would garnish the plates the chocolate cake would be served on. Suddenly I hated the people sitting out in the dining room — well fed, well dressed, and about to eat the chocolate tart. I wanted to weep from frustration, hunger, and exhaustion. Too bad I wasn't paying closer attention to the frosting of the grapes because at that moment I swung my arm around and smacked my wrist into a grape that only seconds before had been in the 240-degree sugar syrup. It hit my skin with a hiss. The cook next to me in one motion threw my arm under cold water and threw a shot of whiskey down my throat. Two minutes later we were back dipping grapes.

The Rites of Passage

163

I tried to pay attention to what I was doing, but it was hard not to watch in horrible fascination while my skin blistered and swelled. After dinner was served (this was at 1 A.M.), word went out that the kitchen staff could finish off the food that was left over. There were three chocolate tarts left over. I had no shame left. I had been wounded in action because of these tarts. I grabbed a whole one and headed for my car. I ate the whole thing before I drove off — no plate, no fork — I ate it just like pizza — the first food that I had had in almost twenty-four hours was a chocolate dessert meant to serve twenty people. Fortunately, the next day was Sunday, my day off. I spent what was left of that night and the whole next day talking to Ralph on the big white phone (for those of you who don't understand, my delicate euphemism means that I paid for my gluttony by throwing up).

It took many months and many miles between me and the restaurant before I could make that chocolate tart. If you promise to limit yourselves to only three or four pieces, I will share the recipe with you.

Jacques's Tart au Chocolat

SERVES 12

Sweet pastry for a 10- or 11-inch flan ring or quiche dish:

2 cups flour
⅓ cup sugar
Pinch of salt
1 stick (¼ lb.) sweet (unsalted) butter,
  very cold, cut into small pieces

1 extra-large egg yolk
3 tablespoons ice water

Place the flour, sugar, and salt in the bowl of an electric mixer or on a work board. Cut in the butter until it resembles coarse meal. Do not overwork or allow the butter to become soft. Mix the egg yolk with two tablespoons of the water. Blend into the dough. If it appears too dry add the third tablespoon of water. Gently form the dough into a ball, trying not to work it too much, which will make it tough. Cover with plastic wrap and chill 30 minutes.

On a floured work surface roll the dough ⅛ inch thick. Line the flan ring or quiche dish, trim the excess, and prick the dough with a fork. Chill 15 minutes.

Heat the oven to 425 degrees and bake the shell for 15 minutes.

Remove from the oven and prepare the filling. Lower the oven to 350 degrees.

For the filling:

1 cup heavy cream
¼ cup sugar
2 extra-large eggs
½ cup pine nuts
½ cup pistachio nuts (unsalted)

1 teaspoon vanilla extract
Grated rind of one large orange
6 ounces bittersweet chocolate, broken
  into small irregular pieces
¼ cup currants (optional)

Mix the cream, sugar, and eggs. Stir in the nuts, vanilla, and orange rind. Pour into prebaked shell. Dot the top with the chocolate pieces and optional currants.

Bake 18–20 minutes at 350 degrees, until the crust is brown and the custard is set.

Serve either hot from the oven or at room temperature.

Chocolate Cherry Torte

What a combination! Bittersweet chocolate, sour cherries, and marzipan. This is David Brody's all-time favorite.

SERVES 10–12

For the torte:

1 (24 ounce) jar Morello cherries (see
  note)
6 ounces bittersweet chocolate, chopped
1½ sticks sweet (unsalted) butter
⅔ cup sugar
3 extra-large eggs
1 teaspoon vanilla extract

½ teaspoon almond extract (or ½
  teaspoon bitter almond extract, if
  available)
½ cup ground almonds
⅔ cup sifted flour
2 tablespoons confectioners' sugar
8 ounces almond paste or marzipan

Preheat the oven to 350 degrees with the rack in the center position. Butter the inside of a 9- or 10-inch cake pan—you can use either a regular or springform pan. Cover the bottom with a circle of parchment or wax paper, butter the paper, and then dust the pan with flour and shake out the excess flour.

Empty the jar of cherries into a strainer and set them aside to drain. Place the chocolate in a small bowl set over a pan of gently simmering water, stirring occasionally until it melts completely. Remove from the heat. Cream the butter with the sugar in the bowl of an electric mixer until it is light and fluffy. Add 2 of the eggs and mix well. Mix in the vanilla and almond extracts. On lowest speed add the chocolate, the nuts, and the flour, mixing only until they are incorporated, then mix in the final egg, again mixing only until it is well incorporated. Pour and scrape the batter into the prepared pan and bake 45–50 minutes, taking care not to overbake. The cake will look dry on top but should be quite moist inside. Let the cake cool 10 minutes in the pan, then invert onto a rack. Let the cake cool right-side up.

Place a length of wax paper on a flat surface. Sprinkle with confectioners' sugar. Work the almond paste (or marzipan) to make a flat round cake. Place this on the wax paper and turn it in the sugar. Cover with another piece of wax paper. Use a rolling pin to roll the almond paste into a circle approximately the same diameter as the cake and about 1/16–1/8 inch thick — use the cake pan as a guide. Peel off the top layer of wax paper; if the round of almond paste tears, just patch it. Invert the empty cake pan onto the almond paste as a guide and use a small sharp knife to cut a circle. Invert the circle onto the cake and peel off the remaining wax paper. Place the cake on a cake rack for frosting, or on a flat cake plate with four narrow strips of wax paper underneath the outermost edges.

For the glaze:

½ cup heavy cream   **8 ounces bittersweet chocolate, chopped**

In a small saucepan, scald the cream. Off the heat, add the chocolate and stir until it is very smooth. If there are any lumps, strain the glaze. Pour over the cake and spread smooth onto the top and sides with a long metal spatula. Pull out the wax paper immediately — before the glaze starts to harden. Decorate with candied violets.

Note: *Morello cherries can be mail-ordered from H. Roth and Sons (see address on page 3). You can also use other brands of sour cherries, but I would stay away from the kind in the can that people sometimes use for the top of cheesecakes. H. Roth also sells ground almonds, bitter almond extract, and the best marzipan I ever tasted.*

Happy Birthday

Most people think it's just wonderful that my husband and I have the same birthday. Wrong. Whichever god has the task of handing out birthday assignments should have had the good sense to pair up my birthdate with someone who loves celebrations as much as I do. My husband is not into birthdays. That is to say, he doesn't object to the actual celebration, if he isn't called upon to lift a finger to cause it to happen. The mere anticipation, the slightest suggestion, that my (our) birthday is looming near sends him into the Slough of Despond (in which there is not one single department store or jewelry shop), from which only a party arranged by me can rescue him. God only knows what caused this character defect in an otherwise perfect specimen. When I was a kid and living at home, birthdays were a big deal. Now, I don't expect David to make a chocolate cream pie from scratch, but he at least could arrange for my mother to air-express one down to me. Of course, he expects me to make his mother's famous chocolate cake for him.

The first year we were married he really did try. He came home with what looked like a shoe box under his arm. It was a shoe box, from Gucci. Get this, I didn't even know what Gucci was. The shoes were gorgeous. I slipped one on, well, not exactly. I managed to slip four of my five toes into one shoe. There didn't seem to be room for my big toe and heel. Cinderella didn't come from Russian peasant stock. "Don't you wear size seven?" he asked. I did indeed wear size seven, but not in this style. I thanked him profusely and said I would exchange the shoes for a bigger size. That year I gave him a sterling silver razor with his initials engraved on it. He nearly severed his jugular vein and went back to his old razor.

The Gucci store was on Fifth Avenue in the Fifties. All of my Fifth Avenue shopping was done in fantasyland and I had never been in a store with a uniformed doorman before. I marveled at David's bravery as I walked into this Disneyland of Millionaires. I clutched my shoe box and looked around for a saleswoman. They were hard to find because they were so tall and skinny — I felt like a hippopotamus in a herd of giraffes. Once I found one, my troubles were hardly over. It seems at Gucci they only speak and understand English if you're buying something. If you're returning something, it has to be done in Italian. I tried to explain that the shoes were too small and I would like to try on a larger size. The saleslady sniffed (I hope it wasn't me she was smelling) and rang for a manager-type. They both examined my shoes for any sign of wear. Thank God the Rockefellers' house had wall-to-wall carpeting — the shoes passed inspection. I was motioned to sit, so I did. They indicated that I should remove my shoes, which I did (praying that I didn't have any holes in my stockings). The manager looked at my feet and said something to the saleslady in Italian ("She has the feet of a Russian peasant" is most likely what he said). They brought out the shoe in a larger size. I could get my foot in, but I felt like I had scraped all the skin off my heel as I did so. A still larger size had more room, but the bottom of the shoe did in no way conform to the contour of my foot. More examination of both foot and shoe. The manager called over a third person, who picked up my old shoe and with great distaste said I had the wrong type of feet for European shoes.

"We regret that you cannot wear the European 'last,' Madame." This one spoke English. "Can I suggest that you pick out something else in the store?" I was willing to give it a try. The shoes had been $70 — an extravagant amount of money for an impoverished law student to spend on his wife's birthday present. I was thrilled; it was a good sign. I saw a beautiful pocketbook. When I asked the saleswoman the price, she exchanged a not so covertly malicious glance with the manager and said, "Four hundred and fifty dollars. Perhaps Madame would be interested in a wallet or key chain." I was mostly interested in breaking her nose.

"No, thank you. I don't want a wallet or a key chain. I think I would like my money back." I'd get the cash and we could go out for three or four nice dinners.

"That's not possible, Madame. The store policy is no cash refunds. Only credits."

But no one ever told us that.

"It says right here on the back of the sales slip." He pointed to writing so tiny that I thought it was an imperfection in the paper.

"But there's nothing here that I want, or can afford."

"Regrettable, Madame," says the master of snotty obsequiousness, "perhaps you can save some money and add it to your credit at another time."

There was no way I was going to let Mr. Gucci keep our $70 and deprive me of a birthday present. I decided right there and then to fight. Well, at least I decided that I would take an Italian course so that I could argue with them in their own language. (Actually I did begin an Italian course right after that, but the professor called me aside after the first month and said, "Signora, you study-a so hard, but you're-a so stupid" — so much for Italian.) I took my shoes and left in a huff to go home to see my lawyer.

There is no one quite as litigious as a second-year law student. They know some of the tricks of the trade and are dying to use them. When I ran crying home to my resident law student about my treatment at Gucci, he threw on his lawyer-in-training cloak, grabbed his Berlitz Italian handbook and rushed off to Fifth Avenue. He got about as far as I did. No refund. Credit only.

It is a testimonial to the perseverance and dedication of my husband that, in the quest for the return of his hard-spent $70, he had to write (in Italian) a letter to Dr. Aldo Gucci, in Italy, threatening a lawsuit if our money wasn't returned. It took six months, but we finally got a check. I think we used it to get a new muffler. That was the last birthday present David ever bought me. Now he gets convenient anxiety attacks or memory lapses when birthday time approaches.

So, what's a birthday lover to do? Every year I made a big party. I cooked, I baked, I cleaned, and I washed. I should have ordered and hired out, but I was a birthday purist. I kept hoping my undying enthusiasm would one day inspire him to do the same for me. Had I not been the perverse victim of my birthday party martyrdom, I could have had a great time, because the parties themselves were wonderful. We had champagne brunches, Western barbecues, midnight buffets, and best of all, dessert extravaganzas. Every year, as I scraped birthday cake off dishes and rinsed champagne glasses, I vowed this would be the last year. I promised myself that, like the Jewish American Princess in the joke, the only thing I would make for next year's birthday would be reservations.

The day after his thirty-second birthday party and my twenty-ninth birthday party cleanup, I gave him the news: "This is the last time I'm doing this. Next year when I'm thirty, if something supremely wonderful doesn't happen, I'm going to have an extremely expensive nervous breakdown. Either way, it's going to cost you. Take your pick."

A year later he took me to an Italian restaurant — in Rome. We went to Rome not to buy fancy Italian shoes, but to eat my favorite chocolate dessert in the whole world: Tartufo. Ah, Tartufo. The deepest, richest, most heavenly chocolate gelati, shaped into a fist-sized ball, embedded with little pieces of maraschino cherry, then rolled in slabs of bittersweet chocolate. This whole concoction, which is served on a doily fitted inside a little fluted cardboard tray, is crowned with a big dollop of the richest, softest whipped cream, called *panna*. I can tell if someone is a dedicated chocolate lover if he or she has made the pilgrimage to eat Tartufo. The restaurant that serves this heavenly dessert (the Lourdes of chocophiles) is called Tre Scalini, and it's located on the Piazza Navona. The restaurant has two doors at the end of its three steps. If you're going for the Tartufo — go into the gelati door, which is on the left. There is a dark marble bar, behind which is a white-jacketed gentleman waiting to transport you to heaven. At the end of ten days I didn't even have to tell him what I wanted. We'd walk in the door and he'd whip two Tartufos out of the freezer, cover them with panna, and stick in a tiny plastic spoon. We would take our gelati outside and sit near the Fountain of the Four Rivers in the glorious Italian sun and try to eat slowly so they would last a long, long time. There are places in this country that make what they claim is the real Tartufo. I've tasted them and am not impressed. Save your money and go to Rome for the real thing.

It was such a wonderful birthday that I have happily made a party for David every year since. I even created a spectacular birthday cake in his honor. It was for his thirty-fifth birthday. I had originally promised to take him anywhere in the world he wanted to go, but our bank account indicated that we could afford to spend one night in our local Holiday Inn. Poor guy, he wanted to go to India. Instead, I orchestrated a major surprise party to which our friends were invited to come and bring a poem to recite in honor of the birthday boy. Both the literary attempts and the meal itself were a fine birthday tribute. Our friends Howard Shulman and Joyce Myers wrote a masterpiece entitled "The Meringue Mushroom That Devoured Boston." The menu was smoked salmon and blue-cheese cakes served on German black bread, and a huge antipasto to start. The main course (dedicated to fall, since the birthdays are in October) was carbonnade of beef (beef stew braised in stock and beer) baked and served in an enormous pumpkin, wild rice with pecans and currants that had been soaked for days in cognac, homemade Swedish potato bread (full of fresh caraway), and steamed root vegetables. We drank mulled cider and dark beer.

The dessert was an idea that I had been playing around with in my head for a long time. When it comes to chocolate cake, big is better. The trouble with a many-layered cake is that it is often difficult to cut into pretty pieces and the leftovers are usually a mess. I wanted something that would fill up the entire dining-room table — something that would make an impressive happy birthday statement in chocolate. I made eight chocolate soufflé rolls (each one 16 inches in length), sprinkled them liberally with crème de cacao, and filled them with chocolate ganache (a heavy cream and chocolate mixture). I placed each filled roll on a foil-covered plywood board cut slightly wider but exactly the same length as the roll. I then frosted the rolls with chocolate glaze, and starting from the top end of one cake, wrote "Happy Birthday, David" in white royal icing and then, underneath that, I listed the names of all the people at the party (there were one hundred), filling up the rest of the cakes. The cakes on the boards were then placed end to end on the table to form a ten-and-a-half-foot-long chocolate roll. I tucked red rosebuds, white daisies, baby's breath, and ferns between the cake and the board to hide the foil and placed a hundred tiny white candles down the center of the roll (it took six people to get them lit). Although it can be a bit tricky to serve because everybody wants to eat their own name, it was a spectacular and wonderfully delicious birthday extravaganza, which has become a standard part of the birthday, anniversary, Bar Mitzvah repertoire. We call it the Name Cake.*

Another great celebration that culminated in a great chocolate dessert was our housewarming party. We invited fifty of our friends to come and bring a joke. Sounds simple, doesn't it? It's no big deal if you don't mind getting up in front of an audience of half-soused critics, all of whom think their joke is the best one of the evening. We gave everybody whistles and tin horns à la "The Gong Show" so they could make rude noises when they thought a joke deserved it. Several people were so nervous they chose drunken oblivion over public performance. There were some extraordinary jokes told that evening, many of which I have, mercifully, managed to forget, and many which I will treasure always. There were even some food jokes. I told the one about the cannibal whose wife loved chocolate so much he bought her a box of Farmer's Fannies. Someone else told the joke about the cannibal who came late to dinner and got the cold shoulder. Someone else told the one about the cannibal who passed his brother in the forest. Then it was time for dinner.

Since I didn't want to miss a minute of this party, I created a menu that pretty much allowed me to be hostess and guest. I ordered a smoked turkey from a smokehouse in Vermont and a Smithfield (or second mortgage) ham from Virginia, which I glazed with maple syrup, brown sugar, and soy sauce. I served these with a mustard mousse. To go with this I studded peeled Bartlett pears with cloves and poached them in port. They were cooled, sliced, then tossed with cubes of Cheshire cheese, chopped red onion, celery, black walnuts, and brandy-soaked currants, and served on a platter of chicory. I poured a very light vinaigrette over the salad just before it was served. There was black bread, and dill whole wheat rolls with sweet butter and Major Grey's chutney. Dessert was a White Chocolate Trifle.* I am a great fan of regular trifle — but I think this one is better: amaretto-soaked vanilla sponge roll filled with creamy, rich white chocolate mousse. This dessert is no joke.

The Name Cake

This is a big job but the results are spectacular and the effort will make you the most talked-about hostess in town. This cake is made up of a number of chocolate soufflé rolls filled with chocolate mousse and laid on boards placed end to end to form one long roll. I have included an alternative filling made with heavy cream and sweet cherries that is easier to make than the chocolate filling. The cake rolls can be glazed with a sophisticated chocolate ganache, or a chocolate cream-cheese frosting, which children seem to prefer. The individual rolls can be baked, filled, and then frozen, unfrosted. They should be defrosted only partially before frosting. I count on each roll feeding 12 people.

These cakes should be baked in heavy-duty jelly-roll pans measuring 11 x 17 inches. You will need a plywood board measuring 16 x 4 inches for every cake you plan to make. You will also need a roll of heavy-duty aluminum foil.

The following recipe is for one cake.

For the cake:

10 extra-large eggs at room temperature	1 cup sugar
10 ounces semisweet or bittersweet chocolate	Cocoa

Preheat the oven to 350 degrees with the rack in the center position of the oven. Line a heavy-duty jelly-roll pan with a sheet of parchment. (Do not use wax paper.) No greasing is necessary if you use parchment.

Separate the eggs, placing the yolks in the bowl of an electric mixer and the whites in either another bowl of the electric mixer, a copper bowl, or a very clean glass bowl for holding until you are through with the bowl containing the yolks.

Break the chocolate into small pieces and melt it over a pan of simmering water. Take care not to let any steam get into the chocolate. Remove from heat to cool slightly.

Beat the egg yolks with half the sugar until they are very thick and light. In a heavy-duty mixer this takes at least 5 minutes and in a hand mixer 10 to 15.

On the slowest mixer speed, add the chocolate to the beaten yolks. Mix only until blended.

If you plan to use the yolk bowl to beat the whites, transfer the chocolate mixture to a large bowl and wash the mixer bowl with soap and very hot water. Rinse well to remove all traces of grease and soap. Beat the egg whites with the remaining sugar until they hold soft peaks. Do not overbeat to the stage where they are dry and grainy.

Mix a large spoonful of the whites into the chocolate mixture to lighten it. Pour the chocolate mixture into the rest of the whites and gently fold the two together until no traces of white show.

Pour the mixture into the prepared pan and distribute it evenly with a rubber scraper, making sure it gets into the corners of the pan.

The total baking time is 15–18 minutes. Halfway through the baking, reverse the pan front to back to ensure even baking.

The cake will rise up and then fall when you remove it from the oven. Let it cool completely in the pan. To remove and prepare it for the filling, loosen the edge of the cake from the pan with a sharp knife; sift a fine layer of cocoa over the top. Cover the cake with 2 large pieces of plastic wrap. Make sure the wrap extends at least 6 inches beyond the long sides of the cake. Cover with another piece of parchment or overlapping pieces of wax paper, top with a large cookie sheet and invert. Carefully peel the parchment off. It should come off very easily. If you do have a problem with its sticking, simply moisten the parchment with a wet paper towel and then pull it off. Trim the edges of the cake with a pair of scissors.

For the chocolate mousse filling:

This recipe makes enough to fill 1–1½ cake rolls. Do not be tempted to use one whole recipe in one cake roll.

10 ounces Lindt Extra-Bittersweet or a comparable high-quality bittersweet chocolate
3 tablespoons instant espresso, dissolved in ¼ cup boiling water
4 eggs, separated

6 ounces sweet (unsalted) butter at room temperature, cut into small pieces
¼ cup water
⅔ cup sugar

Melt the chocolate with the espresso in a metal bowl set over gently simmering water.

Mix in the yolks one at a time and continue to stir over the simmering water until all the yolks have been added and the mixture has thickened. Do not let the mixture boil.

Off the heat, add the butter bit by bit, stirring until it all has melted.

Place the egg whites in the bowl of an electric mixer and, using the whip attachment, beat on the lowest speed until the whites become opaque. Meanwhile, bring the water and sugar to a boil in a small saucepan. Stir until the sugar dissolves and, using a candy thermometer, boil the syrup until it reaches 225 degrees.

Immediately, turn the electric mixer on high and beat the egg whites while pouring the syrup into them in a slow, steady stream. Continue beating until the meringue is stiff and very shiny.

Remove the bowl from the mixer, add the chocolate mixture, and fold the two together with a large rubber spatula.

Chill completely before spreading on the cake.

For the whipped cream and sweet cherry filling:

This recipe fills one cake roll.

1 cup heavy cream	1 10-ounce package frozen (or canned)
¼ cup confectioners' sugar, sifted	sweet cherries, defrosted and drained
¼ cup Kirsch — optional	of their juice

In a chilled bowl with chilled beaters whip the cream. Add the sugar and optional liqueur. Fold in the cherries.

To fill and roll:

Spread the cake with an even coating of the filling, leaving a ½-inch border all around. There may be filling left over — don't be tempted to use it — it will make the cake difficult to roll. A ¼-inch coating will do the trick. Position the cake so one long end is facing you. Grasp the plastic wrap and, using it as an aid, roll up the cake away from you. Cover with another piece of plastic wrap, forming a tight roll, place on a cookie sheet, and freeze. This makes frosting easier. Prepare one of the two frostings. Each recipe makes enough to frost one cake roll.

For the dark chocolate ganache:

10 ounces heavy cream	4 ounces unsweetened chocolate, cut
⅓ cup dark brown sugar, firmly packed	into small pieces
6 ounces semisweet chocolate, cut into	2 tablespoons sweet (unsalted) butter
small pieces	

Scald the cream and the sugar, stirring until the sugar dissolves and small bubbles form around the rim of the pan. Off the heat, add the chocolates. Stir until they dissolve. Add the butter and stir until it melts in. Cool until the glaze thickens to a spreading consistency.

For the chocolate cream-cheese frosting:

2 ounces unsweetened chocolate, cut	¼ cup sweet butter
into pieces	2 cups confectioners' sugar, sifted
4 ounces cream cheese	Heavy cream

Melt the chocolate and set it aside to cool. In the bowl of an electric mixer, cream the cream cheese and butter. Add the sugar and beat until light and fluffy. Add the chocolate and beat it in. You may want to add a few drops of heavy cream to thin the frosting to a spreading consistency.

To assemble:

Make enough frosting to cover the number of cakes you have made. Remove the rolls from the freezer 15 minutes before you plan to frost them. Cover the plywood boards with heavy-duty aluminum foil and tape the foil to the bottom of the board to hold it in place. Remove the plastic wrap and place one cake on each board. It is easier to place the cakes on the boards while the cakes are still frozen.

Place strips of wax paper between the cake and the board to keep the board clean. Glaze or frost the cakes. Remove the wax paper immediately, before the frosting sets.

To write names on the cake:

You can use the commercial cake-decorating preparation that comes in tubes and is sold in supermarkets, or you can use the cream cheese frosting, above, without the addition of chocolate. Use a small pastry tube with a writing tip. I usually add one or two teaspoons of cocoa to make the frosting a light brown, which I think looks nice on a chocolate cake. I've also tinted the frosting light pink when it was for a young girl's birthday. It's a good idea to practice writing on a piece of wax paper before you tackle the cake.

Start at the top of one cake and write "Happy Birthday" or "Congratulations," etc., the short way across the top, then after that, the name of the person of honor, then list the names of the people at the party, one after another. If there is room at the bottom (count on 12 names to a cake) you can write the date.

I decorate my cakes by sticking fresh flowers — rosebuds, baby's breath, and greens — between the bottom edge of the cake and the board. Then I place candles down the length of the cake. If you do use flowers, choose something that will be okay out of water for a while. In very hot weather the cake should be refrigerated — or it can be stored several hours in an air-conditioned room.

White Chocolate Trifle

This is not your basic, ho-hum trifle. Pinwheels of Amaretti macaroon sponge cake filled with apricot puree surround an ethereal amaretto-spiked white chocolate mousse. This is a bit time-consuming, but most definitely worth the effort. You will need Italian Amaretti macaroons, which are readily available in many gourmet shops and most Italian food stores. If possible, buy the miniature unwrapped kind; they cost less and you don't have to spend time taking the papers off. You will also need amaretto liqueur, or you can use apricot brandy, if you wish.

SERVES 8

For the cake roll:

4 ounces (2 cups) finely ground Amaretti macaroons (use the food processor for this)
6 extra-large eggs at room temperature, separated
¾ cup sugar

¼ cup flour
2 ounces sweet (unsalted) butter, melted
1 teaspoon almond extract
3 tablespoons amaretto liqueur or apricot brandy

Preheat the oven to 350 degrees with the rack in the lower third of the oven but not in the lowest rack position. Cover a 17 x 11-inch heavy-duty jelly-roll pan with parchment and either spray the parchment with Pam (or a like product) or grease it lightly with solid vegetable shortening. Sprinkle the Amaretti over the parchment, being careful to keep the coating thin and even.

In the large bowl of an electric mixer with the machine on the highest speed, ribbon the egg yolks with one half of the sugar until they are thick and light-colored. On low speed add the flour, butter, and almond extract, mixing only until they are incorporated. In a clean bowl, with clean beaters, whip the egg whites with the remaining sugar until they are stiff but not dry. Stir one tablespoon of whites into the yolk mixture, then pour the yolk mixture on top of the whites and fold together. Pour the batter on top of the Amaretti crumbs and spread carefully with a long metal spatula. Some of the crumbs will blend into the mixture; that's okay. Try to make sure the batter is spread evenly. Bang the cake several times on the counter to make sure the crumbs are in contact with the batter (so they won't fall off after baking), then bake for 12–15 minutes, until the top is brown and the cake feels firm. Remove the cake from the oven and let it cool 5 minutes. Cover the cake with another piece of parchment and a cookie sheet. Invert. Carefully peel off the parchment — it may stick on the edges, so peel slowly trying not to rip the cake. Immediately sprinkle the cake with the amaretto liqueur or apricot brandy. An easy way to do this is place your thumb over the bottle top, invert the bottle, and shake out the liqueur. The cake should be fairly well soaked with the liqueur — not only does this make it taste great, but it softens the Amaretti crust so that you can roll it. Spread with the filling.

For the filling:

1 pound dried apricots
Water to cover

⅓ cup amaretto liqueur or apricot brandy

Place the apricots in a small saucepan and cover them with water. Bring the water to a boil and simmer gently until the apricots are tender. Drain off the water and add the liqueur. Puree in the food processor.

Position the cake so that the longest side is facing you and, using the bottom piece of parchment as an aid, roll the cake away from you, rolling as tightly as possible. Cover with plastic wrap and refrigerate for 30 minutes or freeze for 20 minutes — this step, which you may choose to omit, makes the cake a little easier to work with.

Coat the bottom and sides of a 7- or 8-cup soufflé dish with 1 tablespoon of vegetable oil. Line the dish with plastic wrap, allowing the wrap to extend well over the edges of the dish. Using a sharp serrated knife, cut the cake into ⅓-inch slices. Place the cake slices on the bottom of the dish, as close together as possible. Repeat with the sides. You most likely will have a few slices left over. If you have spaces between the slices, cut the remaining slices into little pieces and use them to patch. Prepare the white chocolate mousse.

For the mousse:

½ cup heavy cream
9 ounces white chocolate, cut into
  small pieces (I use Tobler Narcisse.)
1 tablespoon gelatin

¼ cup amaretto liqueur or apricot
  brandy
3 extra-large egg whites
¼ cup sugar

Scald the cream in a small saucepan and add the chocolate. Stir on very low heat until the chocolate melts. The unattractive solid material you see is the milk solids separating out — don't worry. Pour the mixture into the food processor and process until smooth. Good-bye milk solids. In a small saucepan over low heat dissolve the gelatin in the liqueur, then add this mixture to the chocolate in the processor. Process until blended.

Beat the egg whites with the sugar until they are stiff and shiny. Fold the chocolate mixture into the whites and pour the mousse into the cake-lined mold. Cover with plastic wrap and chill until set — 4–6 hours. Slice wedges with a sharp, serrated knife.

Champagne and Chocolate Tasting

Looking for something a little less "down home?" Want some elegance with your chocolate? Allow me to suggest two party ideas that will have the gentlemen dusting off their dinner jackets and the ladies getting the jewels out of the vault: a Chocolate Extravaganza Dessert Buffet, and a Champagne and Chocolate Tasting.

A champagne and chocolate tasting can be either an intimate gathering of 6 to 10 people, or include a cast of thousands. The basic plan is the same, it's just the logistics that change as the crowd gets bigger. The event should be planned with people seated around one (or several) tables. You should plan on tasting 4 to 6 champagnes (or sparkling wines) and 8 to 10 kinds of chocolate. There are many ways to organize your tasting: drink the champagnes first, and then taste the chocolates; chocolates first; intersperse the two; or taste one, have a break, and then taste the other. During the break I sometimes encourage people to talk about their favorite chocolates, and chocolate desserts, or even write down their preferred brand and see how that fares in the blind tasting. Once, we ate the chocolate first, then saw a short film on champagne before we concluded with the wine tasting. In choosing the champagne try to have both a moderate-priced bottle (go for the best for the least) and an expensive bottle. We had both French champagne and American and Spanish sparkling wine. The list below may help you to select wines for your tasting. As for the chocolate, you have the option of being a purist and sampling only dark, or only milk, or only white (although I can't imagine why you would want to eat only white chocolate) or taste 3 or 4 of each. The chocolates listed below are the brands I most often use for a tasting. Each person only needs a very small piece of each kind. A 1½-inch square is big enough. First I list each brand of chocolate, giving it a number (1–12), stating whether it's dark or milk, etc., which country produces it, the ingredients, weight of the bar, and the cost. I use a 12-inch paper plate and write in magic marker around the rim the numbers 1–12 (if we have 12 pieces to taste). I then break up the chocolates, put each into a numbered plastic bag (I stick the wrapper from the chocolate into the bag too, because it's nice to know what to look for when you go to buy your favorite brand). As each type of chocolate is passed around (you don't have to pass it from the plastic bag — that's pretty tacky, but if you do put it on a serving plate, remember to mark the plate with the number so you'll know which brand of chocolate is being served on it), instruct people to take a taste and put the rest down on the corresponding number on the plate, so they can retaste it later if they wish. It is helpful to have pitchers of ice water and glasses on the table. Encourage comments about the flavor, aftertaste, melting ability, and general personality of each piece. When all the chocolate has been tasted (and retasted) surprise your friends by showing them the labels.

This is a list of the champagnes we use when we have champagne and chocolate tastings. It was compiled by my dear friend, wine expert, and chocolate lover Dr. Michael Apstein, who coined the motto we chocolate lovers live by: "There's never enough of a good thing."

These are not all true champagnes, that is, sparkling wine produced and bottled in the Champagne region of France. There is one Spanish and one American sparkling wine. They are listed in the suggested order of serving, from

The Chocolate Diet

───

lightest to heaviest. You can count on getting ten 2½-ounce servings from each bottle. Make sure to give each guest a list of these wines, so they can make notations about them.

1. Freixenet Cordon Negro, or Segura Vuidas, 1977
2. Françoise Monopole Blanc de Blanc, Non Vintage
3. Domaine Chandon Blanc de Noir, Non Vintage
4. Billecart Salmon, Non Vintage, or Deutz Rose, 1975
5. Taittinger, Non Vintage, or Jouet Perrier, Non Vintage
6. Laurent Perrier, or Veuve Clicquot Ponsardin, both Non Vintage

Now, for the chocolate. I usually try to have 6–8 darks (that encompasses bittersweet, semisweet, and sweet), 3 or 4 milks, and 2 whites. Some of these chocolates come in 3- or 4-ounce bars and some are commercial coatings, so some things on this list will be easy to find, and others will offer a challenge. You can try bakery supply shops and candy stores. Some candy makers will sell their coatings, but make sure to find out what kind you're buying. Also, see the list of addresses in the back of the book.

I tell my guests that they should judge the chocolates on several things: appearance, aroma, melting characteristics, taste, and aftertaste. They should note whether or not they have to chew it, and whether it tastes like it smells. I tell them to place a bit of the chocolate in their mouths and, without chewing, see if it melts quickly. It's always very interesting to see how many people's preconceived ideas of what is "good" chocolate are changed in this blind tasting. I also stress that this is an entirely subjective exercise. If someone loves the taste and texture of one kind — then that's great chocolate.

I will list more than my recommended number just in case you can't find some brands.

Dark chocolates:

Baker's German Sweet
Callebaut Semisweet
Ghirardelli Bittersweet and Semisweet
Godiva Cooking Chocolate
Hershey Special Dark
Lanvin

Lindt Excellence
Maillard Eagle Sweet
Nestlé's (Peter's) Burgundy
Poulain Cooking Chocolate
Tobler Tradition or Tobler Bittersweet

Milk chocolates:

Cadbury Dairy Milk
Callebaut Milk
Feodora Milk
Lindt au Lait

Nestlé's (Peter's) Swiss Heritage
Tobler Swiss Milk
Carma Gianduja
Perugina Gianduja

White chocolates:

Callebaut White   Tobler Narcisse
Lindt Blancor

You may find other brands available in shops near you. Go ahead and add them to your list. Just remember to use pure chocolates without fillings or flavorings. Save the wrappings so people will know what to look for when they go shopping. I always include a sample of compound coating and carob — it's amazing how people react to them. You can buy coating in cake decorating shops and carob in health food stores.

Chocolate Extravaganza Dessert Buffet

A Chocolate Extravaganza Dessert Buffet birthday (or anniversary, graduation, Bar Mitzvah, christening) party should include a cast of thousands — when we orchestrate one of these parties we not only invite everyone we know and many people we don't (friends of friends) but relatives and acquaintances we haven't seen in years. The other essential ingredient (besides the desserts — I'll get to them in a minute) is kitchen and dining room help. We usually hold this party on a Sunday afternoon. Saturday night sounds great in theory, but the reality is that people have either eaten and aren't that hungry, or they expect dinner — or at least some hors d'oeuvres — and will be disappointed, but who wants to make liver puffs when you can make chocolate mousse cake? Avoid July, August, and September like the plague (for obvious reasons). We usually throw our bash in February — around Valentine's Day — when everyone is cuckoo from winter and ready to have some serious fun and not yet thinking about thighs and bathing suits. Make sure the invitation states the important facts: CHOCOLATE DESSERT BUFFET and EAT in big letters. This discourages those would-be dieters from attending and casting a pall over the affair.

    There are two ways of handling the food preparation: you can ask your guests to bring their favorite chocolate dessert, or you can be a masochist and do all the work yourself. I suppose there is a third way: ordering out, but that lacks a certain je ne sais quoi. If you choose to do all the cooking yourself, the first thing you have to do is sit down with a pen, some paper (big pieces), and your favorite chocolate recipes. Make two columns: one with the desserts that can be frozen (Make sure. Don't guess. Don't freeze anything with gelatin and if the cookbook tells you that you can, throw it — the cookbook — away) and another list of things that cannot, with a notation next to each about how long it will remain delicious after it's baked. List everything — every chocolate dessert that you ever dreamed of making. Make sure there is an even representation from all possible categories: tortes, layer cakes, cheesecakes, (easy-to-serve) pies, cookies, bars, mousses (gelatin-based and frozen), meringues, dipped fruit, Bavarians, etc. Obviously, it's not necessary to have each category, just make sure that you don't make 14 different kinds of brownies and one layer cake and then call it a day. Ice cream takes little planning, and nothing beats great homemade chocolate ice cream with hot fudge sauce. Put a star next to those recipes you have made before and that are really worth making again. Cross off all but two recipes that require more than four hours of preparation, and if these two recipes cannot be frozen cross off one more. Put another star next to those recipes that can be doubled. Cross off all recipes that don't serve easily, that is, cut into small pieces; they fall apart. Chocolate Cream Pie is divine, but cutting it into little wedges makes an unsightly mess (consider individual Chocolate Peanut Pies*). The recipes with the stars next to them should be considered the top contenders. Do not plan to make anything the day of the party. Remember that you'll be frosting cakes and arranging platters and spending time on the phone giving people directions to your house, unless you had the foresight to include a map with the invitation. As you make each dessert, check it off on the list and write down the maximum number of little servings you can get from it. To make the menu planning really simple, the dessert list (all recipes are in this book) from our last bash follows the next, very boring but essential paragraph on logistics.

Be prepared for each person to want a small taste of everything. So, if one cake normally feeds 10, figure you can get at least 20–25 tastes from it (if it cuts evenly without dissolving in crumbs). Cookies should be made smaller than the recipe suggests, but watch the baking time; it won't be as long. Cut squares and bars much smaller, so that if a normal batch makes 2 dozen, cut them to make 4 or 5. If you were to invite 20 people plan to make not less than 10 and not more than 15 different things — one of each would do it. If you have more people, say 40, still make the same 10–15 things, but make two of each thing. You will probably have stuff left over, but that's better than running out. It is very important to have one (two is better) server at the buffet table, cutting the cakes and what-have-you. If guests help themselves, the pieces will be too large and they won't finish what they've taken and you'll run out of food. Count on each person using at least two and probably three plates and two wine glasses. One coffee cup each is usually enough unless you serve only coffee and not wine or champagne (why you'd do that I cannot imagine). Pitchers of ice water are a good idea, too. Get three times the number of napkins (nice big ones, not those skimpy cocktail jobbies) as guests. Don't put ashtrays out; invite smokers to go outside, because smoke is terrible for chocolate (and other things). Do not serve skim milk or sugar substitute with the coffee. Silver cake servers are lovely to look at, but sharp kitchen knives do the best cutting job. It's a nice touch to have the dessert labeled, so people can know what they are eating. Serve the cakes, tortes, pies, and mousses from the buffet table along with several platters of assorted cookies and chocolate-dipped fruit; also have someone passing around trays of cookies and, perhaps, truffles. It is nice to have some savory things to eat like salted nuts or cheese and crackers in addition to a platter of cut-up fresh fruit.

Chocolate Extravaganza Dessert Buffet Menu Suggestions

Can be made ahead and frozen, or can be made two days before and refrigerated:

Rum Nut Balls

Chocolate Phantoms

Chocolate Praline Strudel

Rigo Janci

Champagne and Raspberry Truffles

Chocolate Hazelnut Torte

Chocolate Soufflé Roll

Judy's Frustration Torte

Chocolate Mousse Cake

Coup de Grace with White Chocolate
Sauce

Ginger Cheesecake with Chocolate
Crust

Can be made two days before:

Bête Noire *(Don't refrigerate)*

Can be made the day before:

Chocolate Trifle

Mocha Velvet

Chocolate Peanut Pies

Chocolate-dipped dried apricots,
orange slices, and candied ginger
(Don't refrigerate)

Must be made that day:

Chocolate-covered strawberries *(Don't
refrigerate)*

Also have on hand:

Mixed salted nuts

Fresh fruit platter

Brie and French bread or crackers

The cakes should not be frozen after they are glazed, and they should be completely defrosted before they are glazed. Otherwise the chocolate glaze will be dull. Let them defrost still wrapped in plastic wrap so the moisture collects on the wrap, not the cake.

Chocolate Peanut Pies

What could be better than the combination of peanuts and chocolate? These individual little tartlets are just the thing for fans of Reese's Peanut Butter Cups.

MAKES 25 INDIVIDUAL PIES

For the pastry shells:

2½ cups all-purpose flour
Pinch of salt
½ cup sugar

1¼ sticks of sweet (unsalted) butter,
  very cold or frozen
2 extra-large eggs plus two yolks

In a food processor, blend the first four ingredients until the butter is in pieces the size of peas.

Add the eggs and yolks and process briefly until the mixture is uniform but does not form a ball.

Place the crumbly dough on a board and incorporate the ingredients by pressing the mass with the heel of your hand until all the dough has been kneaded this way. A second kneading may be necessary to make sure the dough forms into a ball easily. Using a metal scraper or spatula, push and scrape dough into two balls. Cover with plastic wrap and chill for about an hour.

To form the tarts:

Preheat the oven to 400 degrees with the rack in the center of the oven. Using butter or vegetable shortening, grease 20 shallow 3-inch tart pans. Roll out the dough to ⅛-inch thickness and cut circles with a 3½-inch round cutter. Place the circles of dough in the tart pans and press the dough down with your fingers, creating a tiny ridge all the way around the edge of the pan. Prick the bottoms with a fork and place the shells on a heavy-duty baking sheet. Refrigerate for half an hour. If you don't have 20 tart pans, bake a few at a time — you can roll out the dough, cut the circles and chill them, and then pop them into the pans after the previous batch is baked.

Bake the shells for 12–15 minutes, until the edges are brown. Remove from the pans and cool on a rack.

When the shells have cooled completely, spread a tablespoon of Skippy Super Chunk Peanut Butter in the bottom of each one. Prepare the chocolate glaze.

For the glaze:

1 cup heavy cream
10 ounces semisweet chocolate, cut
  into very small pieces

In a small saucepan scald the cream. Off the heat, add the chopped chocolate. Stir very gently with a rubber scraper. When the mixture is combined, strain it through a fine sieve to get rid of any lumps.

Pour the glaze over the shells up to the very edge. Let them sit in a cool place until the glaze becomes firm.

Chocolate Praline Strudel

If you love flaky, moist strudel, then this is the dessert for you. Loaded with chocolate, caramelized nuts, and a special combination of marzipan and cocoa, this wonderful recipe is easy to prepare using store-bought filo or strudel leaves. If you've never worked with filo or store-bought strudel before, remember to keep it frozen until an hour or so before you plan to use it, and always keep it covered with a slightly damp cloth or plastic wrap. Since this recipe calls for approximately half a package of leaves, you can afford to mess up a few. Don't be intimidated by the thinness of the leaves — I've taught this recipe to some confirmed klutzes and now they whip out strudels like pros.

The best commercial strudel dough I've ever used is available by mail from H. Roth and Sons (see address page 3).

It is very important to read through this recipe (especially the notes at the end) before you begin to cook.

SERVES 8

For the praline:

2 cups sugar
½ cup water
1 teaspoon lemon juice

14 ounces (1½ cups) slivered almonds
or chopped pecans

Coat a baking sheet with a thin film of vegetable oil. Combine the sugar and water and lemon juice in a one-quart heavy-bottomed pan. Stir over medium heat until all the sugar is dissolved and the syrup is clear. Turn the heat to high and bring the syrup to a boil without stirring. Wash down the sides of the pan with a pastry brush dipped in cold water to prevent sugar crystallization. Cook until the syrup is a golden caramel color. Add the nuts and swirl the syrup to coat them. Pour the mixture onto the prepared baking sheet and allow it to cool completely. Break up the praline with your hands or a hammer and process through a food processor in small batches until it is dustlike praline powder. Store in a covered plastic container.

For the filling:

7 ounces almond paste or marzipan
¾ cup cocoa, sifted
½ cup golden raisins
3 tablespoons cognac
½ package (approximately 12 sheets)
filo or strudel leaves

8 ounces (2 sticks) sweet (unsalted)
butter, melted
8 ounces bittersweet or semisweet
chocolate, chopped fine
3 ounces bittersweet or semisweet
chocolate, melted

Place the almond paste in the bowl of a food processor and add the cocoa, processing until all the cocoa has been mixed into the almond paste. Roll the almond paste out between two sheets of plastic wrap or wax paper to the same size as a sheet of strudel. You may wish to roll the almond paste without using the plastic wrap or waxed paper by simply sprinkling your board and rolling pin with confectioners' sugar.

To assemble the strudel:

Preheat the oven to 350 with the rack in the center position. Brush a heavy-duty jelly-roll pan with melted butter. It's best to use a pan with sides as the filling may leak. Toss the raisins in the cognac in a small saucepan set over low heat. When the cognac begins to simmer turn off the heat and leave the raisins to soak in the cognac. On a dish towel place one sheet of filo dough with the long side closest to you. Brush it with the melted butter, then place a second sheet on top of it, and brush it with butter. Repeat with a third sheet. Sprinkle liberally with praline powder and cover with two more sheets of filo, brushing each with butter. Place the sheet of almond paste on top and cover with two more sheets of filo, brushing each with butter. Sprinkle the top sheet with the chopped chocolate and the raisins. If there is any cognac that has not soaked into the raisins, sprinkle it on as well. Top this with one more layer of filo and butter, then sprinkle with praline. Using the towel to help, start rolling the edge closest to you and continue until you have a roll of strudel inside the towel. Use the towel to transport the strudel to the prepared pan and unroll it there. Paint the roll with the remaining butter and bake it for 35–40 minutes or until it is browned. Drizzle the melted chocolate over the hot strudel and serve it warm, cut into 2-inch slices.

Note: *If you don't want to bother making praline, you might want to try substituting chopped walnuts or pecans.*

Note: *The homemade strudel leaves from H. Roth come 2 or 4 to a box. Use only 2 full sheets for each recipe of strudel, following the directions on the box.*

Note: *I usually double this recipe since it freezes beautifully. If you do freeze it, leave off the chocolate on top and make sure to cool it completely before freezing, and defrost it wrapped. Pop it into a moderate oven for 15–20 minutes and then drizzle on the chocolate.*

Petite Dacquoise

These little, melt-in-your-mouth petit fours are fun to make and create an exquisite picture when presented on a silver platter. This recipe is an adaptation of one created by pastry master Albert Kumin.

MAKES 18

For the layers:

5 egg whites measuring about ¾ cup   **1⅓ cups ground almonds**
⅔ cup superfine sugar

Preheat the oven to 250 degrees. Space the racks so that they are as near to the center of the oven as possible. Cover two baking sheets with parchment, and draw eighteen 2½-inch circles on each one.

Beat the egg whites until foamy; continue beating, adding the sugar gradually, until the whites are firm and shiny. Fold in the nuts. Place the meringue into a pastry bag with a number 4 round tube and pipe meringue into each marked circle, completely filling the circle. Smooth with a spatula to ⅓-inch thickness. Bake for 35–45 minutes or until the meringues are firm and beginning to brown. Remove the meringues from the baking sheet and let them cool on a clean piece of parchment. While they cool prepare the butter cream.

For the butter cream:

2 ounces bittersweet chocolate, cut   **12 ounces (1½ sticks) sweet (unsalted)**
  into small pieces   **butter at room temperature, cut into**
4 extra-large egg whites   **small pieces**
1¼ cups superfine sugar   **Toasted slivered almonds**

Melt the chocolate in a small bowl set over gently simmering water. Stir gently and when completely melted, set aside.

Place the egg whites in the bowl of an electric mixer. Set the bowl in a basin of simmering water and start beating with a wire whisk. Gradually add the sugar, beating rapidly with the whisk. Continue beating until the mixture is somewhat thickened (105 degrees on a candy or instant-read thermometer). A ribbon should form when the whisk is lifted. Transfer the bowl to the electric mixer and start to beat at high speed. Continue beating until the meringue is at room temperature — this will take from 15–20 minutes. Gradually add the butter, beating constantly. Beat in the chocolate.

To assemble:

Spread half of the meringues with about 1 tablespoon of the butter cream. Top with the other layers. Use the remaining butter cream and a number 4 star tip fitted into a pastry bag to pipe little rosettes on top of each Petite Dacquoise; top with a few slivers of toasted almonds. These freeze beautifully: place them on a baking sheet, uncovered. When they are frozen solid, cover them well with plastic wrap. Defrost covered. I serve these in little flowered, fluted paper cups on a silver tray. You have to flatten the paper cups to make the little cakes fit in.

The Thin Ladies

Doesn't It Have Calories

I think it would be more than fair
If my chocolate and I could share
Room in my clothes somewhere,
Oh, doesn't it have calories!

Lots of chocolate for me to eat,
White and dark, milk and bittersweet;
It would make my life complete
To take away the calories.

Once that loverly smell of chocolate has hit my nose,
Moderation's only something done on the TV shows.
Chocolate shavings and chocolate chips,
Chocolate cake dipped in chocolate chips;
Just keep them off my hips
And take away the calories.

With the miracles of technology we have today,
It should not be long till some great scientist finds a way.
Helium seltzer to make egg creams;
Goosing mousses with laser beams.
We'd pay for any schemes
To take away the calories.

(Melody: "Wouldn't It Be Loverly." Lyrics by Dr. Howard Shapiro for the Mohonk Mountain House Chocolate Binge Chocolate Operetta, "Cocoaphony.")

I loved teaching. In theory. In practice it made me crazy. I'm compulsive — I wanted my students to feel they were getting every bit (if not more) of their money's worth, both in information and in samples. As any good and conscientious cooking teacher will tell you, the preparation for a class is a tremendous amount of time and work. There is the planning and shopping, and the advance preparation of certain dishes that cannot be started and finished in one class. Since many classes take place in the teacher's home, he or she also has to deal with spouses (who want dinner), offspring (who look like they're coming down with chicken pox), baby-sitters and dishwashers (who decide at the last minute not to show).

I loved sending out the brochures for my chocolate classes and loved getting registration forms and checks back, but as the classes got nearer, I got more anxious. I insisted on teaching brand-new recipes each term, so there was a flurry of kitchen activity as I tried out new ideas and got hysterical when I couldn't make them work. The entire house was cleaned and the kitchen scrubbed until it shined. Woe to the child who laid a sticky fingerprint on the gleaming cabinet or the husband who left a dirty plate in the sink. The recipes and resources sheets were Xeroxed (and the typos agonized over). Quarts of heavy cream and pounds of sweet butter were jammed into every available inch of the refrigerator. Sour cherries, bitter-almond extract, and ground almonds and hazelnuts arrived from H. Roth and Sons in New York City. Circles of parchment, cardboard rounds, and cocoa butter came from Maid of Scandinavia. In my classes I used many different chocolate products from many fine manufacturers: ground chocolate from Ghirardelli, chocolate liquor (unsweetened chocolate) from Van Leer, Tobler Tradition (bittersweet), Lindt Excellence (also bittersweet), Lindt and Carma gianduja (milk chocolate with hazelnuts), Nestlé's milk chocolate and chocolate chips, Guittard Maxi Chips, Cadbury Fruit and Nut bars, and Poulain cocoa.

But each year I grew more ambivalent about the classes. Part of this came from anticipating the work involved and the other part had to do with the invasion of my kitchen. The space defined by the sink and the two Thermadore ovens is my sanctuary. Like a maestro conducting an orchestra, I know where all my instruments are. The knives are arranged just so, blades all facing the same direction, whisks in one crockery pot, rubber spatulas in another. The drawers filled with pastry tubes, pie crimpers, sugar thermometers, and my collection of rolling pins may look cluttered and disorganized to the casual observer (like my mother who gasps every time she opens one), but I know exactly where everything is. While I seem able to share information and recipes without a problem, I have trouble sharing this space. When you invite ten students into your kitchen to teach them how to make chocolate desserts you just have to grit your teeth and share.

This was the other problem: The Thin Ladies. You know who they are, perhaps you are one yourself. To be a Thin Lady you have to be over 5 feet 5 inches and weigh under 112 pounds. Even when they buckle their belts on the last hole, it's still too big for their waists. Hands, one of which bears a diamond ring that could put all of my kids through an Ivy League school, are meticulously manicured, not a chip to be seen in the red polish, not a stray cuticle to be found. Stomachs concave and hips nonexistent, they come to class in clothes that go to the dry cleaners after they've been worn once. The Thin Ladies once bought something that was wash and wear, but that was by accident — now the cleaning lady owns it. They have a collection of handknit sweaters that look divine on them, but would make me look like the Michelin Man, and their slacks have pressed creases and are never never wrinkled. Do they Scotchguard their clothes, or does someone else pour the catsup on the kids' hamburgers? Even in the worst winter slush, they come to class in designer shoes (that never seem to get wet) carrying matching handbags that are big enough for only the important credit cards. Makeup. They wear eye shadow (subtle, but there) and mascara, blusher and lipstick. I once owned lipstick and mascara, but the baby used them to construct something with Play-Doh. Some other child mixed Vaseline in the blush to create a Halloween monster. I was the monster he created. The Thin Ladies make noise. Their solid gold bangle bracelets clank together and make it hard for them to write. They chew gum, or suck mints, so they won't be tempted to taste anything.

Now, wait a minute. These women have each laid out fifty bucks to learn the hottest new thing in chocolate desserts, and they won't even take a tiny taste? Carefree Sugarless Gum versus double chocolate cheesecake. Yes indeed! Folks, step right up and meet the Thin Ladies. Up before sunrise to run ten miles, then they don their leotards and leg warmers to sweat and stretch to Olivia Newton-John singing "Let's Get Physical" in aerobics class, then off to the tennis courts for a fast set or two. If there's time left a couple of laps in the pool or a quick round of the Nautilus equipment. Lunch is celery sticks and V8 or, if it's been a naughty weekend, black coffee and six glasses of Perrier. They greet each other with body assessments: "Gee Sherri, your hips look really firm. Say, did you lose any weight with that seaweed wrap? You look much thinner." In the exercise classes they eyeball one another's bodies with intense scrutiny because the weight thing is incredibly competitive. When the Thin Ladies are happy with what the health club scale says, they leave the little weights in place indicating 104 or 107. And of course, all the other Thin Ladies check it out. If they move the weights quickly after the weigh-in then that indicates trouble: "This goddammed scale is off again.

It's five pounds heavy. For all the money I pay to work out here, you'd think that the scale would be accurate." It was easier to be a Thin Lady ten years ago when it was okay to smoke cigarettes and take amphetamines. Now we know these things can kill you, so you are left with constant exercise and self-denial. Here's the tremendous irony: these hipless, perfect-thighed wonderwomen are fabulous cooks. The time not spent in exercise class or on the tennis court is spent in cooking classes. They've learned how to whip out Chinese banquets, French Provincial buffets, forty different kinds of hot appetizers using puff pastry made from scratch, crêpes, stocks, and hundreds of assorted breads. They flock to cheese tastings (and never taste, but take copious notes). While the other students are wolfing down the egg rolls they've made, the Thin Ladies are wrapping theirs up "to save for later." Guess they must be stuffed from the head of lettuce they ate for dinner. They collect cooking lessons like we collected trading stamps, and keep beautiful fabric-covered notebooks full of recipes from the classes. They use these recipes to throw lavish dinner parties with course after course of delicious and beautifully prepared dishes. The guests are so wildly impressed with the magnificent food that they never even notice that their hostess doesn't eat anything. When they do eat they know the exact caloric value of everything they place in their mouths. Years of reading diet books have implanted on their brains an indelible diet chart and turned their tongues into little scales. When the tiny scale registers five hundred calories, the mouth automatically seals shut. They are able to sublimate their desire to eat by feeding others. The gratification they receive from slaving away over a hot oven to turn out megacalorie meals that their friends and family consume with gusto quells any hunger pangs they may feel. The only place the Thin Ladies feel really comfortable eating a meal is a sushi bar where an entire sashimi dinner can be worked off in ten laps in the pool.

Since, in the spirit of competitive entertaining, all the Thin Ladies are making the same rounds of cooking courses, there is an active pursuit of the latest "in" thing to cook. When desserts became the new frontier the Thin Ladies almost broke their perfect fingernails dialing my number. My classes were filled only days after the mailing went out. Although there were students from other dietary persuasions, the Thin Ladies usually outnumbered them two to one. They never come alone, usually in twos, sometimes in threes. They rarely talk to the other people in the class. Perhaps they think weight is catching. While the other students fight over who will get in there and knead the dough, roll the pie crust, or pipe the butter cream, the Thin Ladies are quite happy to let the other members of the class mess around in the ingredients. When all the desserts are finished and it's time for Le Grand Tasting everyone gets their goodies on a china plate, except the Thin Ladies, who want theirs in a Baggie to go.

It only sounds like I hate the Thin Ladies. My feelings about them are warped by the enormous hostility they evoke in me. You see, I am a failed Thin Lady. Oh yes, I did time in the gym and on the track, doing the pinch test after every workout. I ran ten miles before dawn and denied myself the pleasures of carbohydrates and starch. I can still tell you the number of calories lying in wait in an Oreo cookie, and how many sit-ups it takes to work off a piece of deep-dish apple pie. After making a cake I would immediately pour soap into the mixing bowl of chocolate frosting, lest I be tempted to take a lick. How many breakfasts of grapefruit and vitamin E capsules, how many celery stick, bouillon, and diet Jell-O lunches, how many Stillman dinners did I suffer through only to have to come face to face (or should I say hip to hip) with the bitter truth? I love to eat. I could not assuage those mighty hunger pangs by feeding lasagna and cheesecake to my best friends. I couldn't watch my kids eat ice cream sundaes and be satisfied with Perrier and Lime. Oh, Thin Ladies! From whence cometh your iron will? I hate lumpy thighs as much as you do. I want to slip into those size sixes (and have them hang loose). I want people to gasp at my bony shoulders and protruding cheekbones and ask, solicitiously, if I've been sick. But, as much as I want to crawl out of bed in the morning and have the scale greet me with a cheery 105, I want to eat too. Jelly doughnuts, pepperoni pizza, un-Diet Coke, French toast slathered with butter and soaked with maple syrup, brie, saltines spread with crunchy peanut butter topped with raspberry jam. And most of all chocolate. I want to eat brownies, Hershey's Golden Almond bars, Mallomars, and Toblerone. Chocolate frappes, malteds, egg creams, and ice cream sodas. Thin Ladies, I salute you! I envy you! I watch you in my cooking classes, so neat and trim (my slacks never saw a crease and my designer insignia is a splotch of misdirected butter cream), taking notes instead of tastes, and curse the day my gold bangle bracelet was eaten by the disposal. I wish I could trade my support hose for your dainty patterned stockings, and my canvas carry-all for a six by six-inch real leather clutch bag. But I can't and still be a cook with soul. So, Thin Ladies, now that you know its background, please forgive my hostility and the covetous glares I direct at your streamlined torsos. I forgive your unwavering dedication in refusing to taste my desserts. Please feel free to inhale deeply as you pass me the fudge sauce.

Rigo Janci

Although many desserts are called the ultimate chocolate thrill, this one has to be a frontrunner for the title. There is definitely enough chocolate in this classic Hungarian confection to satisfy anyone's craving. This excellent recipe comes from the *Cooking of Vienna's Empire* volume in the Time-Life cooking series.

For the cake:

3 ounces unsweetened chocolate	½ cup sugar
¾ cup sweet (unsalted) butter at room temperature	4 extra-large eggs, separated
	½ cup flour, measured after sifting

Preheat the oven to 350 degrees with the rack in the center position of the oven. Line an 11 x 17-inch jelly-roll pan with a sheet of parchment, or coat it with butter, then dust lightly with flour. Knock out the excess flour.

Melt the chocolate in a small metal bowl set over a pan of gently simmering water. Set aside to cool.

Cream the butter and ¼ cup of the sugar until the mixture is light and fluffy. Add the melted chocolate and the egg yolks and stir until blended.

In a clean mixing bowl, beat the egg whites with the remaining sugar until they are firm but not dry. With a rubber spatula, stir about ⅓ of the whites into the chocolate mixture, then pour the chocolate mixture over the rest of the whites. Sprinkle the flour on top, then fold the flour into the mixture until no white streaks are visible.

Pour the batter into the prepared pan, spreading it evenly with a rubber spatula. Bake for 12–15 minutes or until the cake shrinks slightly away from the sides of the pan. Remove the cake from the oven and let it cool for 10 minutes before inverting it onto a rack or cookie sheet and peeling off the parchment. If the parchment sticks, simply moisten it with a wet paper towel.

For the filling:

1½ cups heavy cream	4 tablespoons dark rum
10 ounces bittersweet chocolate, chopped into small pieces	1 tablespoon vanilla extract

In a heavy 1-quart saucepan, scald the cream, then add the chocolate and stir over low heat until the chocolate melts. Continue to simmer over very low heat for one more minute, stirring constantly, until the mixture thickens slightly. Pour into a bowl and refrigerate for at least one hour or until the mixture thickens. When the mixture is very cold, place it in the bowl of an electric mixer, add the rum and vanilla, and beat with the wire whip attachment until the filling is smooth and creamy and forms smooth peaks when the beater is lifted from the bowl.

Cut the cake in half to make two layers, each 8½ inches wide. Place one layer on a cake rack, then spread the filling on it. The filling will be about 2 inches thick. Set the other layer on top and refrigerate for one hour. Make the glaze.

The Thin Ladies

For the glaze:

1 cup sugar
⅓ cup water

7 ounces bittersweet chocolate,
chopped into small pieces

In a heavy 1-quart saucepan, combine the sugar and water and bring them to a simmer. Lower the heat and add the chocolate, stirring constantly until the chocolate is melted and the mixture is smooth. Cool to room temperature.

Set the rack holding the cake on a jelly-roll pan and, holding the saucepan with the glaze 2 inches above the cake, pour the glaze over it. If necessary, spread the glaze smooth with a metal spatula. Refrigerate the cake for 20 minutes or until the glaze is firm. Serve by cutting the cake into 35 small squares, 5 in each row across and 7 in each row down. Use a sharp knife that has been dipped in hot water. Rinse the knife and dip it again before each cut.

Coup de Grace

Every year at Mohonk I demonstrate a new chocolate dessert. The pressure is really on me from the amassed world-class chocophiles to come up with something that will knock their socks off. The chosen dessert of the 1984 Chocolate Binge was this amazingly intense frozen chocolate gelati. The addition of orange gives it an unusual and delicious taste, and the accompanying sauce adds a wonderful accent. The name of this dessert was coined by chocolate bard Howard Shapiro. If you wish you can substitute lemon rind for the orange rind for a really interesting taste.

MAKES 1 QUART

For the gelati:

6 ounces unsweetened chocolate,
  chopped
¼ cup Dutch process cocoa
2 tablespoons powdered instant espresso
6 extra-large egg yolks

¾ cup sugar
2 cups milk
½ cup heavy cream
Finely grated rind of one large orange
  or lemon

Melt the chocolate in a small metal bowl placed over a pan of gently simmering water. Off the heat, stir in the cocoa and instant espresso. Stir to blend.

In the bowl of an electric mixer beat the egg yolks with the sugar until the mixture is thick and light yellow in color. In a medium-sized saucepan, scald the milk and cream together until little bubbles appear around the rim of the pan. With the mixer on lowest speed, add the hot milk/cream mixture to the eggs and stir until blended. Return the mixture to the saucepan, and cook over low heat, stirring constantly, until the mixture thickens slightly and coats the back of a spoon. Make sure the mixture does not boil. Strain through a fine mesh sieve and then stir in the chocolate and the orange rind. Cool slightly and then freeze in an ice cream machine.

For the sauce:

1 cup sugar
½ cup water
½ cup Grand Marnier

Rind of one large brightly colored orange or lemon, pith (white part) removed, cut into very fine strips (a lemon zester is perfect for this job)

Combine the sugar, water, and Grand Marnier in a small shallow skillet. Bring the mixture to a boil and add the orange or lemon rind. Boil vigorously until the mixture begins to thicken and the rind is soft. Cool completely.

To serve:

Place a scoop of the gelati on a plate or a shallow saucer, pour a little of the sauce on top and garnish with the orange rind.

White Chocolate en Tulipe

A crisp, delicate cookie cup holds an airy white chocolate mousse. A deep, rich raspberry sauce adds color and contrast. This outstanding recipe is another creation of pastry chef Betsy Bisberg.

It is essential to weigh the sugar, egg whites, and flour for this recipe.

MAKES 1½ CUPS

For the cookies:

⅔ cup plus 2 tablespoons sweet
 (unsalted) butter
8 ounces sugar
8 ounces egg whites

8 ounces flour, sifted
1 teaspoon vanilla extract
Finely grated rind of one orange

Preheat the oven to 400 degrees with the rack in the upper third of the oven. Cover a heavy-duty baking sheet with a piece of parchment. Trace two or three 5-inch circles on the paper, leaving as much space as possible between the circles — these cookies spread about 3 additional inches. Have ready 8–10 cups or small bowls (1½-cup size), placed upside down. These will serve as molds for the tulipes.

Beat the butter until it is soft. Add the sugar and beat until the mixture is light and fluffy. Beat in the egg whites and then, on low speed, the flour and vanilla. Mix in the orange rind. The batter will have a pastelike consistency. You can either paint the batter onto the parchment with a brush or drop with a teaspoon onto the prepared baking sheet, and with the back of the spoon spread it into a 5-inch circle. The batter will be thin, but be careful not to leave any holes, or make it too thin at the edge. These cookies spread, so don't make more than a few at a time, and place them far apart on the sheets. Bake for 4–5 minutes, or just until the edges turn brown. Remove the cookies from the baking sheet with a metal spatula and place them over the upside-down cups. Use your hands to press them around the cups to form the tulip shape. The cookies must be removed from the parchment right away, or they will harden and become impossible to bend. If they do harden, return them to the oven for a few seconds. Leave the tulipes on the cups until they are completely cooled. Repeat the process with the rest of the batter. Prepare the mousse and the sauce.

For the mousse:

8 ounces high-quality white chocolate, cut into small pieces (Tobler Narcisse is delicious in this recipe.)	1 cup very cold heavy cream
	3 tablespoons amaretto liqueur
3 extra-large egg whites at room temperature	

Melt the chocolate in a small metal bowl placed over a pan of gently simmering water. Whisk the chocolate occasionally until it is melted and very smooth. Turn off the heat, but don't remove the bowl from the pan. The chocolate must stay warm, but not hot. Beat the egg whites until they are stiff but not dry, and set them aside. Combine the cold cream and liqueur and beat until very stiff. Fold the egg whites, and then the whipped cream into the warm chocolate. This mousse is best made, spooned into the tulips, and served immediately. If it is not stiff enough, refrigerate it briefly. Don't let it get too cold.

For the sauce:

10 ounces frozen raspberries	¼ cup Framboise or Grand Marnier, optional
⅓ cup seedless raspberry jam	
1 tablespoon lemon juice	Fresh raspberries, optional

Place the above ingredients in the bowl of a food processor or blender and process until the puree is very smooth. You may, if you wish, strain out the seeds. I rarely use fresh raspberries to make this sauce — it's better to eat them whole.

To assemble:

Place the tulipe on a small dish, or in a shallow cup. Spoon some mousse into the tulipe and pour the raspberry sauce over it. Garnish with a few fresh raspberries.

The Best Chocolate Soufflé

That is not a humble title for a dessert, but this is no ordinary soufflé. I used to hate chocolate soufflés. They never tasted chocolatey enough, and there was never enough substance to them — just fluff — they always looked suspiciously raw in the middle. And they were always too sweet. Not this chocolate soufflé! Rich and substantial, it's unadulterated chocolate heaven!

THIS SOUFFLÉ WILL SERVE 4 CHOCOLATE FREAKS OR 6 NORMAL PEOPLE

For the soufflé:

1 cup sugar
½ cup milk
2 teaspoons instant coffee (if you hate coffee, leave this out)
1 tablespoon instant or quick-mixing flour (Wondra)
4 ounces bittersweet or semisweet chocolate, cut into very small pieces

4 ounces unsweetened chocolate, cut into very small pieces
1 tablespoon sweet (unsalted) butter
4 extra-large eggs at room temperature, separated

Preheat the oven to 400 degrees with the rack in the upper third — but not the highest position — of the oven. Butter a 6-cup (the size is important) or 8 x 2½-inch soufflé dish. Sprinkle the inside with sugar and knock the excess sugar out.

In a medium-sized saucepan combine the sugar and milk and optional coffee. Bring the mixture to a rolling boil and add the flour, stir it in, and cook one more minute. Off the heat, add the chocolates. Stir until melted. Add the butter and stir until melted. Add the egg yolks one at a time, stirring after each addition before adding the next.

Beat the egg whites until they are stiff but not dry. Stir a large spoonful of whites into the chocolate mixture in the pan to lighten. Pour the chocolate mixture over the whites and fold together gently but thoroughly. Pour into the prepared pan.

Bake for 20 minutes. Turn the oven down to 350 and bake 5–10 more minutes. This soufflé will not rise dramatically, but the top should be very crusty and the soufflé should be firm — not too wiggly when you shake the pan. Remove from the oven and serve with the following sauce. The soufflé should be eaten immediately — but it's also delicious at room temperature.

For the crème anglaise:

2 cups milk
1 cup heavy cream
⅓ cup sugar

1½ tablespoons flour
5 extra-large egg yolks
3 tablespoons rum or other liquor of
  your choice

In a medium-sized saucepan bring the milk and cream to a simmer. Place the sugar, flour, and egg yolks in a mixing bowl and stir briefly just to blend. Pour the simmering milk over them. Whisk until blended. Return mixture to the saucepan and cook over low heat, stirring constantly, until the sauce thickens slightly. Add the rum and serve warm. I pass this sauce on the side when I serve the hot soufflé — some people like their chocolate unadulterated.

Frozen Chocolate Ginger Truffles

This unusual ice cream dessert features little scoops of heavenly ginger ice cream encased in a crumbly chocolate coating. If you don't want to bother with the coating part, the ice cream is fabulous by itself or served with the 5-Star Hot Fudge* (page 22). It is important to refreeze the ice cream after you take it from the machine so that it is very solid when you scoop the "truffles."

MAKES 20–30 TRUFFLES, DEPENDING ON THE SIZE OF YOUR SCOOP

2 cups milk
5 extra-large egg yolks
¾ cup sugar
2 teaspoons vanilla extract
1 teaspoon ginger flavoring (extract),
  optional
1 cup candied ginger, chopped into
  very small pieces (don't use the food
  processor to do this — it makes the
  ginger gummy)

1 cup heavy cream, whipped
4 ounces bittersweet chocolate
1 cup unsweetened Dutch process cocoa

Place the milk in a medium-sized saucepan set over moderate heat. While the milk is heating, place the egg yolks and sugar in a mixing bowl and whisk until the mixture is thick and light. When the milk begins to simmer pour it slowly into the egg/sugar mixture, whisking to combine the ingredients. Return the mixture to the saucepan and cook over low heat, stirring constantly with a rubber spatula or wooden spoon until the custard begins to thicken slightly and a clear line forms when you run your finger over the spoon or spatula. Pour the custard through a strainer into a metal bowl and add the vanilla, ginger extract, and the chopped candied ginger. Refrigerate until cold. Fold the whipped cream into the custard and freeze in an ice cream maker.

Place the ice cream in a metal bowl and freeze until it is very hard.

Chop the chocolate and cocoa together in the bowl of a food processor until the mixture is powdery with tiny lumps of chocolate remaining. Place this coating in a small, deep bowl. Line two cookie sheets with plastic wrap. Using a small (⅛–¼ cup) ice cream scoop, scoop a small ball of ice cream and drop it into the coating. Shake the bowl vigorously, tossing the ice cream ball to cover it completely with the chocolate coating. Remove the ball from the coating with a rubber spatula and place it on the plastic-lined cookie sheet. Repeat with the rest of the ice cream. It is important to work fast so the ice cream doesn't melt. If there is any remaining coating, sprinkle it over the truffles. If the ice cream gets soft, return it to the freezer until it is hard. Place the truffles in the freezer until they are hard.

To serve:

Place three truffles on each plate.

Fanny's Special Chocolate Kuchen

People can be so funny about recipes. I get asked for mine all the time and have no problem sharing them. This act in no way diminishes me, or makes me the lesser cook, and it certainly doesn't cut into my business. It really warms my heart to know that someone would like something I made well enough to want to make it too. Besides, there are a million recipes — some already discovered and made into classics, and others still waiting to be created. Why make a big deal about passing along an admired one? I know that some pastry chefs are firm in their nonsharing policies, and it's easy to respect that position since one can understand their not wanting their "signature" creations appearing at every corner bakery and restaurant. On the other hand, there are some recipes that are so fantastic (like the Trianon) that people are driven to distraction trying to figure them out.

Let me tell you about my aunt Fanny's Special Chocolate Kuchen.* It was called "special" kuchen, as opposed to "regular" kuchen, because it only made appearances on occasions (happy or sad) when the whole family would get together. Each Rosh Hashonah, Thanksgiving, and Hanukah, Fanny would retire to her kitchen and close the door behind her only to emerge several hours later, her cheeks aglow and her brow damp, hair frizzing out of her bun, smiling triumphantly with kuchen in hand. It made stellar appearances at Fourth of July barbecues, the cousins' Bar Mitzvahs, and even several weddings (the caterers had to be talked into serving one dish that wasn't theirs). It eased the pain of the mourners sitting shiva and it welcomed each baby's birth. What a dish was Fanny's kuchen! All the aunts and grandmothers agreed that there was nothing to rival it in all the world. As proud as they were of their culinary achievements, they had to admit that Fanny was the Kuchen Queen. The dish was always served right from the oven; the aroma of the yeasted dough was enough to make you drunk with desire to tear into it. The filling, which melted in your mouth, was studded with pieces of sweet chocolate, nuts, and something Fanny called "my secret ingredient." Now, it was ironic that she would refer to only one ingredient as "secret," because all the ingredients were secret. Fanny would not give out that recipe. She had been stubbornly unmoved in her attitude for so many years that the aunts and grandmothers had stopped begging, pleading, or even asking a long time ago. At one point they commanded her not to bring it to family functions if she would not give out the recipe, but the men and children in the family went wild at the idea of being deprived of their much-beloved dessert, so it was reinstated. When Fanny would set her dish upon the table the other ladies would exchange exasperated looks, while barely managing to suppress the murderous rages that were welling up in their usually gentle bosoms.

My grandmother always said that if Fanny were really smart, she would use that kuchen to catch a husband, then she would have something really important to brag about and then she could share the recipe. Much to the amazement of everyone in our family old enough to appreciate its significance, Fanny did indeed, in her fifty-second year, find the man of her dreams. The wedding arrangements proceeded with great dispatch (lest the gentleman have second thoughts, or Fanny decide that spinsterhood was, after all, preferable to such a great change in her life-style at her age). The ceremony and reception were to be held at my aunts' house with refreshments supplied by the local four-star Kosher caterer. The crisis came when Fanny realized she could not be both cook and bride at the same time. In order for her famous kuchen to appear at this most important event, she had to spend the hour just before the ceremony in a hot kitchen. What to do? The aunts and grandmothers watched Fanny with great amusement and not a little self-righteousness as she agonized over her situation. What would her wedding be without the kuchen? But how would her husband feel about a sweaty, disheveled bride? Finally, just a week before the wedding, she took her elder sister aside and said she would give her the recipe if she would (a) agree to make the kuchen for the reception and (b) promise to never divulge the recipe to anyone else. "No thanks," said my aunt, who wasn't about to subject herself to the jealous rages of her female relatives. If Fanny was going to share the recipe, it had to be shared with everyone. Fanny agonized yet a few more days. At last, the Thursday before the wedding, while there was still time to run out to the Crown Market for ingredients, Fanny acquiesced. The ladies were invited into the kitchen to watch Fanny make the kuchen. Six months later, at Thanksgiving dinner, Fanny presented a new dish — a dessert she called Lemon Surprise, her new secret recipe.

Fanny's Special Chocolate Kuchen

My friend Judy Samuelson has for years tried to crack the recipe of a chocolate cake made in a bakery in Denver, where she grew up. Now that she lives in Boston and can't just whip around the corner to pick it up, she offers anyone who will bring her home one of these cakes (if they happen through Denver), a ride home from Boston's Logan airport. The cake is called the Chocolate Torte and is sold at Vollmer's Bakery on East Colfax. The recipe originated at another bakery called Bauer's, but they went out of business, and although many bakeries claimed they made the REAL Chocolate Torte, Judy said that only the one from Vollmer's was the authentic item. The cake consists of two 1-inch layers of chocolate cake with a 2-inch filling of the most heavenly smooth and rich dark chocolate fudge. The whole thing is frosted with chocolate ganache, and then a thin layer of compound chocolate is poured over that to give it a beautifully smooth, shiny surface. The top is then decorated with elegant chocolate swirls. Judy beseeched me to help her figure out the recipe so she wouldn't have to rely on the Denver connection to get her fix. I called in Carol Pollak, my friend and pastry expert, for a consultation. We had no trouble figuring out the cake layers — they were pretty straightforward American-style sour cream cake. The frosting and the shiny glaze were also no problem. It was that smooth, fudgy 2-inch interior, which made the cake so special, that had us baffled. As luck would have it, I had to travel to Denver for a consulting job. I promised Judy I would return with two cakes and as much information about them as I could shake loose from the bakery. She promised to meet my plane at Logan. When I told the people at the consulting job about my other reason for coming to Denver, they graciously offered to assist me. It seems they were enamored of the cake themselves. We drove to the bakery and ordered two cakes to be picked up the next day. I casually asked if the cakes were made on the premises, and was told that they were made in the bakery's kitchen directly across the street. We hotfooted it across the street and knocked at the screen door that stood ajar inviting flies in and good smells out. Someone answered in Spanish. We went in to find a young man supervising several hundred gallons of chocolate goo going around at high speed in an enormous industrial mixer. I thanked God I was less stupid at Spanish than Italian and asked if he were the baker. "Sí, Señora." Did he make the famous chocolate torte? "Sí, Señora." Was it hard to make? "No, no. Muy fácil." I didn't think it would be too bright to ask him if the recipe was a secret, so I told him how much I enjoyed the cake and how (stretching the truth a bit) I had come from Boston just to buy some to bring home. That impressed him a lot. When I told him my favorite part of the cake was the filling, he pointed to the huge mixer and indicated that that was what he was making as we spoke. Here was my big chance. "What's it made of?" I asked — no use beating around the bush. "Fifty pounds of chocolate, four gallons of water, and twenty pounds of sugar." He rattled this off in rapid Spanish. At least that's

The Chocolate Diet

202

what I thought he said — numbers were never my forte, even in English. He explained that the chocolate, sugar, and water were melted together and then allowed to cool. The mixture was then mixed at high speed for four hours. "Four hours?" I gasped. "Quatros horas, sí." He went on to say that many people have wanted to make the cake at home, but it's just not possible. (When I got home I tried cutting down the ingredients to an amount small enough to be held by my five-quart industrial mixer, but after beating it for only one hour the machine became so hot I couldn't put my hand on it). Judy met me at the airport and was delighted with the two cakes I had brought from Denver. She took the bad news like a champ and I promised to make her a reasonable facsimile of the cake, which I did, and which we called "Judy's Frustration Cake.*"

Sometimes, when you ask for a recipe, the cook obliges you, but gives you only part, or leaves out an ingredient or technique. We had a fabulous chocolate cake in a restaurant located in a tiny hill town near Avignon in the South of France. The cake's presentation didn't make my heart go pitter-pat — it looked like a thin wedge of nutless brownie — but the taste and texture were a ten on the Richter scale. It tasted like a baked chocolate truffle with the thinnest crust on top. We polished it off with dispatch and ordered another serving. Only after I was absolutely sure I couldn't figure out how it was made did I ask the chef for the recipe. At first he hesitated, explaining that the procedure was difficult, but I persevered. As he dictated in French, I realized that the first part of the recipe was a brand-new (at least for me) way of working with chocolate, but it made sense. The last part of the recipe, however, was obviously bogus. "Just beat the cup of flour into the four eggs until the mixture is smooth" makes something the consistency of something the puppy left on the carpet. It took over a year and about two hundred attempts to figure out the last part of the recipe (which in no way resembled what the chef had told me), but the persistence paid off in the creation (or should I say "re-creation"?) of the Bête Noire.*

Now, the question is, because I was given one part of a recipe and figured out the other part on my own, is this now "my recipe"? There is a fine line between creating a new recipe from an existing one by substantially changing the original and blatantly stealing another person's recipe. I see my recipes in other people's cookbooks without credit and my back goes up. The author changes one ingredient, or an amount of something, and feels that he or she has created something new. That just isn't so. Obviously, exactly how much one would have to change the original is entirely subjective; some people think that even if the basic ingredients are the same, it's still their recipe.

There are so many great recipes, why not share what you have? If it makes you crazy to think other people are getting credit for something that is really yours, make it a point to ask that the borrower always identify the recipe with your name: Hazel MacDonald's Veal Bonny Prince Charlie, or Donald Q. Stubbles Prune Paella. Giving out that recipe won't make the dish taste not as delicious next time you make it — be a sport — like Aunt Fanny, you can always come up with yet another secret recipe.

Besides the recipes for the illusive kuchen and the Bête Noire, I've included here some other wonderful chocolate recipes from people who were not only delighted to share theirs, but were amazed to hear not everyone felt that way.

Fanny's Special Chocolate Kuchen

It seems like there was more than one "secret" ingredient in Fanny's kuchen. The aunts were surprised at the addition of coffee to the dough, and certainly raised their eyebrows when they learned about the bourbon kicker in the apricot glaze. We could hardly wait for the kuchen to cool off — more than once I burned my mouth in my impatience.

MAKES ONE 15-INCH PASTRY

For the dough:

½ cup water
1 tablespoon powdered instant coffee
1 tablespoon sugar
1 package dry yeast
2 extra-large eggs
2 egg yolks

½ cup sour cream
1 teaspoon salt
1 cup butter, melted
4–5 cups flour
1 cup raisins, soaked overnight in ½
    cup bourbon

Heat the water and dissolve the coffee in it. Cool to skin temperature.

In the large bowl of an electric mixer, mix the coffee, sugar, and yeast. Make sure the yeast is dissolved before proceeding. Add the eggs, yolks, sour cream, salt, and butter. Mix well. With the mixer on slow speed, add the flour gradually until four cups are incorporated. Mix on medium speed until the dough no longer sticks to the sides of the bowl. You may need to add some more flour. Mix for at least 5 minutes. Mix in raisins.

Cover the dough with plastic wrap and set in a warm, draft-free place to rise until it has doubled in volume. This will take approximately 1½ to 2 hours. At the end of the rising, punch down the dough, cover with plastic wrap, and place it in the refrigerator until it is thoroughly chilled. The dough may be prepared in advance up to this point and will keep in the refrigerator up to three days. Make the streusel topping.

For the topping:

¼ cup sweet butter, melted
¼ cup brown sugar
1 tablespoon cinnamon
½ cup ground almonds (Ground
  almonds can be purchased by mail
  from H. Roth and Sons. See page 3
  for address.)
½ cup flour

Combine the butter, sugar, cinnamon, and almonds. With your fingers, work in the flour until the mixture has small lumps. Assemble the filling ingredients.

For the filling:

3 tablespoons cinnamon mixed with ½
  cup granulated sugar
1½ cups apricot preserves
3 tablespoons bourbon
1 cup chocolate chips

To form the kuchen:

Butter a 15-inch pizza pan (make sure it fits in your oven before you start! If it doesn't, make two smaller kuchens using 9-inch cake pans). Place the cold dough on a floured surface. Sprinkle it with flour and roll it out into a 16-inch circle. Drape the circle over the rolling pin and place it on the prepared pan. Fold the edges over and crimp them to form a 1-inch border. Sprinkle the dough with cinnamon sugar. Heat the preserves slightly to soften, mix in the bourbon. Spread the warm mixture over the dough — up to but not on the border. Sprinkle with the chocolate chips and finally with the streusel. Let the kuchen rise in a warm place for 30 minutes.

Preheat the oven to 400 degrees with the rack in the center position of the oven. Place the kuchen in the oven and bake for 5 minutes. Then turn the oven down to 350 degrees. Bake the kuchen 35–40 minutes, or until the crust is browned. Cool slightly and cut into wedges.

Judy's Frustration Cake

The raspberry glaze is my addition.

SERVES 12–14

For the layers:

5 ounces semisweet chocolate, chopped
¼ cup boiling water
5 extra-large eggs at room temperature
5 ounces (¾ cup) sugar
3 ounces (¾ cup) cake flour, unsifted
Pinch of salt

Preheat the oven to 350 degrees with the rack in the center of the oven. Grease a 9-inch cake pan with 3-inch sides. You may use a springform or regular cake pan, but it must have high sides. Line it with a round of parchment, then grease and flour the parchment. Knock out the excess flour.

Place the chopped chocolate and the boiling water in a small bowl set over a pan of gently simmering water. Stir gently until the chocolate has melted.

Beat the eggs and sugar in an electric mixer, using the whip attachment, until the eggs have tripled in volume and are very light yellow in color and form a thick ribbon. Combine the flour and pinch of salt in a strainer or sifter and in three additions add it to the egg/sugar mixture. Between the additions fold very carefully until all the flour is incorporated. Be careful to scrape the bottom of the bowl when folding.

Pour the chocolate into the egg mixture in two stages and fold gently but completely until the two mixtures are totally incorporated. Pour the batter into the prepared pan.

Bake 40 minutes, or until a cake tester comes out clean and the sides begin to pull away from the pan. Invert at once onto a wire rack to cool. Remove the parchment.

When the cake has cooled completely cut it into two layers using a very sharp serrated knife. Brush the cut side of each layer with the glaze.

For the glaze:

1 cup seedless raspberry preserves
2 tablespoons lemon juice

Heat these two ingredients in a small pan until the mixture is spreadable.

For the filling and frosting:

2¼ cups heavy cream **⅓ cup light corn syrup**
2½ tablespoons instant espresso
24 ounces (1½ pounds) bittersweet
  chocolate, chopped into very small
  pieces

Scald the heavy cream with the instant espresso in a large heavy-bottomed saucepan.

Off the heat add the chopped chocolate. Add the corn syrup. Stir gently with a rubber scraper until the mixture is smooth and glossy. Allow to cool for a few minutes. This filling/frosting will be very thick.

To assemble:

1 cup heavy cream, whipped **Fresh raspberries (optional)**

Place a piece of wax paper on top of the glazed side of one layer. Place a cookie sheet on top of the wax paper. Flip the layer over onto the cookie sheet. Cover this layer with two crisscrossed pieces of plastic wrap. The wrap should extend well beyond the edges of the cake. Place the clean cake pan in which you baked the cake over this plastic-covered layer. Using the cookie sheet, turn the whole thing over so that the layer is now glazed-side up in the plastic wrap–lined cake pan. Press the layer gently down into the pan and arrange the plastic wrap so that it covers the inside edges of the pan and flows out over the edges. No plastic wrap should cover any part of the top of the cake. Remove the wax paper and scrape any of the raspberry glaze on it back onto the cake. Pour two-thirds of the chocolate filling/frosting on top of this layer. Place the cake in the freezer for 30 minutes to firm the filling. Place the other layer, glazed-side down, on top of the filling and gently press the top layer down to seal the cake together. The top layer may not fit all the way into the pan — this is okay. Pull the plastic wrap up and around the top of the second (top) layer. Chill very well.

When the cake is well chilled, gently heat the rest of the filling/frosting in either a double boiler or carefully over a low heat and set aside. Remove the cake from the pan (the plastic wrap should make this easy to do) and place a cake plate on top of it. Flip it over, so the cake plate is now on the bottom. Remove the plastic wrap. Place strips of wax paper under the cake to catch the excess frosting. Pour the filling/frosting over the cake and using a long straight flexible cake spatula, frost the top and sides. Pull out the strips of wax paper immediately after frosting. Serve at room temperature garnished with whipped cream rosettes and the optional fresh raspberries.

Bête Noire

When I give cooking demonstrations, this is the dessert that I love to teach. It is a chocoholic's dream dessert — easy to make and you hardly have to wait any time at all to eat it. With a thin crispy top and a creamy smooth inside — it's like eating a slice of chocolate truffle. The wonderful name, which literally translated means "black beast" and, idiomatically, "nemesis," was coined by master of the *bon bon* mot Howard Shapiro. The name really fits — it took hundreds of tries to perfect this wonderfully intense chocolate masterpiece. You can serve this practically hot out of the oven (try not to burn your mouth in your haste to eat it), warm with whipped cream, or cooled with white chocolate sauce. It does not freeze, but will keep, refrigerated, for a week.

SERVES 8–10

8 ounces unsweetened chocolate
4 ounces semi-or bittersweet chocolate
½ cup water
1⅓ cups sugar

½ pound (2 sticks) sweet (unsalted) butter at room temperature, cut into small pieces
5 extra-large eggs at room temperature

Preheat the oven to 350 degrees with the rack in the center of the oven.

Butter a 9-inch cake pan (not a springform) and place a circle of parchment or wax paper on the bottom, covering it completely. Butter the paper.

Chop both the chocolates into fine pieces and set them aside.

Combine the water with 1 cup of the sugar in a heavy 1½-quart saucepan. Bring to a rapid boil over high heat and cook about 2 minutes.

Remove the saucepan from the heat and immediately add the chocolate pieces, stirring until they are completely melted. Then add the butter, piece by piece, stirring to melt it completely.

Place the eggs and the remaining ⅓ cup sugar in either the bowl of an electric mixer or a regular mixing bowl. For a cake with a crunchy crust: beat the eggs and sugar in the electric mixer until they have tripled in volume. For a smooth top (better for frosting): mix the eggs and sugar only until the sugar dissolves.

Add the chocolate/butter mixture to the eggs and mix to incorporate completely. DO NOT OVERBEAT! — this causes nasty air bubbles.

Spoon and scrape the mixture into the prepared pan. Set the pan into a slightly larger pan or a sturdy jelly-roll pan. Set both in the oven and pour hot water into the larger pan.

Bake for 25–30 minutes. Let cool in the pan for 10 minutes and then run a sharp knife around the sides to release the cake. Cover with plastic wrap and unmold onto a cookie sheet. Invert a serving plate over the cake and flip it over, so the plate is on the bottom and the cake on top. Serve with either a chocolate ganache glaze or a white chocolate sauce (both recipes follow).

Chocolate Ganache

1 cup heavy cream
10 ounces bittersweet chocolate, cut into small pieces

Scald the cream. Add the chocolate off the heat, and stir very gently until smooth. Cool slightly and pour over cake.

White Chocolate Sauce

1 cup heavy cream
9 ounces Tobler Narcisse, cut into small pieces

½ cup Drambuie

Scald the cream, then off the heat, add the chocolate. If milk solids do not dissolve, process for a few seconds in a food processor or blender. Add the Drambuie.

Processor Bête Noire

Just recently it occurred to me that this already ridiculously easy-to-make dessert could be done faster and easier (fewer steps and fewer dishes to wash) in our space-age friend the food processor. So, I gave it a try. Not only does it work — it's so easy to make that it has replaced instant chocolate pudding as an easy dessert in my circle of we-want-it-now chocolate lovers.

Use the ingredients that are listed in the Bête Noire recipe and follow that recipe's directions for preparing the pan and preheating the oven.

Place both chocolates in the bowl of the food processor and process until the chocolate is in tiny pieces. Place ALL the sugar (1⅓ cups) and the ½ cup of water into a small saucepan and bring it to a rolling boil. Cut the butter (which has to be at room temperature) into pieces. Crack the eggs into a measuring cup or a small bowl with a spout. With the processor on, add the boiling sugar syrup to the chocolate, then add the butter piece by piece. Finally, add the eggs. Process only until the mixture is very smooth. Pour the batter into the prepared pan and bake according to the Bête Noire recipe.

Jason Lamb's Chocolate Amaretto Terrine

The brand-new Windsor Court Hotel in New Orleans has to have one of the most beautiful and elegantly decorated lobbies I have ever seen. Every afternoon a sumptuous high tea is served there accompanied by the sweet strains of a young couple playing duets. The dining room is stunning — both in terms of decor and menu. The high point of our delicious meal was this amaretto terrine served on a plate on which chocolate scrollwork had been piped. Dedicated dessert lovers should make a pilgrimage to New Orleans to see and taste the delights created by the talented young pastry chef Jason Lamb.

SERVES 12

12 ounces semisweet chocolate, chopped into small pieces
1½ cups sugar
½ cup water
12 ounces (3 sticks) sweet (unsalted) butter at room temperature
2¾ cups cocoa

2 extra-large eggs
3 extra-large egg yolks
¼ cup amaretto
2 teaspoons almond extract
2 cups sliced toasted almonds for garnish (see note)

Grease a 6-cup loaf pan (Jason uses a 3 x 11-inch enameled metal terrine mold) and line it with a large piece of plastic wrap, pressing the plastic into the pan to conform tightly with the sides and corners. Let the excess wrap hang down over the outside of the pan; this gives you something to grip when you remove the terrine from the mold.

Place the chopped chocolate in a bowl set over a pan of gently simmering water and stir occasionally until it melts. Remove from heat and set aside. Place the sugar and water in a small saucepan over high heat. Whisk briefly until the sugar dissolves, then let boil without stirring for three minutes. Remove from heat.

Place the butter in the bowl of an electric mixer and mix at high speed until the butter is fluffy. On slowest speed, add the cocoa and mix well. Mix in the eggs, egg yolks, amaretto, and almond extract. Add the chocolate and half of the sugar syrup and mix at high speed. Turn off the mixer and, using a rubber scraper, scrape down the sides of the bowl. Place the bowl back on the mixer and with the machine on high speed, add the remaining syrup. Scrape down the sides of the bowl once more. Pour the mixture into the prepared pan, cover with plastic wrap, and refrigerate overnight. Unmold the terrine and set it on a serving dish.

To serve:

Cut thin slices with a sharp knife that has been dipped in hot water and garnish with the toasted almonds.

Note: *To toast the almonds, place them, sliced, in a single layer on a cookie sheet in a 350 degree oven. Cook for 5–8 minutes, watching them carefully. Shake the pan several times, or stir the almonds with a spoon during the toasting. Allow them to cool completely before storing in an airtight container.*

Chocolate Hermits

Traditional hermits are made with raisins and flavored with cinnamon, nutmeg, allspice, and cloves. This rather untraditional version, based on a recipe from Norrie Chadbourne, my favorite photographer's mom and a wonderful baker, has chocolate instead of raisins and none of the traditional spices. The cookies, however, have that wonderful chewy texture of old-fashioned hermits — with, of course, the addition of your favorite food — chocolate.

½ cup solid vegetable shortening

1 cup firmly packed brown sugar

2 eggs

¼ cup molasses

2 cups flour

1 teaspoon baking powder

½ teaspoon salt

¼ cup unsweetened cocoa, not Dutch process

12 ounces bittersweet or semisweet chocolate bits

1 cup walnuts or pecans, broken into large pieces

Cream the shortening and brown sugar until smooth. Mix in the eggs and molasses and beat until the mixture is smooth. Sift the flour together with the baking powder, salt, and cocoa, then add to the other mixture, bit by bit, mixing until it is all incorporated. Mix in the chocolate chips and nuts. Scrape down the sides of the bowl and cover the batter with plastic wrap, pressing the plastic directly onto the batter. Refrigerate for at least one hour — or longer.

Preheat the oven to 350 degrees. Lightly grease two heavy baking sheets. Divide the dough into fourths and roll one portion between your hands to form a thick band. Set it onto the baking sheet and press it with your hand to form a flat 10 x 3-inch rectangle. Do the same with the remaining dough, placing two portions on each baking sheet.

Bake the hermits for 20–25 minutes or until they are firm to the touch. Switch the baking sheets in the oven from top to bottom and back to front halfway through the baking time.

Remove the baking sheets from the oven and let the cookies set for a few minutes. Then use a large knife to cut each rectangle horizontally into 6 even bars, making 24 cookies. Allow the hermits to cool completely before storing them in an airtight tin.

Bobbie Geismer's Chocolate Squares

You can thank Cleveland's top chocolate lover for these tasty goodies. If you like brownies you'll love these!

MAKES 6 DOZEN SMALL SQUARES OR 4 DOZEN LARGE

For the squares:

8 ounces unsweetened chocolate, chopped

8 ounces (2 sticks) sweet (unsalted) butter

4 extra-large eggs

2 cups sugar

1 cup all-purpose flour, measured after sifting

2 teaspoons vanilla extract

2 teaspoons orange extract (optional)

3 cups pecans, finely chopped

Preheat the oven to 350 degrees with the rack in the lower third, but not the bottom, of the oven. Coat a 17 x 11-inch heavy-duty jelly-roll pan with butter. Melt the chocolate and butter together in a small metal bowl set over a pan of gently simmering water. Stir to mix, then cool to room temperature.

In the large bowl of an electric mixer, beat the eggs until foamy, gradually adding the sugar. When the mixture is thick and holds a ribbon when the beaters are lifted out of the bowl, place the machine on the lowest speed and add the flour, flavorings, and nuts. Mix only until incorporated. Stir in the melted chocolate.

Spread the batter in the prepared pan and bake 15–18 minutes. While the squares are baking prepare the icing.

For the icing:

3 tablespoons milk
1 teaspoon vanilla extract

10 ounces (2 cups) sifted confectioners' sugar

Mix the milk and vanilla into the sugar and stir until smooth. Ice the squares while they are still hot. Cool completely before cutting.

Hazelnut Creams

These elegant and sublimely delicious pastries are the creation of Beverly Jones, who teaches cooking in Andover, Massachusetts. They take time and a bit of patience to make — but the result is well worth the effort. See notes on page 87 for toasting hazelnuts.

MAKES 34 PASTRIES

For the cookies:

½ cup sweet (unsalted) butter
½ cup dark brown sugar, firmly packed
½ teaspoon vanilla extract
¾ cup flour

¼ cup ground, toasted hazelnuts
1 generous tablespoon candied ginger, finely chopped

Preheat the oven to 350 degrees with the rack in the upper third of the oven. In the bowl of an electric mixer or food processor, cream the butter and the sugar until the mixture is light and fluffy. Mix in the vanilla, then the flour, nuts, and ginger. If the mixture is too sticky to handle easily, chill 30 minutes, then shape into balls the size of walnuts. Place the balls about 1½ inches apart on an ungreased cookie sheet and flatten slightly with the palm of your hand. Bake 10–12 minutes, or until the cookies are just beginning to brown. Cool on a rack and store in a tightly covered container until ready to assemble.

For the filling:

½ cup sweet butter
½ teaspoon vanilla extract
4 tablespoons heavy cream

2 cups sifted confectioners' sugar
⅓ cup ground, toasted hazelnuts

In the bowl of an electric mixer or food processor, cream the butter, vanilla, and cream. Gradually add the confectioners' sugar, then the ground nuts.

For the glaze:

8 ounces semisweet chocolate, chopped   2 teaspoons solid vegetable shortening

Place the chocolate and shortening in a small bowl set over a pan of gently simmering water. Stir occasionally until melted and smooth.

To assemble:

Working with 8 cookies at a time, place one generous tablespoon of the hazelnut buttercream on each cookie and spread the filling, mounding it high in the center, sloping toward the rim. (An easy way to spread the filling is to use an ice cube inside a piece of plastic wrap.) Set the frosted cookies on a cake rack that is sitting on a wax paper–covered jelly-roll pan, or other pan with sides. Carefully pour some glaze over each cookie, then tap the rack to make the glaze flow and cover the filling. Place the pastries (still on the rack) in the refrigerator for a few minutes until the glaze hardens, then lift them off with a metal spatula. Repeat with the remaining cookies.

Lynne Bail's Gillie Whoppers

These chocolate walnut bars with chocolate marshmallow topping and the delicious hot fudge sauce recipe that follows are creations of my neighbor and dear friend Lynne Bail.

MAKES 24 SQUARES

For the bars:

¾ cup sifted all-purpose flour,
  measured after sifting
½ teaspoon baking powder
¼ teaspoon salt
2 tablespoons unsweetened cocoa
¾ cup sugar
½ cup (1 stick) sweet (unsalted) butter
  at room temperature, cut into small
  pieces

2 extra-large eggs
1 teaspoon vanilla extract
½ cup walnuts, chopped
1½ cups (approximately) miniature
  marshmallows

Preheat the oven to 350 degrees with the rack in the center position of the oven. Grease an 8 x 8-inch baking pan with either butter or Crisco. Sift together flour, baking powder, salt, and cocoa and place them in a medium-sized mixing bowl. Add the sugar. Blend in the butter, eggs, and vanilla and mix well. Stir in the nuts. Spread in the prepared pan and bake for 20 minutes. While the bars are baking, assemble the ingredients for the topping. At the end of the baking time, remove the pan from the oven, but do not turn the oven off. Sprinkle the marshmallows on top of the bars, trying to keep them away from the edges. Return the pan to the oven and bake three more minutes, or until the marshmallows melt. Spread the melted marshmallows over the bars leaving a ½-inch border at the sides of the pan.

For the topping:

½ cup dark brown sugar, firmly packed   3 tablespoons sweet (unsalted) butter
¼ cup water   2 teaspoons vanilla extract
2 ounces baking chocolate, chopped   1½ cups confectioners' sugar, sifted

In a small saucepan combine the brown sugar, water, and chocolate. Boil for three minutes. Off the heat, add the butter and stir until it melts, add the vanilla and confectioners' sugar, mix well. Spread this topping over the marshmallows, right up to the sides of the pan. Cool completely before cutting into bars.

Lynne's Great Hot Fudge Sauce

MAKES 1½ CUPS

¼ cup butter   ¾ cup sugar
1 ounce unsweetened chocolate,   ½ cup evaporated milk
  chopped   Pinch of salt
¼ cup cocoa   ½ teaspoon vanilla extract

In a small saucepan set over very low heat, melt the butter and chocolate together. Add the cocoa and sugar and blend thoroughly. Add the evaporated milk, salt, and vanilla very gradually, stirring continuously. Store in a covered glass container in the refrigerator. If you need to soften it, place the glass container in a pan of hot water.

Betsy's Chocolate Nut Pie

Thanks and love to Sue and Phil Strause.

MAKES ONE 10-INCH PIE

1 10-inch unbaked pie shell (see
  Chocolate Cream Pie, page 11)
12 ounces bittersweet chocolate
2 tablespoons sweet (unsalted) butter
1 cup dark corn syrup
½ cup sugar

1 teaspoon vanilla extract
3 extra-large eggs
Pinch of salt
1 cup pecans or walnuts, coarsely
  chopped
Unsweetened whipped cream

Preheat the oven to 350 degrees with the rack in the center position of the oven. In a medium-sized bowl set over gently simmering water, melt the chocolate with the butter. Stir until blended. Combine all the other ingredients in a mixing bowl and blend in the melted chocolate. Pour into the unbaked pie shell and bake 35 minutes. Serve at room temperature with unsweetened whipped cream.

Commander's Palace Chocolate Fudge Sheba

New Orleans is a city that celebrates great food. I have eaten some of the finest meals of my life with some of the finest people I've ever known in that beautiful city — and how they love chocolate! My meal at Commander's Palace was in every respect a fabulous experience. Ella Brennan's warm and exuberant hospitality, chef Emeril Lagasse's magnificent food, and the elegant surroundings combined to make a most perfect evening. Chef Lagasse generously shared his recipe for this most outstandingly delicious and devilishly rich chocolate dessert.

SERVES 12–15

20 ounces (1¼ pounds) semisweet
  chocolate, chopped
6 extra-large egg yolks at room
  temperature
6 ounces sweet (unsalted) butter at room
  temperature

7 extra-large egg whites at room
  temperature
½ cup sugar
1 cup pecans, chopped

Lightly coat an 8-cup mold with melted butter. Melt the chocolate in a small metal bowl placed over a pan of gently simmering water. Remove from the heat and let it cool to room temperature. Beat the egg yolks until they triple in volume and form a ribbon when the beater is lifted from the bowl. Cream the butter until it is light and fluffy (you can do this in the food processor). Use a rubber spatula to fold the chocolate into the butter, then fold the yolks into the chocolate mixture until smooth. Whip the egg whites with the sugar until they are stiff but not dry, and then fold them into the chocolate mixture. Pour into the prepared mold and sprinkle the top with the chopped pecans. Lightly press the pecans into the chocolate. Cover with plastic wrap and refrigerate until hard. Unmold by very briefly dipping the mold into hot water — remember to quickly dry the mold before inverting onto the serving plate.

To serve:

Use a long, thin knife dipped in hot water to cut thin pieces.

Heavenly Oatmeal Bars Jordan Pond House

Once, on a trip to Bar Harbor, Maine, David and I had delicious dinner in Acadia National Park at the beautiful Jordan Pond House Restaurant. What a memorable meal that was! We loved every morsel — especially the wonderful homemade strawberry ice cream accompanied by the most scrumptious crisp buttery oatmeal bar covered with a thick creamy layer of chocolate. The people at the next table made a bet with us that the cookies were a secret recipe that wouldn't be shared, which only made me more determined to get it. I flagged a passing waiter and asked if the baker was in the kitchen. Yes, she was, he said. Could I see her? I asked. She couldn't come out to the dining room, he told me. Could I go into the kitchen? Before he could answer I was in the kitchen congratulating the young woman who had baked the cookies. Her name was Robin Piskura, and she was delighted to share this recipe that has been a favorite of the Jordan Pond House's clientele for years.

MAKES 60 2 x 1-INCH BARS

For the bars:

1 cup (2 sticks) sweet (unsalted) butter	¾ cup light corn syrup
1⅓ cups dark brown sugar, firmly packed	5⅓ cups quick-cooking oats
	2 teaspoons vanilla extract

Preheat the oven to 350 degrees with the rack in the center position of the oven. Coat a 9 x 13-inch baking pan with butter or vegetable shortening or spray it with Pam. (I have also used an 11 x 7-inch pan to bake these bars — it's sort of a tight squeeze, but it works. If you do use the smaller pan it helps to unmold the bars before cutting — but after cooling — and then spread the glaze.)

Cream the butter and sugar until light and fluffy. Mix in the corn syrup, oats, and vanilla. Spread in the prepared pan and bake 16 minutes. Cool until lukewarm and then spread on the glaze.

For the glaze:

12 ounces semisweet chocolate chips   1 cup peanut butter

Place the chocolate chips and peanut butter in a small saucepan and stir over low heat until the chocolate melts and the mixture is smooth. Spread over the warm bars, then cool completely or refrigerate until cold, then cut into bars.

Chocolate Consultant?

When I was a cook it was much easier to answer the question "What do you DO?" Now, when I state my profession, people either roll their eyes in disbelief, or immediately write me off as a lunatic. "A chocolate consultant? Are you kidding? What do you do, test-market bonbons and do quality control on chocolate fudge layer cakes?" When I finally manage to convince them that, in fact, I do make a living teaching, researching, and promoting chocolate, they have to admit that I have their fantasy job.

I must confess that when the idea of becoming a chocolate consultant first came to me I wasn't really certain what the job entailed, or even more important, if I could make a living at it. Would anyone really be willing to pay me for my expertise? Well, there was only one way to find out, and hell, wasn't it worth a try? Imagine being able to make a living working with the thing I loved best. It wasn't really such a long shot. After all, the American public had joined me with wild enthusiasm in my love affair with chocolate. They loved to eat it, cook with it, give it as gifts, talk about it, read about it, and brag about their latest chocolate "find." In an economy that inhibited most of our frivolous spending, chocolate had become an affordable luxury. It tastes wonderful, looks beautiful, makes you feel terrific, and has all the class of a Ferrari for a fraction of the cost. The same people who flocked to adult education classes to learn the difference between Bordeaux and Beaujolais were now happily paying $50 for one of my classes to learn the difference between Tobler and Hershey. Wouldn't a career as a chocolate consultant be the inevitable outcome of a life spent on The Chocolate Diet?

So, how did I become a chocolate consultant? First let's deal with how I became a consultant. There are several ways of becoming a consultant. You can send out several thousand business cards to all the men in your old-boy network, or all the women in your old-girl network, then sit back and wait for the phone to ring, or you can start charging for all the free advice you've been giving away for years. I leaned toward the latter school of thought, but to be safe, sent out business cards. The phone lines didn't exactly melt with the overload of calls, but I did get several interesting propositions, one of which was illegal.

A lucky break, preferably with a large and very wealthy corporation, was what was needed, I told myself. While I waited for the break I did a little catering and a lot of food styling (working with photographers and advertising agencies, getting food photo-perfect for ads). Then I got a phone call from San Francisco from a woman named Sandra Brod.

"I got your name from Adrianne Marcus," she said. (Let's hear it for the old-girl network.) "I'm organizing a huge chocolate convention in San Francisco and would like you to do a cooking demonstration."

"You would?"

I was hysterically trying to figure out how I could afford to get to California when she said, "Of course we would fly you to California and pay your hotel expenses."

"You would?"

"What kind of fee would you want for the demonstration?"

"Huh?"

She repeated her question. And all I could say was, "You want to pay me, too?" Some consultant. David immediately taped a little card to the telephone table with my fees on it, just in case I had another memory lapse.

My husband has separation anxiety. It really has nothing to do with who will drive the carpool, fix the breakfasts, or do the laundry. We can hire someone to do all that. He just likes me to be around. It's amazing, however, how the prospect of a check big enough to pay the summer camp tuition for one-and-a-half boys can cure even the most severe separation anxiety. So that conflict was resolved. The other conflict involved my fourteen-month-old baby, whom I wasn't ready to wean, even if it did mean a week in sunny California.

No one ever told me that when you're flying with a baby you should request only clear liquids for you and the child. The rule of thumb seems to be "Eat it and wear it." The other thing I wasn't warned about was the stimulating effect of pressurized cabin air on a toddler. We're talking marathon screaming, interspersed with the Baby Decathlon: aisle running, cracker spitting, and juice spilling. I arrived in California on my first business trip dressed to kill in my sweet child's breakfast and dinner. The La Leche League owes me a Purple Heart.

The chocolate festival was held in a building called the Galleria in San Francisco. An enormous main floor and four balconies were filled with booths and stalls representing every form of chocolate: candies, ice cream, cookies, cakes. There were chocolate themes and logos on T-shirts, mugs, and calendars. Portraits in chocolate, sculptures and molded objects of every sort imaginable — and some you never imagined. Chocolate books, cards, and banners were displayed. When the doors opened at noon, there were already several thousand people in line. They couldn't plunk down their $7 admission fee fast enough to get inside to spend yet more money buying things from the vendors operating the booths. Chocophiles of all ages and shapes jammed the aisles, filling their shopping bags and mouths with foods made with their favorite ingredient. They sprayed chocolate perfume, painted themselves with chocolate lipstick, and watched with awe as a man immersed himself in a bathtub full of melted chocolate. They wandered around in utter bliss with brown tinging the corners of their mouths, their eyes glazed over in happy delirium. Perfect chocolate bliss was created that day.

The demonstration area was in the center of the main floor. Never before had I given a class to so many people who wanted to stand so close to me. No one seemed to mind getting splattered with any of the ingredients. They asked the usual questions, and because I was in California, I felt I could be a little more freewheeling with the answers.

"How did you get into the chocolate business?"

"I flunked vanilla."

"How do you stay so thin?"

"I take drugs."

We all had a swell time. I had brought three cakes with me from Boston, so that everyone could have a little taste. Dividing three nine-inch chocolate tortes by one thousand chocolate freaks is no easy task. When I ran out of cake I let people lick the bowls and utensils. The audience was fantastic — but I wasn't sure if it was me they loved, or my chocolate. After the class was over, a young man came over to me and pulled out his wallet. He said, "I have something to show you." For a minute I was afraid it was going to be a seamy photo of him doing something dirty with chocolate. He pulled out a well-worn newspaper clipping and gently opened it up, lovingly smoothing out the creases. He said, "I've been carrying this around for five years. I knew that one day I would meet you and be able to thank you in person for my favorite chocolate dessert." It was my ginger cheesecake recipe from the *New York Times*. I gave him a chocolate kiss.

One of the most ego-gratifying experiences I ever had was when the saleswoman in the gourmet department of Henri Bendel recognized me as being the "chocolate lady" on the "David Susskind Show." I was sure that only my mother had watched. The producer of the program had called only a week before the taping. They were doing an hour-long show on chocolate and had four men lined up, but were in desperate need of a woman chocolate expert who had a good "media personality." I think the producer wanted me to give him a list of names, but I gave him a sales job instead. Before he knew it, he had asked me to join the four men.

I am terrified of flying. I only get on airplanes if they're going to Paris or if I have to be in New York to be on network TV. It's hard to justify my usual dose of two Seconal when I'm riding the shuttle for only forty-five minutes. Besides, I end up weaving around LaGuardia like a drunk. I was able to appear calm and composed on national television because I had used up all my terror flying the shuttle sober.

The other guests on the show were Rudi Sprüngli, representing the sixth generation of the Lindt family and the product manager for Lindt and Sprüngli Ltd. in the USA; Albert Pechenik, who is said to be the genius behind the success of Godiva Chocolates and currently the importer and promoter of Michele Guerrard Chocolates; Milton Zelman, creator and publisher of the *Chocolate News;* and Tom Kron, the most controversial and, in many ways, the most important person in the current chocolate craze in this country.

The studio was crammed with chocolates in all shapes and sizes: trays of bonbons, boxes of truffles, huge ten-pound bars, a solid chocolate leg, rulers, calculators. The smell of chocolate was so intense that one inhale made your mouth water and your hips widen. I added the two special chocolate things I had brought from Boston: a Trianon made with Tom Kron's cooking chocolate and an assortment of my favorite chocolates made by Harbor Sweets in Marblehead, Massachusetts. The TV staff were alternately slapping snitching hands and sneaking little tastes for themselves. Even though this was not a live show, there was a palpable tension in the air as the crew got ready for the filming. First we all got "made up" by this guy who waved cream and brushes around my face and transformed me into a blemishless streetwalker. I was afraid to smile or talk because I thought I would crack the makeup. (I washed it off in the ladies' room.) Then there was a big to-do about where we were going to sit. Tom Kron didn't want to sit next to any of the competition, but David Susskind put him at the end next to Rudi. Then all the chocolate was arranged on a coffee table in front of us. We each tried to move our own product into a better position. Then David Susskind read the introduction around twelve times, until the producer was happy with it, and then the show started. We were each invited to talk about the current wild chocolate mania in the United States. Al spoke about how Americans were discovering the delights of European chocolates and were finally willing to spend money for quality. Rudi, a handsome and eloquent spokesman for his family, which has been making fabulous Swiss chocolate for over one hundred years, of course agreed, but pointed out that many generations of Americans had been enjoying quality Swiss chocolates. Milton spoke about worldwide chocolate consumption and about the European taste and the American taste. He agreed the tastes were indeed different, but not that one was better than the other. I said that I thought the chocolate craze was in part a snob thing — the "new kiwi" — and in part a result of great marketing and the very active advertising campaigns undertaken by chocolate companies in this country. I said it warmed my heart that now Americans were realizing that this country had chocolate products that rivaled Europe's.

Then there was Tom Kron. I think Tom Kron is single-handedly responsible for the incredible love affair this country is having with chocolate. Malcolm Blue, my revered and adored chocolate mentor at the Nestlé Company, calls Tom Kron the Henry Ford of chocolate. Before Tom Kron, candy came in cellophane-wrapped boxes that stood on dusty pharmacy shelves for months. Before Tom Kron, dedicated chocolate lovers had to travel miles to the handful of candy stores that made hand-dipped chocolates from quality ingredients, or made do with mail order (which means good stuff, but delayed gratification). Before Tom Kron, who ever heard of chocolate-dipped orange sections and strawberries? Who knew what a chocolate truffle was? Or had seen a solid, pure chocolate leg or golf ball? Sure, these things are commonplace now. Chocolate tennis rackets are a dime a dozen and your aunt Tilly turns out fifteen different kinds of truffles with her eyes closed. But when you think back, you'll have to agree that it wasn't always this way. Tom started in a basement shop and within a year had moved upstairs on Madison Avenue. When you wandered into his store he would offer you a plate upon which were some irregularly shaped dark chocolate–covered lumps. When you took a bite an explosion of flavor would happen in your mouth and a little stream of sweet juice would run down your chin as you savored the amazing combination of the taste of bittersweet chocolate and succulent, tangy orange. My husband said I spent more money there by the minute than he made by the hour. The truffles were refined to the point of perfection. Irregular squares no bigger than a thumbnail, they were so much classier than the humongous ostrich eggs that are sold today. You knew they were made with real ingredients because they didn't keep for more than a week. He made thick dark and milk chocolate bars laden with toasted hazelnuts, chocolate birthday cards and initials made out of REAL chocolate, not that compound fake stuff that tastes like a tongue depressor. It wasn't just the chocolate that made Tom's stuff special. The packaging, designed by his wife, Diane, was innovative and elegant. All in all a very special treat. The guy was eccentric, but he believed passionately in his product and himself. Other people obviously believed in his ideas too, because they started copying him like he had invented legal counterfeit money.

Kron became THE status chocolate. Soon, chocolate boutiques became as prevalent as pizza parlors. Every hostess worth her salt learned how to make chocolate-covered strawberries and kept a pound of Kron truffles in the freezer to wow her guests. It breaks my heart and makes me furious to hear people who should know better berate Tom for his eccentric behavior while conveniently forgetting that he paved the way for their success.

To say the show was lively and controversial was an understatement. The Susskind crew loved it because it was right up their alley. I loved it because I got to say on TV that I was a chocolate consultant — whatever that was.

The second time I was on national television I had little time to prepare. The "Today" show had come to Mohonk to cover the Chocolate Binge, a chocolate convention that I ran in New York State. When it was over they asked if I could return to New York to be on the show the next morning. This meant David would have to make the four-hour drive back to Boston alone with the baby (whom I was still nursing and who had a raging ear infection) and hold down the fort until I returned. Of course I said yes. They asked me to please bring a chocolate cake so that Jane Pauley and Bryant Gumbel could taste it on the air. No problem. Well, actually it was a problem because it meant I had to find a place in New York City to bake the cake. I called my friend Sara Lee Singer, who owns a fabulous cookie shop called Betsy's Place (she wanted to call it Sara Lee's but you-know-who wouldn't let her) and asked if I could use her kitchen after she closed up for the day. Sara Lee, bless her heart, said "sure." I show up with my ingredients at 8 P.M. — I am only slightly exhausted after running the Chocolate Binge for four days — and get to work. It's very quiet in the bakery except for the occasional stray noise on the stairway, which, I am sure, is the sound of the deranged lunatic on his way up to rob and molest me. I'm not used to the equipment and I don't know where any utensils are kept. I flounder around and waste an hour getting set up. I get the cake into the oven. It bakes for a half hour. It has to cool (in the freezer) for another hour before I can frost it. Now it's 11 P.M. and I haven't had lunch or checked into the hotel. I frost the cake and then, in a moment of gratitude, write "I Love David" in big letters across the top of it. I grab a cab and hotfoot it over to this very fancy hotel, where I take a shower, pump my breasts, and crawl into the biggest bed I've ever seen, then with my last bit of energy call and order fourteen out of the possible eighteen things on the room service menu.

The limousine picks me up at 5:15 A.M. How does Jane Pauley do it? The weather forecast is for a terrific snowstorm, due to start at 8 or 9 A.M. I arrive at the studio and am met (once again) by a makeup man who wants to turn me into someone who doesn't look at all like me. I try to be a good sport. The producer flips out when she sees my cake. "Oh, Jesus. Why the hell did you write that on the cake?" I tell her that it's a Valentine to my husband, St. David-Sent-from-God, who is directly responsible for my appearance on this show. She says, "Everyone will think you mean David Hartman and he's on the other network." I was tired of being such a good sport but promised that I would tell the 30 million people watching the show, who could not have cared less, which David I meant.

I am joined by the chocolate psychiatrist and his wife who teach you how to share your feelings and not your chocolate. The three of us are positioned behind a long table filled with unlabeled boxes of chocolate candy. In the center is my cake. I am amazed to find that I'm not nervous. I guess my feeling was: I'll only get one shot at this, why waste energy being terrified? Live TV is like a cross between feeding time at the zoo and rush hour in an air traffic controller's tower. The tension is off the scale. People want things done instantly and done right. The hierarchy is readily apparent because people yell at people directly under them and no one yells at Bryant or Jane. While we stand behind the table waiting for our two-minute spot, a man I have never met before starts slipping a wire down my sweater and pulling it out from under my skirt. "Just wiring your mike, honey." I've heard that one before. . . . Jane and Bryant come over to get ready and we're introduced. I hope they start soon because I think I'm about to get nervous and I'm sweating like a pig. The camera lights go on and the producer signals them to begin. We all flash 1000-watt smiles as they do the intro. The first thing Bryant Gumbel does is ask me to tell him about all the chocolates on the table. This is the unlabeled chocolate that I had never seen until I walked into the studio an hour before. I felt like I was on the "G.E. College Bowl." Fortunately, I recognized most of them; where chocolate is concerned, I have instant recall. Then he went on to talk to the chocolate shrink. To do so he sort of had to step over and push in front of me. I knew my parents (and other fans) were not getting their money's worth — they could look at Bryant Gumbel anytime — so I sort of kept pushing back, so I would be in front. He is much bigger than I and didn't notice. Then it was time to eat the cake. I had a knife and while I cut said very loudly that this cake was a Valentine's Day present to my husband, David BRODY, who was home taking care of the kids so I could be on the show. Jane Pauley says that she has such an addiction to chocolate that she doesn't allow herself even the smallest taste lest she go nuts and eat everything in sight. So, no cake for Jane. I cut a piece for Bryant, the pusher. He then responds with the singularly finest straight line I have ever been handed in my life: "Gee, no thanks. I only like to eat white chocolate." My friends who watched the show said they thought I was going to have an apoplectic fit trying to swallow the retort that would have finished my public life right then and there. I was through with being a good sport. I wanted to go home and nurse my baby. When I left the studio to race across town to make what turned out to be the last shuttle out for two days because of the snowstorm, the crew of the "Today" show, minus the hosts, were devouring my chocolate cake.

I was grateful for the opportunity to be on the "Today" show. It was super for my business, and I must confess that I am grateful to Bryant Gumbel for providing me with a terrific story — after I calmed down, I realized how hilarious it was. So, Bryant, I dedicate this recipe to you:

White Chocolate and Chestnut Soufflé

SERVES 8

6 ounces Tobler Narcisse, broken into small pieces
1 stick (4 ounces) sweet (unsalted) butter at room temperature
½ cup dark brown sugar, firmly packed
6 eggs at room temperature, separated

2 teaspoons vanilla extract
7 ounces unsweetened chestnut puree (available in cans)
⅓ cup granulated sugar
Confectioners' sugar

Preheat the oven to 400 degrees with the rack in the center of the oven.

Butter and sprinkle with sugar eight individual 1-cup soufflé or charlotte molds.

Melt the chocolate over simmering water, being careful not to let the water touch the bottom of the bowl or steam get into the chocolate. Stir to remove lumps and off the heat continue stirring until it is room temperature.

In the bowl of an electric mixer, cream the butter with the brown sugar, then add the egg yolks one at a time, beating until they are incorporated. Add the vanilla and the chestnut puree and mix until smooth. Add the white chocolate and mix only until incorporated. If you stir too much and the mixture gets warm it will separate.

Beat the egg whites with the granulated sugar until they are shiny and hold soft peaks. Fold a spoonful of whites into the other mixture to lighten and then pour the chocolate chestnut mixture into the whites. Fold very gently. Pour the mixture into the soufflé dishes and cook for approximately 20 minutes until they are puffed and brown. Sift some confectioners' sugar on top and serve.

Not Quite to Die for

As much as I love chocolate, I am not quite ready to give up my life for it, which was what almost happened. When *National Geographic* magazine was doing a story about chocolate as a commodity, they sent a photographer to Boston to take pictures of some of my work. The photographer, a sensationally talented Danish woman named Sisse Brimberg, spent a week at my house with her baby son, Calder, and they soon became our very special friends. She turned our dining room into a studio filled with lights hung on jerry-rigged scaffolding, cameras of all shapes and sizes, and wires and extension cords strung around the remains of the dining-room furniture. The walls were covered with huge pieces of pastel poster held up by masking tape, and the windows were covered to keep out the light. I baked and decorated and Sisse photographed while Calder and my son Sam destroyed the rest of the house. We wore out three baby-sitters that week. I made a five-tiered chocolate wedding cake, decorated with hundreds of white gold-leafed chocolate roses; enormous dark and milk chocolate leaves and flowers; dark and white chocolate roses spilling out of a chocolate vase; and hundreds of meringue mushrooms, which we piled into an enormous straw basket and decorated with tiny dried flowers. Sisse's head was full of ideas about chocolate work she wanted, and I was in heaven trying to please her and her camera. We worked around the clock, stopping only to soothe a crying baby or order out for more pizza. Halfway through the week Sisse decided that she wanted a picture of a great cascade of chocolate bonbons spilling out of a chocolate sack. I made the sack (This isn't hard to do — the secret is to melt enough chocolate in a very narrow but very deep container, stick your hand into the bag — I used one of those tall, narrow heavyweight fancy bags used for gift wine and trimmed the top with pinking shears — and stick the bag into the chocolate, keeping your hand inside. Make sure the chocolate coats the whole bag, then let the excess drip off. The real trick is not to remove the bag. Obviously, no one will get to eat it, but if you fill it with great things, no one will miss eating the bag. If no one eats it, then you can use compound chocolate, which you don't have to temper). So, the bag is done and Sisse says, "I think we need to go to New York to buy chocolate." I told her that there were fine chocolate shops in Boston. For her picture, Sisse wanted New York chocolate. Who was I to argue?

The decision to go was made so fast that I didn't even have time to get into my usual state of preflight anxiety. Sisse, Calder, and I boarded an early morning Boston–New York shuttle. Sam was banned from airplanes after a certain incident involving him, a westbound American Airlines flight, and several intolerant childless businessmen. It was a cloudless April day — perfect flying weather, I assured myself. Calder fell asleep in his mother's lap a few minutes into the flight. Sisse and I made a long, long list of all the chocolate shops we had to visit to collect props for her photograph. The flight usually takes forty minutes from takeoff to landing. I realized that we had been up in the air over an hour and the ground was nowhere in sight. Must be a wait at the airport, I comforted myself. Then the turbulence started. I always sit next to the window (so I can see if we're going to crash). All I could see was gray mist. Sisse, who knew how I felt about this whole business of flying, engaged me in conversation while we bumped and rocked about. The stewardess wasn't acting like there was anything wrong, so I tried to relax. We were seated in the very front of the plane (thank God), so when the pilot telephoned the stewardess we could see her face as the color drained from it and her shaking hands as she quickly strapped herself into a seat. At this point there were sheets of rain pouring down the windows. The pilot's voice came over the loudspeaker. He said that he apologized for the (increasing) turbulence. We were caught in an unexpected storm, with very high winds. He couldn't say how long it would take to land, but he did say it was probably going to get worse. I waited for him to say that we were in no danger — that everything would be okay — that we weren't going to crash. The only other thing he said was to secure all objects under the seat. Sisse and I looked at Calder, sound asleep in her arms. We grabbed each other's hands and held on tight. The plane began to twist and shudder as the wings caught the powerful gusts of wind. As a photographer for the *National Geographic,* Sisse had flown all over the world in tiny planes held together with string and elastic bands. She had never been afraid. I could tell by the look on her face that she was scared now. Someone screamed for a doctor. A man had had a heart attack. The turbulence was so bad the stewardess couldn't walk down the aisle. I knew we were going to crash. All around us businessmen were vomiting and calling for the stewardess, who was powerless to help them. I started to cry. I really wanted to be brave, but there was no energy left to hold terror in. Sisse and I put our arms around each other and the baby, and I made God a lot of promises that you can bet that I kept. How Sisse had the strength to comfort me and contain her own fear I'll never know. Finally after what seemed like hours, the black clouds parted just enough so that one could see the runway. The problem was that we were very low and the wind prevented the pilot from lining up the wings for the landing. I think the most horrifying moment of all was watching the wing, like a staggering drunk trying to get through a door, parallel, then angle off the runway . . . another two-thousand-year minute.

Well, since I'm here telling you this story, you know I made it. Paramedics rushed about the plane to deal with the man who had had the heart attack and assist those poor souls who were seated in the back, where the turbulence was much worse than it was where we sat. Several people had passed out from fright. The plane emptied, but Sisse and I just sat there, watching Calder, who had slept through the entire nightmare, and felt thankful that we were alive.

We got off the plane with roaring headaches. We told the cab driver that he would get a big tip if he would drive into the city without going over forty miles per hour. A stiff drink and some chocolate were what we needed — in that order. It had to be good (you-almost-lost-your-life-for-this) chocolate.

We made straightaway for Neuchatel on Sixth Avenue between Fifty-fifth and Fifty-sixth streets. Krikor and Patricia Yepremian listened to our tale of misfortune and fed us their exquisite champagne truffles. We began to feel better. Our next stop was the Trump Tower, 725 Fifth Avenue, at Chocolaterie Corné Toison d'Or, where Alvin and Merle Lewis gave us divine bonbons made of sweetened crème fraîche from Brussels. The headaches were clearing. Next, to Serendipity (East Sixtieth Street between Second and Third avenues) for two frozen hot chocolates. Calder, who didn't understand the reason for this chocolate windfall, wasn't asking any questions. He just kept smiling and eating. After that we went to what I think is the most beautiful chocolate shop I have ever seen: Le Chocolatier Manon, located at 872 Madison Avenue. A rounded glass case displays candies in a way that makes you think you stumbled into Cartier instead of a chocolate shop. The salespeople are nice, whether you buy one piece or a dozen. My favorite piece is called *bouchon*. It's shaped like a champagne cork, filled with chocolate and marzipan, and decorated with a tiny dot of gold leaf. Then we stopped by Betsy's Place (236 West Twenty-sixth Street), where my friend Sara Lee Singer comforted us with a dozen kinds of chocolate cookies and her famous rugulah.

Next, to Greenwich Village to Li-Lac (120 Christopher Street) for maple walnut creams and their magnificent pralines (our only nonchocolate departure). While we ate we picked out pieces for the shot, examining each one to make sure it was picture perfect. Soon Calder's stroller was hung with dozens of elegant shopping bags from the best chocolate shops of the city. And soon the Mamas were feeling good as new.

For two days we toured the chocolate dens of New York, neither of us wanting to face the fact that we had to get this final picture shot and that meant getting back to Boston. Sisse was adamant about returning on the shuttle. She pointed out that it was just like falling off a horse. It was important to get right back on again. I pointed out that while a fall from a horse can sometimes result in serious injury, it's nothing like the injury you get falling out of a crashing plane. She wouldn't be swayed. No, we wouldn't rent a car. No, we couldn't take the train. No, the bus was out of the question. Never argue with a stubborn Dane.

Fortified with several pounds of champagne truffles, we boarded the plane. The flight, of course, was uneventful. Every time there was a mysterious bump or noise, Sisse fed me another truffle. I did just fine. The picture appeared in the November 1984 *National Geographic* and was a huge success.

The Chocolate Diet

So, you've been inspired by the story of my life and now you want to go on The Chocolate Diet. It isn't difficult and it's loads of fun. You must begin by committing the following rules to memory and promise to obey them always:

Only eat and cook with real chocolate. Forget that stuff that's made with palm kernel or coconut oil instead of real cocoa butter. You'll know the difference as soon as you put the bogus item in your mouth — it never melts, but just sits there like a piece of tofu, waiting to be chewed. Because of the magical properties of cocoa butter, real chocolate melts at body temperature — which, unless you've been sucking ice cubes, is the same as mouth temperature.

Don't you dare even think of using carob. Not only does it taste terrible, it isn't even good for you. It's got as much sugar as real chocolate, and it's made from highly saturated fats! Talk about coating your arteries. Real chocolate is made with cocoa butter, which is a far less saturated fat. There are even tests that show that real chocolate has a certain substance that slows down the bacteria that cause tooth decay that carob doesn't have.

Yes, it's difficult to do things like coat truffles, strawberries, and candy with real chocolate. That's because you can't just melt it and go to town. The cocoa butter that makes real chocolate so special is a temperamental son of a gun. That's because there are two different crystals in the cocoa butter and they melt at different temperatures. It is necessary to heat and cool the chocolate at very specific temperatures to ensure the stabilization of these crystals. If you don't perform this annoying and, unfortunately, time-consuming task, the chocolate will not harden properly, and will not shine. Many people throw up their hands at the thought of tempering (temper tantrum) — after all, it's so easy to use coating chocolate, which, because it contains no cocoa butter, doesn't have to be messed around with. There are thousands of "candy ladies" (and gentlemen, I suppose) who make a pretty penny melting down this glop, pouring it into plastic molds (usually in the shape of lollipops, or Smurfs), and selling it to the uneducated public. Gee, don't people become sort of suspicious when they have to chew the stuff as if they were eating a pepperoni pizza? Take heart, chocolate lovers! Help is here. There are several books (listed below) that, with a little patience on your part, will help you learn how to temper chocolate. If you're really serious about it, and want to do quantity work, you can buy a tempering machine from Hilliard's Chocolate System, Inc., 275 East Center Street, West Bridgewater, Massachusetts 02379 (617) 587-3666.

Only eat the good stuff. Come on now, all that stuff that you keep stashed in the back of the third drawer down on the right next to the kitchen sink for low-sugar time adds inches to your figure without giving you the chocolate thrill that you deserve. Get serious. Buy quality and eat only one. Permit me a brief digression here. Please don't get sucked into assuming that if it's imported and it's expensive, it must be great. More on that later. Can't eat just one? At $10–$25 a pound I'll bet you can learn to ration yourself.

Sure, generic chocolate ice cream is cheap. But if you're serious about entering the big time and sharing the stage with real chocophiles, spend more for the great stuff (or make your own) and be satisfied with less. Remember, this is one time that even though less probably costs more, the calorie count is the same as the cheap stuff.

Cook with the best ingredients available. If you use garbage chocolate, stale eggs, no-name butter or — spare me — margarine when you bake, then you're going to end up with something that even the most desperate dessert craver will refuse. Yes, most of these desserts are expensive to make. If you can't justify the expense, then satisfy yourself with reading the recipe and eating a bowl of cornflakes. If you're going to make them, then do it right. Use one of the high-quality chocolates recommended either in the recipe or in the list in the back of this book. And treat chocolate with respect. Never, never put it in the refrigerator for storage. It will develop a film of moisture and eventually turn moldy. It will also pick up the odors of things like fish, strong cheese, and salami — you don't want to make a chocolate/salami torte, do you? Some people say it's okay to freeze chocolate if it's very well wrapped in several layers of plastic wrap and foil. I'm not wild about this idea. If you keep it in a cool, dry place, out of sunlight, dark chocolate will keep for well over a year, and milk and white chocolates for at least six months. I store my chocolate for cooking in large heavy-duty plastic containers with firmly sealed lids in what used to be our wine cellar. Now that I have all this chocolate, we can't afford to buy wine anymore. If the chocolate gets too warm, the cocoa butter will separate and rise to the top, forming a whitish cast. This is called blooming. The chocolate doesn't look so great, but it is fine for cooking. I have a big No Smoking sign in my kitchen; not only do I hate the smell of smoke, but the odor can be absorbed by the chocolate, as can the smell of strong perfume. If I buy cocoa in paper boxes, I put it in plastic containers for storage.

Eggs should be used well before the date stamped on the carton. Always be careful to check the date of supermarket eggs; I buy mine at a local farm, just to be sure they're fresh. To test an egg for freshness, float it in a bowl of water. If it rises to the top, discard it. Always, unless otherwise specified, use sweet — that's unsalted — butter. Keep it in the freezer until you need to use it. (I always keep five pounds of sweet butter in the freezer in case I feel like making something and don't want to shop.) The salt acts as a preservative, so the shelf life of sweet butter is much shorter than salted butter. There is also a higher water content in salted butter. Check the dates carefully on containers of cream and milk and always smell them before you add them to a recipe. If heavy cream smells sour, pour the cream into another bowl and then resmell. Sometimes the cream on the sides of the container is spoiled, but not the entire contents. I don't like to use frozen cream — especially for whipping. Nuts should always be kept in the freezer. They turn rancid very fast and can wreck the flavor of a dessert. I always keep several pounds of ground nuts in my freezer. Both ground almonds and hazelnuts can be ordered from H. Roth and Sons. (For the address see page 3.)

Same goes for utensils. Now that I've sounded off about ingredients, allow me a word about utensils and equipment. Cake pans, jelly-roll pans (for the soufflé rolls), and cookie sheets should be of high-grade, heavy-duty aluminum. These can be purchased in most gourmet cookshops, department stores, or ordered through Maid of Scandinavia (address on page 3). Using these high-quality items will give you consistently good results. NEVER PUT YOUR CAKE PANS OR COOKIE SHEETS IN THE DISHWASHER. Never, never use steel wool to clean them. Dishwasher detergent and steel wool (abrasive cleaners too) leave tiny scratches in the surfaces of the pans and sheets that will make it impossible to get the cakes out and the cookies off. Use hot water, a sponge, liquid detergent, and elbow grease to clean your pans. If you prepare your pans properly for baking, it will save on elbow grease. I usually use Crisco (instead of butter) to grease my pans. If you're rich, you can use butter. When a recipe says to line a pan with parchment (and dust it with flour) then DO IT. I prefer parchment over wax paper for this purpose. It simply works better. Otherwise, you'll be serving the cake right out of the pan — not too classy. Sheets or circles of parchment can be ordered through Maid of Scandinavia, or purchased at bakery supply stores. I rarely suggest using vegetable cooking spray for cake pans and cookie sheets. I find that it burns too easily, is hard to clean off the pan (when it burns), and occasionally leaves a funny taste. For some things, though, it is terrific — like preparing a loaf pan to hold a marquise or dessert terrine.

An accurate scale for weighing dry ingredients is an essential kitchen tool. I have one that hangs on the wall and closes flat when not in use. There is no way that you can eyeball twelve ounces of flour and come anywhere near the right amount. Standing on the bathroom scale with a bowl full of flour is not the recommended way. Other necessary items are glass liquid measures and a set of dry measuring cups and spoons.

Mixers: if you're a serious baker, then for heaven's sake, invest in a good sturdy mixer. I love my Kitchen Aid and the Kenwood I use for teaching (you get a better view because the head lifts up). You need a machine that can ribbon egg yolks, whip quantities of cream, beat more than four egg whites at a time. You folks who are enjoying this book only for the funny stories are fine with your hand-held mixers.

Ovens: I don't care what kind of oven you have, or whether it's gas or electric (although electric does have a more even temperature, which is better for baking), as long as when the little knob reads 350 degrees that means that inside the oven it is really 350 degrees. If your cakes and cookies are raw, or burnt, then it's a good bet that your oven temperature is screwy. Get a good oven thermometer — a mercury one — and use it. If your oven temperature is off you have three choices: you can pay the serviceman a small fortune to fix it, you can buy a new stove, or you can keep that thermometer in the oven and compensate on the dial. So, if you know your oven's 50 degrees low, and you want to cook something at 300 degrees, set the knob for 350. Don't forget to take a reading before you put your cake in the oven. Please pay attention to baking directions; when I say put the cake in a water bath on the middle rack, don't improvise and put it on the top rack, and then curse me when the top gets burnt.

Speaking of directions — permit me a brief digression. I got a call from a man who was trying to make the Bête Noire and found that there was a mistake in the recipe. Let me tell you, before I go on, that the cake in question was tested over two hundred times, and as the recipe was printed there were no mistakes. Considering it's so simple that a monkey could make it, I was pretty surprised to hear this man say he had had trouble. He said he had too much batter for the cake pan. Did he use a nine-inch pan like the recipe called for? "Oh, yes," he said. Did it have two-inch-high straight sides? "Oh, no," he said, "I didn't have a pan like that, so I used a nine-inch pie plate." That's not bad enough. He said he didn't have five extra-large eggs, so he substituted seven large eggs. The "mistake" was that he just figured that he could casually improvise on my recipe. Wrong, mister, wrong. You're not cooking a roast beef — baking is a scientific process, with precise steps. I wrote the recipe that way because that's the way I wanted you to do it. Think of it this way: if you took a Red Cross first-aid course and the instructor told you that if a person was drowning you should pull him out of the water before you started giving him mouth-to-mouth resuscitation, would you even consider changing the order of the procedure? Would you improvise by offering him a martini before you started pounding his chest? Of course not! So don't screw around with my recipes. They say what I mean.

The lesson here is pretty straightforward. Leave well enough alone. *The other thing you should do before you even turn on the oven is sit down and read the recipe beginning to end.* Make certain you have all the ingredients you will need on hand. If the recipe calls for softened butter, don't wait until the last minute to pull it out of the freezer. (If you have frozen butter and need softened butter, cut it into pieces, place half in the bowl of an electric mixer or food processor, melt the other half and pour it over the still-frozen part. Mix, or process, until you have softened butter.) Dark corn syrup is not light corn syrup. Condensed milk is not evaporated milk. Make sure you know which equipment you will need and get it out so it's right there when you need it. Use a ruler to measure pans and if a recipe calls for a two-quart pot and you're not sure how big your pot is, use your liquid measure and pour eight cups of water into the pan. If only six cups fit then you'll know it's not big enough.

Okay, now I've invited you to spend money on good equipment and quality ingredients. I've yelled at you about following directions. There is a purpose to all this strident bossiness. If you do use the right equipment and the best ingredients, not only will you turn out great-tasting (and good-looking) food, everything will work. There are two bonuses in having everything work. First, you won't waste time and money and your cooking ego will soar, and second, your reputation as a convert to The Chocolate Diet will be forever insured.

There's more . . .

You really should go to The Chocolate Diet spas: All chocophiles worth their salt know that THE place to be the first week of February is Mohonk Mountain House in New Paltz, New York. That's when and where the Chocolate Binge takes place. Four days and three nights of nonstop chocolate madness, including seminars, workshops, and hands-in demonstrations. Capped off by the Nestlé Brown and White Ball (where you come dressed as your favorite piece of chocolate) and the chocolate operetta. It's the biggest chocolate event of the year.

If you prefer to attend a chocolate spa in a warmer climate, I suggest you join me on the *Queen Elizabeth II* when it sails from Boston each November for the Chocolate Cruise: ten days and nights in the fabulous Caribbean and chocolate too. While this program isn't nearly as intense as Mohonk's (after all, you need time to swim and snorkel), it would make most chocolate lovers very, very happy.

Let your friends go off to the Rancho la Puerta, or the Golden Door. Now you know the ultimate spas for loyal practitioners of The Chocolate Diet.

Recommended reading for people on The Chocolate Diet: Maida Heatter's four dessert volumes are required reading whether you are just starting to cook desserts or have been doing it with great success for many years. Beginning with the first book, *Maida Heatter's Book of Great Desserts,* the series includes a volume dedicated to cookies, *Maida Heatter's Book of Great Cookies;* a fabulous chocolate collection, *Maida Heatter's Book of Great Chocolate Desserts;* and last, but never least, *Maida Heatter's New Book of Great Desserts.* (All published by Knopf.) Not only are the books chock-full of the most mouth-watering temptations, but each recipe is crafted in a clear and easy-to-understand style that guarantees success.

Jacques Pepin's two volumes *La Technique* and *La Methode* (Times Books) have a number of beautiful and unusual chocolate presentations accompanied by easy-to-follow directions and photographs.

I think all the books Michael Field ever wrote are extraordinary. The chocolate recipes in his volume *All Manner of Food* (Ecco) include classics, like a great chocolate soufflé, and unusual ideas: figs stuffed with chocolate and almonds.

For good, simple, down-home goodies, turn to Mabel Hoffman's *Chocolate Cookery* (H. P. Books). It is a great resource for quick and easy chocolate treats. It's also a great book for children to use. Filled with beautiful color photos, which were styled by Mabel Hoffman, the book itself looks good enough to eat.

Naomi Turner, the Candy Queen of Cape Cod, has a valid criticism of most candy cookbooks. As one who is a real expert in this field, Naomi points out that most of the books just skim the surface of the complex art of candymaking. The recipe failure rate can be very high if the areas of temperature and technique are not carefully explained to the cook/reader. Beware of any book that says, "Cook the sugar syrup until the bubbles look big," or "Melt the chocolate and dip the centers." Every candymaker knows that exact temperature is critical, and because of the instability of cocoa butter, one cannot just melt chocolate without tempering it.

There are, happily, two candy cookbooks that deal not only with in-depth technique but also with the art of making fine chocolate candy. One is *Candy,* a volume in the Time-Life Good Cook Series, and the other is *Anita Prichard's Complete Candy Cookbook* (Harmony Books). Both these books are filled with clearly written information and recipes, plus hundreds of photographs that assist and inspire the cook.

Elaine Gonzales's masterpiece, *Chocolate Artistry* (Contemporary Books), is in a class by itself. Years of research went into this fantastic book, which deals with every aspect of chocolate candymaking. I give this book my highest recommendation, and if you ever have the opportunity to see Elaine demonstrate her chocolate work, run, don't walk.

The chocolate craze has spawned two magazines created for those of you who love to buy, eat, and cook with your favorite ingredient. *Chocolate News* (The World's Favorite Flavor Publication) is the brainchild of its publisher, Milton Zelman. For subscription information write to Zel Publishing, P.O. Box 1745, FDR Station, New York, New York 10150 (212) 750-9289. The second magazine, *Chocolatier,* is a glossy, upscale, full-color tribute to our favorite food. Full of great recipes and beautiful photographs, it is a treat to the eye and an inspiration to the palate. For information: *Chocolatier* Magazine, 45 West Thirty-fourth Street, #407, New York, New York 10001 (212) 239-0855.

Several years ago a young woman in New Haven, Connecticut, put pen to paper and created a birthday card featuring birds, hippopotamuses, and sheep singing "Hippo Birdie Two Ewes," and a star was born. Several hundred million cards, posters, note paper, mugs, stuffed animals, T-shirts, and stickers later, Sandra Boynton, who combines incredible talent, staggering prolificacy, and delicious wit, has won the hearts of a worldwide adoring public. When a talent as tremendous as this one turns to chocolate, the possibilities are too delicious to contemplate. Her book *Chocolate: The Consuming Passion* (Workman) is a tongue-in-cheek reference book for everyone who loves chocolate, loves to laugh, or both. Cavort with hippos and turkeys while you learn about chocolate personality profiles. Find out the answers to vital questions like "Sex or chocolate, which is better?" and "Does the notion of chocolate preclude the concept of free will?" There is even a page on starting your own cocoa plantation. For those of you who can stop laughing long enough to walk to the kitchen, there are some terrific recipes. I would find it difficult to believe you don't already own this book. In our house we have six copies — one for each kind of chocolate personality — including our dog, Hershey.

Chocolate Diet Classes and Workshops. Most people who want to create great chocolate desserts need only to be able to read a recipe and follow directions. If you want to learn everything that there is to know about chocolate from botany to chemistry to production and manufacture, save your money and travel out to Hayward, California, where Terry Richardson, a world-class chocolate authority, gives an intensive four-day course on every aspect of our favorite ingredient. For information write: Richardson Researches, Inc., 26046 Eden Landing Road #1, Hayward, California 94545.

If you are looking for inspiration as well as instruction in the basic (and advanced) techniques of baking with and molding chocolate, then go see Rose Levy Beranbaum at her school, Cordon Rose, at 110 Bleeker Street, New York, New York 10012 (212) 475-8856. Ask for the "Special Intensive Chocolate Workshop." This delightful and fantastically talented lady is one of the finest cooking teachers I have ever met. She overflows with enthusiasm and love for her medium. Her unique ideas and creations seem to set the style for the legions of cooks whom she inspires.

When I turn forty a trip to Rome for Tartufo is not going to fill the bill. I want to spend a week at Gaston Lenôtre's Chocolate Class, which is held in his bakery outside of Paris. Too bad our kids will have to give up their college tuition for this birthday present because I hear that M. Lenôtre doesn't give scholarships. I also hear it's conducted entirely in French. Well, maybe another week in Rome won't be so bad. If you find yourself in Paris and want to enjoy Lenôtre's magnificent desserts, you can do so at any number of locations around the city. If you would like to enjoy your dessert sitting down in one of the most elegantly beautiful restaurants in the world, then have dinner at Pre Catalan, Patrick Lenôtre's showcase in the Bois de Boulogne.

Staples of The Chocolate Diet. Everyone has his or her favorite chocolate. That's good. Lots of people I meet are very curious about what my favorite chocolate is. The truth is that I don't have one single favorite kind — since I believe nothing exceeds like excess, I have a whole list of favorites. I find that there is a strong tendency for consumers to automatically assume that European chocolate is better than American chocolate. The fact is that both America and Europe manufacture all grades of chocolate from the stuff that you die to eat to the stuff that you won't feed to your dog. Keep in mind that if what you have in your mouth tastes wonderful to you, then it IS wonderful chocolate. The names here are a totally subjective list of my favorites. The addresses for these chocolate companies, as well as suppliers of less than bulk quantities, can be found in a listing in the back of the book. First the cooking category. These are, of course, also wonderful to eat: Lindt Excellence, Tobler Tradition, and Tobler Narcisse (white chocolate). These three-ounce bars are available in most specialty food shops. Ghirardelli Queen (ten-pound bars available from Madame Chocolate), Ghirardelli Eagle baking (semisweet, bittersweet, and unsweetened) chocolate, and Ghirardelli ground chocolate (for fabulous hot chocolate and ice cream). Harder to find in the East but worth the hunt is Guittard chocolate. Peter's (Nestlé) Burgundy (ten-pound bars available from Madame Chocolate). The Van Leer Chocolate Company makes a wonderfully delicious and elegant line of dark and mild chocolates that can be ordered in bulk from the company. If you do happen to place an order, give my love to my special friends Malcolm (Mo) Campbell and his wife, Jean (daughter of the company's founder). (See addresses, back of book.)

My favorite cocoas are Poulain and Droste, which are both available in specialty food shops. Lindt makes a magnificent cocoa that's, unfortunately, not imported — yet.

Now, getting right down to serious matters, what follows is an abridged list of the chocolate candies, confections, and desserts that make it a breeze to stay on The Chocolate Diet. This list is comprised of chocolates that I would throw myself in front of a five-ton semi doing eighty m.p.h. to get.

Cote d'Or Chocolate Bar (gold wrapper)

Tobler Milk Chocolate Bar

Nestlé's Crunch Bar. The American version is delicious, the Swiss version, heaven.

Nestlé's Semi-sweet Chocolate Chips. The best friend a chocolate chip cookie could ever have.

Reese's Peanut Butter Cups

Hershey Golden Almond Bars

Hershey Golden Pecan Bars

Carma Swiss Hazelnut and Almond Gianduja and their chocolate sprinkles, made from real chocolate. Write for their beautiful catalogue. (See address in the back of the book.) You'll be tempted to buy everything they sell.

Sweet Sloops, from Harbor Sweets, 85 Levitt Street, P.O. Box 150, Marblehead, Massachusetts 01945 (617) 745-7648

Michel Guerrard Raspberry Truffles, available in many major department stores.

Neuchatel Chocolatier Champagne Truffles, 1369 Sixth Avenue, New York, New York 10055 (212) 489-9320

Valentine's Chocolate-Dipped Raspberries. Daria Baranoff uses the very special chocolate that her parents manufacture in Kobe, Japan, to make these divine treats. Her marzipan is homemade and superb. Valentine's Cosmopolitan Confections, 1112 Fourth Street, San Rafael, California 94901 (415) 456-3262

Brandied Pecan Truffles made by Sara Bancroft, who owns and operates Silver Elegance, 1450A Oddstad Road, Culver City, California 94063 (415) 368-3533

Everything made by See's Candies. For the shop nearest you call toll free (800) 325-4149

Maple Walnut Creams and Hazelnut Truffles made by Li-Lac Chocolates, 120 Christopher Street, New York, New York 10014 (212) 242-7374

Truffle Glacées from Chocolaterie Corné Toison d'Or, The Trump Tower, 725 Fifth Avenue, New York, New York 10022 (212) 308-4060

Tom Kron's truffles and chocolate-covered orange sections

Coffee/Orange Truffle Tartlets from The Chocolate Box, 1375 Massachusetts Ave, Arlington, Massachusetts 02174 (617) 646-7575

Chocolate Pecan Logs, Fanny Farmer

Anything chocolate from Christian Constant, 26 Rue du Bac, Paris, France. Tel. 296-53-53

Mill Acres' Chocolate Truffles, 1295 Penn Avenue, Wyomissing, Pennsylvania 19610 (215) 373-2988

Chocolate Champagne Corks from Le Chocolatier Manon, 872 Madison Avenue, New York, New York 10021 (212) 288-8088

Another chocolate treat can be found at Ferrara's, 195 Grand Street, in New York's Little Italy. A company named Motta makes a confection called Connetti —hazelnut and milk chocolate filling enrobed with more rich Italian milk chocolate. This treat also comes in the form of shrimp, mushrooms, and snails. They are gorgeous and are available from Bloomingdale's, Neiman Marcus, and John Wanamaker.

Chocolate-covered Peanut Butter Sticks and Dark- and Milk-layered Truffles made at Jagielky's, 5115 Ventnor Avenue, Ventnor, New Jersey 08406 (609) 823-6501

Chocolate Pecan Turtles hand-dipped at the Chatham Candy Manor, Main Street, Chatham, Massachusetts 02633

"Needhams" and the best chocolate-dipped strawberries I ever tasted. Available from Downeast Candies, P.O. Box 514, Boothbay Harbor, Maine 04538

For your sweetie, how about a real chocolate Ferrari or custom-designed mink coat from Chocolate Designs, 1712 Post Oak Boulevard, Houston, Texas 77056 (713) 622-5990?

Rachel's Brownies, Great Valley Center, 81 West Lancaster Avenue, Malvern, Pennsylvania 19355 (215) 296-2198

Chocolate Chewies from Gottlieb's Bakery, 1601 Bull Street, Savannah, Georgia 31401 (912) 236-4261

The White Chocolate Curl Torte made by Pâtisserie Lanciani, 271–275 West Fourth Street, New York, New York, and sold at the various locations of Pasta and Cheese in New York City.

I happen to be a David's Cookie freak. If you're lucky enough to be within commuting distance of one of David Liederman's over 130 stores, you can enjoy the ethereal delight of one (or, if you're like me, a dozen) of his cookies still warm from the oven, chock-full of big chunks of Lindt chocolate. No, they don't mail well — we tried it.

If you're ever in Hollywood and dying for a great hot fudge sundae, head straight for C. C. Brown's, 7007 Hollywood Boulevard, Hollywood, California 90028 (213) 462-9262. They also sell their hot fudge sauce in cans to go.

White Chocolate Mousse from the Ambria Restaurant, Beldon Stratford Hotel, 2300 North Lincoln Park West, Chicago, Illinois 60614 (312) 472-5959. Everything else they make is wonderful too!

Betsy's Place, 236 West Twenty-sixth Street, New York, New York 10001 (212) 691-5775. All the things that owner Sara Lee Singer makes are delicious, but her chocolate cookies (all of them) are tops. She's a fabulous lady, so introduce yourself when you stop by. Tell her Lora sent you.

The Postilion Luscious Chocolate Sauce made by Madame Kuony, 615 Old Pioneer Road, Fond du Lac, Wisconsin 54935 (414) 922-4170, is the very finest I have ever tasted. It is available by mail order or at Neiman Marcus, and at fine food shops across the country.

Schrafft's Ice Cream Company has brought back an old favorite — their heavenly hot fudge! It's the original formula that we loved as kids. Available at Bloomingdale's in New York City. For other locations write: John LeSauvage, Schrafft's Ice Cream Company, LTD, 333 Fifth Avenue, Pelham, New York 10803 (914) 738-5511

In Boston and surrounding suburbs, Bailey's Ice Cream Shops supply devotees with sundaes dripping with dark and creamy rich hot fudge sauce.

If you're feeling very rich, see Jack Singer at Chocolate/Chocolat in Toronto. He will build you a solid chocolate castle — to live in or eat. Chocolate/Chocolat, 626 King Street W, Toronto, Ontario, Canada M5H1B2 (416) 366-5263. If you're not feeling rich, the other chocolate treats in his store will do just fine.

Last, but never least, there is a restaurant on Christie Street in New York City's Lower East Side. The name of this restaurant is Sammy's Rumanian Steak House. On each table is (besides a maple syrup container full of schmaltz — rendered chicken fat to pour on slices of black bread) a seltzer bottle, a quart of milk, and a jar of Fox's U-Bet Chocolate Syrup. What could be better to wash down your kasha and varnishkas than a chocolate egg cream?

Well, now you hate me, right? You think it's my fault your hips are round and dimpled and your dog calls you Spot. You think if you run right out and eat all the above-mentioned you will look like the before photo in the Mr. Weight

Watchers meets Miss Clearasil ad. Relax, we're coming up to the last and probably most important rule of The Chocolate Diet.

How to Eat on The Chocolate Diet. The second thing people want to know when they meet me is why I'm not fat. The first thing they want to know is how can they get a job like mine. I am 5 feet 5½ inches tall and usually weigh 114 pounds. In the summer I weigh slightly more because I run farther. I eat chocolate every day of my life, and so, unless you're a diabetic or violently allergic to chocolate, you can relax with the knowledge that tests have shown chocolate does not cause acne. That's the good news. The bad news is that you can't be a disgusting, out-of-control oinker about it. No matter what you may think, I am convinced that there is no such thing as a chocoholic. The very name offends me. The person who thinks he or she is, indeed, a chocoholic could in a different set of life circumstances be a pizzaholic, chain smoker, or compulsive turkey on rye with Russian dressing eater. The thing these people have in common is the inability to stop eating their favorite food. It is BAD BAD BAD to eat too much chocolate. (a) While it is somewhat nutritious, it's not a substitute for a well-balanced meal, even though it is a great source of pleasure. (b) It can make you fat. (c) The more you eat at once (that is, within a twenty-four-hour period) the less you are able to appreciate the fine points of it. (d) The more you eat, the more likely it is that some will get on your clothes and it's hard as hell to remove. In other words, too much of this good thing can ruin your health, your shape, your clothes, and your mind. That's pretty heavy. You will be too if you don't heed my advice. ONE IS ENOUGH! Take one piece, one scoop, one slice, and put the rest away — far away. When I find my resolve slipping, I have one of my children hide the tempting item. Eat it slowly and think about it — not about the rest of it waiting there — while you enjoy. EAT QUALITY! When I was a kid I used to get my chocolate high by eating Hershey's chocolate syrup with a teaspoon right out of the can. When I was a kid I could put any amount of any high-caloric thing into my mouth and my twelve-year-old metabolism would zap it. Now it ain't so. I have right now three hundred pounds of chocolate in my house. I wouldn't dream of tearing open the cartons and stuffing my face because I know that in my refrigerator is a box of crème fraîche truffles spiked with raspberry eau-de-vie and there's a Hershey Golden Almond Bar stashed behind the tuna in the pantry. I'd rather get my chocolate high on this good stuff — and so should you. If, in late March, you discover Junior Mints left over from your child's Halloween haul, you can be sure that they are stale. Trust me — flush them fast and enjoy a fresh champagne truffle or small slice of chocolate cheesecake instead. SOMETHING HAS TO GO! If you eat chocolate and don't want to gain weight, then you have to give up something else. Cottage cheese instead of cream cheese on your bagel, yogurt for lunch instead of a burger and fries, stock instead of cream-based soup. Come on, you've deprived yourself of worse things: Robert Redford, a sable coat, a cruise down the Nile. Chocolate's worth it! If you absolutely cannot give up anything then you have another choice: WORK OUT! One hour of running entitles you to a piece of chocolate fudge cake, swim a mile and eat some fudge, ride your bike and refresh yourself with a chocolate ice cream soda. If you've done all these things and really deserve your chocolate treat then for God's sake DON'T FEEL GUILTY. For years you've associated pleasurable things with guilt. Don't wreck a sublime chocolate experience by feeling guilty. Chocolate isn't like premarital sex. It will not make you pregnant. And it always feels good. It won't give you a disease that has to be registered with the board of health. What you are doing is 100 percent socially acceptable — and (hopefully) you've earned the right to do it. Millions of people wish they could do what you are doing. Take a bite. Close your eyes. Isn't chocolate divine? A true gift from the gods? Don't you feel wonderful? Beautiful? Happy to be alive and eating chocolate? Congratulations! You're on The Chocolate Diet.

Gloria's Northern Comfort

This recipe, created by Gloria Weiss, won first prize in the 1983 Mohonk Dessert Recipe Contest.

SERVES 8

2 cups (1 pint) whipping cream
1 tablespoon instant coffee powder —
  not granulated or freeze-dried
1 cup Hershey's Chocolate Syrup

1 tablespoon rum
1 teaspoon almond extract
½ box cinnamon graham crackers

Place cream and instant coffee powder in the bowl of an electric mixer or medium-sized metal bowl. Place the bowl in the refrigerator or freezer to chill while you prepare the pan.

Line a 5 x 9-inch loaf pan with waxed paper. The easiest way to do this is to grease the pan first with solid vegetable shortening and then line it with the paper, which will stick to the shortening.

Remove the chilled bowl from the refrigerator or freezer and whip at high speed, adding the chocolate syrup gradually.

Fold in the rum and the almond extract.

Coat the sides and bottom of the prepared pan with the chocolate/cream mixture.

Alternate layers of graham crackers and cream mixture, ending with cream mixture after filling the pan right to the top.

Freeze. Then turn out onto a serving dish and refrigerate until ready to serve.

Resource List

Catalogues

Madame Chocolate
1940-C Lehigh Avenue
Glenview, Illinois 60025
(312) 729-3330

Maid of Scandinavia
3244 Raleigh Avenue
Minneapolis, Minnesota 55416
(800) 328-6722

Publications

Chocolate News
Zel Publishing
P.O. Box 1745
FDR Station
New York, New York 10150
(212) 750-9289

***Chocolatier* Magazine**
45 West Thirty-fourth Street
New York, New York 10001
(212) 239-0855

Chocolate Companies

For information on buying in bulk (usually 500 pounds or more — it varies with
each manufacturer) or to locate a wholesaler or retailer in your area:

Nestlé
Malcolm Blue (Bulk Division)
100 Bloomingdale Road
White Plains, New York 10605
(914) 697-2812

Lindt of Switzerland
777 West Putnam Avenue
Greenwich, Connecticut 06836
(203) 629-2380

Tobler Suchard USA
1400 East Wisconsin Street
Delavan, Wisconsin 53115
(800) 558-5022

Felchin
E. A. Tosi Company
P. O. Box 265
Braintree, Massachusetts 02184
(617) 848-1040

Van Leer Chocolate Corporation
110–114 Hoboken Avenue
Jersey City, New Jersey 07302
(800) 526-3161

Ghirardelli Chocolate Company
1111 139th Avenue
San Leandro, California 94578
(415) 483-6970

Guittard
416 West Eighth Street
Fleet 330
Los Angeles, California 90014
(213) 622-9424

Bloomer Chocolate Company
600 West Kinzie Street
Chicago, Illinois 60610
(312) 226-7000

Ambrosia Chocolate Company
1133 North Fifth Street
Milwaukee, Wisconsin 53203
(414) 271-2089

Carma
Albert Uster Imports
9201 Grovemont Road
Gaithersburg, Maryland 20877
(301) 258-7350

Other Resources

Motta Chocolates (Connetti and other wonderful chocolates)
Rossario J. Caponetto
Ferrara Foods and Confections
195–201 Grand Street
New York, New York 10013
(212) 226-6150

H. Roth and Sons
1577 First Avenue
New York, New York 10028
(212) 734-1110

Postilion Luscious Hot Fudge Sauce
Madame Kuony
615 Old Pioneer Road
Fond du Lac, Wisconsin 54935
(414) 922-4170

Mozart Liqueur
Berentsen Company (Importers)
4444 Riverside Drive
Burbank California 91505
(213) 842-6112

Index

Milk chocolate:
    (chip) initiation cake, 96–97
    fondue, Toblerone, 81–82
    hazelnut (Gianduja) sauce, 123–24
    ice cream, 32
    See also Gianduja
Mocha velvet (refrigerator cheesecake),
    98–99
Mom's:
    brownies, 40
    chocolate chip cookies, 9–10
    chocolate cream pie, 11–12
    fudge squares, 12–13
Mousse:
    cake, chocolate, 127–28
    filling for name cake, 173
    Gianduja for cannoli, 158
    Simone Beck's Marquise glacé au
        chocolat, 66
    torte, Mozart, 142–43
    white chocolate, 177
    white chocolate en tulipe, 195–97
Mozart mousse torte, 142–43
Mun kickel (poppy seed cookies), 41–42

The Name cake, 172–75; Simone Beck's
    filling for, 66
Northern Comfort, Gloria's (prizewinner),
    242–43
Nut chocolate pie, Betsy's, 215

Oatmeal bars, heavenly, Jordan Pond
    House, 216–17
Old-fashioned peppermint stick ice
    cream, 21–22
Oranges, chocolate-dipped fruit, 82–83

Pasta, chocolate, Peggy Glass's lasagna,
    158–59
Pastry, chocolate-filled brioche, 138–39
Peanut butter chocolate balls, 39
Peanut butter chocolate cake, Sue
    Small's, 153–54
Peanut chocolate pies, 183–84
Pecan chocolate ice cream roll with
    bourbon caramel sauce, 46–48

Peppermint stick ice cream, old-fash-
    ioned, 21–22
Petite dacquoise, 186–87
Phantoms, chocolate (cookies), 140–41
Pie(s):
    Betsy's chocolate nut, 215
    chocolate angel, 106–7
    chocolate peanut (individual), 183–84
    Mom's chocolate cream, 11–12
    See also Tarts
Pistachio chocolate cake, Carole Wald's,
    155
Poppy seed cookies (mun kickel), 41–42
Praline strudel, chocolate, 184–85
Prunes, chocolate-dipped, Armagnac-
    soaked, 60–61

Quiche, Jacques's tart au chocolat,
    164–65

Raspberry truffles, 123
Refrigerator cheesecake, mocha velvet,
    98–99
Refrigerator roll, famous chocolate, 10
Refrigerator roll, Gloria's northern
    comfort, 242–43
Rigo Janci (Hungarian cake), 192–94
Rum nut balls, chocolate, 39

Sauce(s):
    bourbon caramel, 47
    chocolate ganache, 208
    chocolate rum (for caramel baked
        bananas), 133
    5-star hot fudge, 22–23
    hazelnut Gianduja, 123–24
    hot fudge (for Brownie tart), 30
    hot fudge, Lynne's great, 214
    white chocolate Drambuie, 82, 208–9
Sherbet, granite de chocolate Amer, 97
Soufflé, the best chocolate, 197–98
Soufflé roll, the name cake, 172–75
Soufflé, white chocolate and chestnut, 225
Spiced chocolate dacquoise, 87–89
Squares. *See* Brownies, Cookies
Straight "A" layer cake, 53–54